INTEGRATING
COMPUTERS
INTO THE
ELEMENTARY AND
MIDDLE SCHOOL

INTEGRATING COMPUTERS INTO THE ELEMENTARY AND MIDDLE SCHOOL

NANCY ROBERTS
RICHARD C. CARTER
SUSAN N. FRIEL
MARGERY S. MILLER
Lesley College

Prentice Hall, Englewood Cliffs, New Jersey 07632

Library of Congress Cataloging-in-Publication Data

Integrating computers into the elementary and middle
  school.

   Includes bibliographies and index.
   1. Computer-assisted instruction—United States.
2. Education, Elementary—United States—Data processing
I. Roberts, Nancy, (date)   .
LB1028.5.I545   1988   372.13'9445   87-11751
ISBN 0-13-468794-9

Editorial/production supervision and
   interior design: Cyndy Lyle Rymer
Cover design: Ben Santora
Computer art: Brian W. Starkweather, age 11
Manufacturing buyer: Carol Bystrom

Printed in the United States of America

10 9 8 7 6 5 4 3 2 1

ISBN 0-13-468794-9 01

Prentice-Hall International (UK) Limited, *London*
Prentice-Hall of Australia Pty. Limited, *Sydney*
Prentice-Hall Canada Inc., *Toronto*
Prentice-Hall Hispanoamericana, S.A., *Mexico*
Prentice-Hall of India Private Limited, *New Delhi*
Prentice-Hall of Japan, Inc., *Tokyo*
Prentice-Hall of Southeast Asia Pte. Ltd., *Singapore*
Editora Prentice-Hall do Brasil, Ltda., *Rio de Janeiro*

To our students, the practitioners who continuously share with us their creative ideas.

CONTENTS

CHAPTER SEVEN
LOGO PROGRAMMING IN THE CURRICULUM   *152*

CHAPTER EIGHT
CREATING AN INTERDISCIPLINARY CURRICULUM   *173*

CHAPTER NINE
NEXT STEPS   *187*

RESOURCE SECTION   *194*

INDEX   *218*

PREFACE

Integrating computers into the ordinary activities of elementary and middle school classrooms is the current goal of most educators—it is also the theme of this book. The authors are all faculty members at Lesley College, a school with a long tradition of educating pre- and in-service teachers. Our graduate program in Computers in Education dates back to 1978, about the time of the appearance of the personal computer. As an education faculty located in Cambridge, Massachusetts, one of the high-technology areas of this country, we began exploring the use of computers for education in the early 1970s. We have become increasingly convinced of the contribution technology has made and will continue to make to the teaching-learning process in and out of the classroom.

We have so far worked with more than 2,000 teachers around the country, most of whom have completed about 1,000 hours, under our direction, of study in educational applications of technology. Teachers' adaptability, creativity, and general stick-to-itiveness continue to amaze and delight us. Coming from classrooms ourselves, we have learned about technology along with our students—as we recommend they do. The constant intellectual excitement of muddling through things together, achieving successes along with the failures, and continually being challenged by a stream of new developments has made these years in the field of computers in education our most rewarding ones.

The purpose of this book is to share our convictions, enthusiasm, and discoveries with as many current and future teachers as possible. The futuristic scenario described in the last chapter, "Next Steps: School Days 1999," is quite implementable today. This book is our contribution to making it happen. The other eight chapters describe ways of getting to the technology-rich and educationally challenging classroom of 1999.

Chapter 1 looks at educational innovation and the process most schools go through when attempting to institute a new curriculum. Bringing computers into the classroom creates a unique set of issues considered in Chapter 2. These include software evaluation, managing a changed learning environment, and then evaluating the impact of the change. Chapters 3, 4, 5, and 6 describe in careful detail ways to integrate computers into social studies, language arts, mathematics, and science. The Logo language has held a special position in bringing computers into the classroom. Chapter 7 looks at the many different ways of integrating Logo programming into the discipline areas. Chapter 8 reviews the history of the interdisciplinary approach to teaching and suggests ways computers can enhance this strategy.

Our book ends with Chapter 9's vision of the future, a future only a decade away. Join us in getting our schools there.

NANCY ROBERTS
RICHARD CARTER
SUSAN FRIEL
MARGERY MILLER

CREDITS

We would like to thank the following sources for permission to reprint:

Figure 3-4 on page 53 used with permission of Grolier Electronic Publishing.

Figure 4-1 on page 63 reprinted from a discussion by Susan H. Lena and Ezra Stieglitz, "Tooling Up with a Data Base to Teach Reading in the Content Areas;" paper presented at the 37th Annual New England Reading Association Conference, October 25, 1985, Hartford, CT

Figure 4-3 on page 65: Photo courtesy of IBM.

Figure 4-8 on page 71 reprinted with permission from the author, Shelley Wepner.

Table 4-1 on page 78, "Selecting Word Processing Software," from *Writing On-Line,* edited by James L. Collins and Elizabeth A. Sommers and appearing in the chapter "Selecting Word Processing Software" by Michael Spitzer. Reprinted by permission of Boynton/Cook Publishers, Inc.

Figure 6-3 on page 134 used with permission of HRM Software.

Figure 6-4 on page 135 courtesy of Technical Education Research Centers.

Section entitled "School Days 1999" by Ricky Carter in Chapter Nine reprinted by special permission of *Classroom Computer Learning* (formerly *Classroom Computer News*).

All computer screen photos not otherwise credited courtesy of Andrea Roberts.

INTEGRATING COMPUTERS INTO THE ELEMENTARY AND MIDDLE SCHOOL

ONE
EVOLUTION
OR REVOLUTION?

The introduction of microcomputers into the elementary and middle school classroom is considered by some a revolution. Perhaps it appeared as such in its initial years. However, at this time it is more useful to think of the process of absorbing technology into education as evolutionary.

To the best of our knowledge the first computer was brought into a precollege setting in 1964 by a teacher at a private school in Connecticut who convinced one of the leading computer companies to donate a machine to the mathematics department. The machine was used to teach computer programming to secondary-level students. This use of computers—teaching programming as part of the mathematics curriculum—spread throughout secondary education across the country. It was not until the advent of the much less expensive microcomputer, in 1978, that any inroads were made below the secondary level or to subject areas other than mathematics.

From 1978 to about 1982, the inclusion of computers in schools was primarily a grass-roots movement, often led by a single teacher. This usually resulted in only one teacher in a building using computers. As computers dropped in price and more software became available, pressures built in each community to ensure that all students were computer literate, causing administrators to become involved in the microcomputer move-

1

ment. From 1982 to 1985 a great deal of money was spent on computer products. Many more people from both the schools and local communities participated in decision making and long-term planning around technology in the schools. Educating teachers to use computers became a concern.

Trends during the next few years will show a leveling off of expenditures for computers, less community pressure for student computer literacy, and less concern about teacher computer literacy. Computers will continue to be pervasive but they will receive no special attention. Computer environments will become far more accommodating. People will require less specific computer training. A similar trend will occur with educational software, making the time needed for teachers and students to learn to use a new piece of software less significant. While the "computer revolution" has been occurring for a good twenty years, it appears that we have entered more of an evolutionary phase that focuses on the integration of computers into the schools.

PERSPECTIVES ON TEACHING, LEARNING, AND COMPUTERS

The purpose of this book is to present this evolutionary process from a teacher's perspective, focusing on how the teacher can use the machines to make his or her teaching more effective. Effective teaching can be considered from two perspectives: the strategies or process chosen by the teacher for presenting a particular lesson, and the learning environment created for the student. Let's look first at the possible roles of the computer in the teaching process.

Computers can support some of the many strategies a teacher may choose. For teachers who organize their lessons into individualized work assignments, there are software packages that can be used for a variety of individual student needs ranging from traditional mathematics drill-and-practice, like *Teasers by Tobb,* to open-ended problem-solving challenges exemplified by *Gertrude's Puzzles* (Chapter 5). Group or whole-class activities are facilitated by simulations such as the *Search Series* that easily accommodate several students using one computer (Chapter 3). For activities that emphasize hands-on discovery, such tool software as databases, simple statistical packages, as well as data-gathering microcomputer-based laboratory equipment are now available (Chapter 6).

Choosing a teaching strategy also involves considering the available resources. The examples presented throughout this book involve a variety of ways any number of computers can be used effectively: from a single computer available for only a few weeks a year, to several computers in a classroom all year, to a computer lab or two in the school available "by appointment," to any combination of these.

Of equal importance is how the teacher chooses to use computers, aside from the number of machines available and his or her teaching style.

> You can use the computer in the same way you use other media—to deliver packaged goods. If you do that, you offer an initially enticing medium that's more fun than most teachers or textbooks. Students respond to even the illusion of control over the learning process. A single student or a group at a computer is doing what kids do naturally in most of their lives—learn without a teacher. But if the content is the same old stuff, they'll catch on and lose interest. That would be a terrible waste.
>
> Because what is new about the computer is that it can be used—in nearly every area of learning—not just to deliver canned knowledge in entertaining ways but to empower the user, to put the learner in charge of the learning process—the only way we really learn. (Naiman, p. 35)

The authors believe in the importance of keeping the student in control of the educational process. This idea can be expressed in several ways:

The student is becoming a *creator* of knowledge rather than a receiver of information. The student can be thought of as a *pilot* of the learning experience rather than as a passive passenger through the twelve school years.

The teacher is becoming a *facilitator* of learning who focuses on the learning process, rather than an instructor whose main function is to ensure the mastery of a certain content area composed of basic facts and skills.

As an illustration, let's look at how one group of third-graders *piloted* their unit on dinosaurs with the aid of a computer. This particular class had a computer housed permanently in their room. The teacher had been developing the concepts of gathering and recording information on a variety of topics during the year. The concept of storing information on their computer using what is referred to as *database software* had previously been introduced. This database software was used to organize the class's research about dinosaurs.

After the initial introduction to the topic the class decided on the kind of information it wanted to collect. The students set up the categories for their database as:

```
Name:
Eat:
Live:
Weight:
Big:
```

Information had been collected and entered for several dinosaurs before the students realized that some of the most interesting information was not being included, so they inserted a new category:

```
Unusual Features:
```

The students went back through their database and added this information for each of the dinosaurs already recorded. In addition, they included Unusual Features for all new dinosaurs they found.

Once the database had a reasonable number of entries, the students began to use it as a resource for reports they wrote using a word processor. The students quickly determined the largest dinosaur they had found, which dinosaurs were meat eaters, and which were plant eaters. They developed hypotheses that related where the dinosaurs lived to their size and eating habits. The class then came up with possible reasons for the dinosaurs' disappearance *based* on the information in their databases.

As a language arts activity, the children used the computer program *Crossword Magic* to create crossword puzzles incorporating their dinosaur-related vocabulary. At the conclusion of this unit, the teacher commented, "The computer isn't another subject, it's enhancing what is already there."

People's teaching philosophy and style undoubtedly bias their choice and use of software. If a teacher wishes to shift the atmosphere in his or her classroom, to organize the presentation of material somewhat differently, he or she can use the computer as a catalyst for experimentation. Thinking about kinds of software in the three categories of *tutor, tool,* and *tutee* can be related to teaching style and classroom atmosphere. *Tutor software,* including all kinds of drill-and-practice, is often chosen for direct instruction. *Tool software,* such as word-processing packages and databases, is effective for creating an atmosphere of shared decision making. *Tutee software* generally has students program the machine to accomplish their own tasks, thus putting them in the *pilot's* seat.

DIRECTIONS IN EDUCATIONAL SOFTWARE

A new type of software that is beginning to appear combines tool and tutee. This software uses the knowledge of the quickly developing field of artificial intelligence, where the computer is programmed to do more and more tasks so that it almost appears to be thinking like a person. As an example, picture all the steps a student writer goes through from the conception of an idea to the final product. Currently at least 50 percent of the student's time is spent in such activities as reading and note taking, outlining, and perhaps writing a first draft without the aid of a machine.

New writing tools are being developed that include ways to do all these activities by means of the computer. Referred to as *electronic learning environments,* these programs include several important themes:

1. The student is able to learn by doing, to play with ideas.
2. The computer has the "capacity to act as mirrors of the mind—that is, as reflectors of a student's own mental processes of reasoning and problem solving."
3. The technology helps "students discover the intrinsic motivation of learning itself" without having to rely on an arcade-type environment for such motivation. (Brown, pp. 2, 3)

Other important changes in educational software incorporate the use of expert systems. An *expert teacher* is someone who:

- takes advantage of the "moment to teach";
- prompts the student with the exact information needed at the most opportune time;
- helps the student avoid pursuing a blind alley by demonstrating a particular algorithm; and
- assists the student by providing new information or suggesting other resources precisely when appropriate.

Such teachers undoubtedly exist, at least in small numbers. But even an expert teacher with a class of thirty students cannot possibly give his or her expert advice to everyone all the time!

Several projects are now underway to incorporate the characteristics of the expert teacher into software. One of these projects is the development of a first-year algebra course that demonstrates how to solve problems when requested by the student, that shows the student how to set up algebra algorithms, that solves equations when requested, and that has the student teach the computer how to do algebra (program the computer) when appropriate (Roberts). These, then, are some of the new learning environments being created to change the curriculum so that it better suits the needs of children who will live as adults in the twenty-first century.

STRATEGIES FOR EDUCATIONAL INNOVATION

How will this all happen? What has the process of integrating this innovation looked like until now and what can classroom teachers expect in the near future? Studies done over several years—studies having nothing to do with computers—have attempted to understand how change takes place in our schools. It turns out that there are both similarities and differences between these studies and what has been observed in introducing computer use in education. Let's first look at this literature of innovation and then how computer integration differs.

The Rand Corporation did a study for the Department of Health, Education, and Welfare back in the mid-seventies to determine the characteristics of federally funded innovative educational projects that either succeeded (were ongoing) or failed (disappeared when funding stopped). Several strategies were identified by Rand as ineffective for causing continuous change and several as effective. Strategies found ineffective include:

- outside consultants
- packaged management approaches
- one-shot preimplementation training
- formal evaluation
- comprehensive projects

The following were effective strategies, particularly when applied in concert:

- concrete, teacher-specific, and extended training
- classroom assistance from project or district staff
- teacher observation of similar projects in other classrooms, schools, or districts
- regular project meetings that focused on practical problems
- teacher participation in project discussions
- local materials development
- principal participation in training. (Berman and McLaughlin, p. viii)

The principal was found to be the key to project success, providing legitimacy for the project and giving moral support when needed. A more recent study in 1985 by Carey and Gall found essentially the same things.

How do the results of this study shed light on the integration of computers into education? As we just saw, the strategies that do not work for integrating computers include packaged management consultants and one-shot preimplementation training. One school system hired a consultant group to help develop a three-year plan for integrating computers into the curriculum. The school system had five previous years of varied experiences with computers at all levels. The management consulting group came with a set of packaged materials for the planning committee to use as a guide. If the school system had followed the consultants' suggestions, it would have taken five giant steps backwards. The school system was between stages 2 and 3 (as described below) and the consultants were starting it back at stage 1.

The amount of training currently needed to make a novice computer-using teacher feel capable of thinking about curriculum change is in the range of 1,000 hours, a long way from a one-shot training session. However, as more teachers are exposed to computers and as computers become easier to use, some day one-time training in educational computer use might be all that is necessary.

Outside consultants might contribute to the integration of computers if they are used for in-service training in which the teachers are paid to participate. However, having worked with about 2,000 teachers across the country in a rather expensive master's program, the authors found that teachers who pay for their own education are more motivated and serious than those who do not.

Formal evaluation is probably quite important to understanding the most effective ways to use computers. Because it is not a narrowly focused project like these studied by the Rand Corporation, but rather a comprehensive one, the integration of computers needs continual study and evaluation.

As for those elements found effective in integrating computers, the only one from the Rand list to eliminate is "local material development," if that means software development by teachers. Software of any innovative nature takes many hours to write: it is a full-time job, not something to do over a weekend. True, there are authoring languages that allow teachers to develop software in a reasonable length of time without being programmers. However, the kind of software these systems are designed to develop is essentially drill-and-practice. There is a place for such programs in the classroom, but a rather small place. Teachers can, however, take a finished piece of software and successfully integrate it into their lessons, as the rest of this book illustrates.

Not all teachers need to use computers—not yet, anyway. Therefore not all teachers need to attend meetings on integrating computers into the curriculum as long as there is a balanced representation of grades in the school. Eventually, given a principal who is a strong instructional leader, some computer use will entice every teacher. Moreover, because of the many facets of integrating computers into schools—from purchasing, maintaining, and cataloging hardware and software, to staff training, to keeping abreast of new developments and technologies—it is critical for each school system (or even each school building) to have a *full-time computer coordinator.*

STAGES OF INNOVATION

The Rand report identifies effective strategies for initiating innovation. Most educators agree that there is some place for computers in the educational environment, but with varying degrees of commitment and enthusiasm. How do these differences in commitment affect what happens in the school? Beverly Hunter has identified three stages of computer use through which most schools seem to pass.

> **Stage 1.** Technology—especially computers—is the object of study. New courses, primarily in computer programming or "computer literacy" are established.
>
> **Stage 2.** . . . . Computers are viewed as tools which can support the curriculum in a variety of subject areas. Curriculum work is aimed towards integrating the use of the tools into existing curriculum in mathematics, science, social studies, and language arts.
>
> **Stage 3.** The focus is less on technology and more on reassessment of curriculum goals and priorities, especially with regard to the relative emphasis on problem solving, information handling, algorithmic thinking, creative communications, and so forth. (p. 3)

Stage 1 behavior was dominant during the period prior to the development of microcomputers and the first few years after the appearance of small computers. This stage is also characterized by limited resources in both hardware and software, and few computer-comfortable teachers in the school building. The principal often has political considerations as his or her top priority, such as making sure that all fourth-graders use computers or all children in the school have at least some amount of hands-on time during the school year. Most teachers do not want to know anything about computers and are sure this bandwagon will go by soon. Only the one or two original, grass-roots teachers are experimenting with the technology. However, as the principal becomes active and decides that, for example, all fifth- and seventh-graders will learn Logo, more teachers are forced to get involved. As a self-protection mechanism, teachers start pressuring for some form of education; thus the number of computer-comfortable teachers in any one building increases. This spread of knowledgeable teachers, increased hardware, and better software begins to move the school towards stage 2.

At stage 2, schools are attending to the process of integrating computers into their everyday curriculum. Moreover, several tools such as word processors, databases, and spreadsheets are now available, or about to be published, that are designed specifically for elementary and middle school students. This software is simpler and friendlier, runs on machines with small memories, and is accompanied by other educational materials such as student booklets and teacher manuals. Moreover, at this stage, tool software is exciting to use rather than nerve-racking. The use of such tools for a year or two generally leads the school toward stage 3.

Success brings a very positive feeling in a school and makes the teachers involved want to share their knowledge with others in their system. The mechanism for sharing is generally a committee. Interestingly enough, committee discussions usually shift from issues around technol-ogy to thinking about general educational goals. What is the purpose of school? What are our fifth-grade mathematics goals and are they still appropriate? How can we beef up our eighth-grade science curriculum? Because the reason for forming the committee was the integration of computers, discussions about curriculum change are closely tied to using technology. Thus computers can act as a catalyst for educational change if the environment is ready.

One stage 2 school system, just at the point of forming its com-mittees, came up with the following statement:

> We the staff of the School of the Future are committed to excellence in education,
>
> - with a strong emphasis on basic skills utilizing technology;
> - shared decision making in matters of policy and curriculum;
> - problem solving as a tool in all academic areas in preparation for life experience;
> - integration of computers in all subject areas as well as the humanities;
> - parents and teachers working together to provide a unified educational partnership; and
> - communication of ideas between this school and liaisons in each elementary school in Cambridge. (*School of the Future*)

The attitudes of the computer-using staff clearly reflect what stage the school is at. At the end of the first year of using computers, the School of the Future teachers said, "We've introduced word processing to grades three through six, introduced Logo to everyone, and played *Geography Search* with the fifth-grade class. We don't know what to do next. We need help." This is a report reflecting a school at stage 1.

By the end of the second year, the progress report included such statements as, "Teachers are engaged in a lot of problem solving with their students. The classes are more student directed than teacher directed. From first grade on up, students can take an idea, program it, and debug it. Computers are now used at many different levels of sophistication." These statements suggest a school at stage 2 of computer integration.

This system is rapidly moving into stage 3, as shown by the forming of several system-wide committees to address issues of teacher training, purchasing additional hardware and software, extending community in-volvement in the schools, and revising the curriculum. These committees, soon to be in full swing, are in close communication with the school board; in fact, a school board member may be on one of them.

Not every individual staff person and individual school building within a system is at the same stage of computer use at the same time. In fact, in most situations, behaviors exhibiting all three stages can usually be found in any one environment. What is important, however, is to have some risk takers, in terms of experimenting with technology, in each building. In addition, supportive communications patterns must be established so that people can progress easily through the stages. The brief history of technological innovation in schools suggests that most people, buildings, and systems go through each stage for some period of time. This is in no sense required; it just seems to be the most usual pattern.

KEY ELEMENTS OF INNOVATION

What are some of the key elements for keeping a school moving toward the more effective use of technology? Four identifiable areas make a difference. These are:

1. support, involvement, and leadership of the principal;
2. teachers educated in the use of computers;
3. an enthusiastic, visionary staff willing to spend the many hours needed to rework the curriculum; and
4. community support, as indicated by the contribution of resources.

As noted by the Rand study, the school principal is a key person in bringing about educational change. He or she should participate in computer training, and his or her office should become a technology-based demonstration work area. The principal should be involved, along with the staff, in all purchasing decisions. Performing in-class computer demonstrations, acting as a public relations person, providing consultants, and encouraging the staff to take computers home with them are some of the ways a principal can provide enthusiastic leadership for the school. It is also very important for the principal to create an atmosphere that *tolerates failure.* Teachers must be made to feel comfortable talking about a disastrous effort and discussing with colleagues the reasons for it.

Many alternatives now exist for teachers to learn about computers, about available software, and about how technology can enhance the classroom. Taking a course designed especially for teachers is strongly encouraged as a safe beginning. If courses are not available, self-learning is recommended for all grass-roots teachers. It is perhaps the most exciting way to learn because it involves the learner in the process of hands-on discovery. The teacher begins by learning to use one piece of software that makes a particular task easier, such as word processing or a computerized grade book. Finding a useful tool package generally convinces a teacher of the value of computers. Once confidence has been built, the teacher uses a computer with students. Experimenting with a few pieces of software in class is the next logical step; the teacher should start with a sure-to-succeed piece such as a simulation recommended by another teacher. Success is a wonderful encouragement for further experimenting. If a teacher becomes frustrated, he or she should share it with colleagues or take a day visiting a classroom where the teacher is excited about using computers.

Once a few teachers have become enthusiastic about computers and the principal has given his or her support for the project, it is time to increase the base of computer-using people in the school and create a *visionary staff*. Several suggestions can be made to facilitate this happening. More money probably needs to be allocated for hardware and software. Visiting days to classrooms where particularly interesting applications are occurring need to be encouraged. Focused in-service, determined by teacher requests, needs to be provided. Small within-school committees can be formed for teachers to think together about specific applications suitable for a particular grade level. Teachers can divide up the work of becoming familiar with new software. In some cases new software might require new ways of thinking about knowledge. For example, software such as *Survey Taker* and databases allow students to create information in the same way social scientists do. Teachers, during their own college education, might never have had the opportunity to *be* social scientists. Most teachers have been exposed only to the lecture model of teaching in college. It is both instructive and fun for a small group of teachers to work through a real problem-solving experience together before attempting it with their own students.

Microcomputer-based laboratory equipment allows data gathering, hypothesis formulation, and problem solving in science. Again, working through some of the experiments with other teachers is an excellent way to compensate for one's own educational gaps. Meeting with colleagues also provides a time to develop classroom support materials and pedagogical techniques. These hands-on staff activities develop an experience base that leads to positive attitudes about curriculum change. Things are accomplished in a timely way and teachers have opportunities to absorb new ways of thinking about education.

Finally, knowing that the community enthusiastically supports its school system is extremely helpful for causing change. Contributions of both hardware and software are an indication of support. Involving parents or other community members as school volunteers can be quite productive. Calling on community members with expertise needed by the staff for more state-of-the-art applications of technologies such as communication networks or videodiscs or in conducting scientific research contributes to teachers' self-esteem and feelings of self-worth. Forming joint committees composed of educators, local politicians, and business people can start the process of community involvement. The idea of community involvement in schools is hardly new; but because of all the recent publicity relating to technology, the community is very aware of what schools are attempting to cope with and is therefore more willing to listen and help. Once again, computers can act as a catalyst for change in another dimension.

The distinction between teachers who use computers like books and worksheets and teachers who are inclined to experiment is often the result of being in contact with someone who can clearly articulate a visionary educational scenario. These people are found in all sorts of places: local universities with a particularly technologically enthused education faculty; at a nearby institution doing state-of-the-art work in technology; among the parent group; or right within the local education staff. These people need to be sought out and involved in local school planning and implementation.

INTEGRATING COMPUTERS INTO THE CLASSROOM

In what ways should teachers think about computers? Following is a summary of how computers are enhancing the classroom scene:

• *Computers motivate students.* This is seen most clearly by the increase that often occurs in time-on-task, especially by children who have an attention problem. Keeping inner-city fourth graders engaged in the writing process was not a problem in a word processing laboratory for 40 minutes per day. Observing the same students in their regular language arts classroom revealed that the teacher engaged in managing/policing activities for 30 out of the 40 minutes of class.

• *Computers help the teacher present difficult concepts through the use of pictures,* especially dynamic pictures. Mathematics and science benefit most from this characteristic. Teaching the concept of *variable* to sixth graders in a prealgebra class using icon (picture)-based software on the Macintosh enriched the teaching task, and was quite an effective strategy.

• *Computers provide students with feedback,* either immediate or delayed, controlling the length of frustration and insuring success in a task. Spelling checks are an excellent example of easing frustration with immediate feedback.

• *Computers can do just about any amount of number crunching in very little time.* This allows simulations and games to have far more sophistication than similar precomputer versions. Working with a social studies teacher who had developed a simulation to give his class active involvement in understanding the reasons for Rockefeller's ability to create an oil monopoly in the 1800s illustrates this point. The students normally entered their financial transactions on paper and figured out their team's worth at the end of each round. The students not only disliked doing the mathematics, but, as we discovered, made continuous errors. Setting up a spreadsheet for doing the math eliminated the least liked part of the simulation, allowed the students much more time for policy discussions and negotiations, and made the game "more honest" by controlling the mathematical errors.

• *Computers can generate events randomly,* whether for research or for simulation and games, providing more interesting environments. The simulation/game *The Other Side,* a game designed to study the value of competition versus cooperation between two countries, provides days upon days of classroom use because of the continuously different scenarios generated by the randomness built into the program.

• *Computers can store and allow the manipulation of large amounts of data,* allowing the user to think interactively and draw his or her own conclusions. The ability of students to both create and access large databases on specific topics allows a reasonably high level of thinking and scientific investigation to occur in the classroom.

• *Computers can provide unlimited numbers of individualized lessons* to students who respond to this kind of teaching. Ongoing research in the use of computer based drill-and-practice and tutorials suggests that impressive gains can be made in the acquisition of basic skills by certain students.

• *Computers have the potential for providing access to both people and information* around the world quickly and inexpensively. A brother and sister, both middle school students, completed sophisticated research projects at home because they had access to on-line news services through their father's work. Laura was researching lycra, a synthetic fiber, and her brother was writing a paper on the black-footed ferret, an endangered species. Both were able to get the information needed, complete references, and write their papers in one evening with the aid of their home computer (Hunter).

• *Computers provide a much richer environment for teaching and give practice in learning problem-solving strategies.* New software and curriculum, now under development, will provide students with an integrated environment for collecting data, forming hypotheses, building simulation models, and asking their "what if" questions. These tools not only replicate the scientific process in the classroom but make problem solving less of an effort than for adults takling real-world problems (Tinker).

Computers, however, are useless without an enthusiastic, forward-looking teacher who takes great pride in his or her profession. The main purpose of this book is to aid such teachers in the evolutionary process of integrating technology into their classrooms as a means for improving the learning/teaching environment.

REFERENCES

BERMAN, P., AND M. W. MCLAUGHLIN. *Federal Programs Supporting Educational Change, Vol. VII: Implementing and Sustaining Innovations.* R-1589/8-HEW. Santa Monica, Calif.: Rand, May 1978.

BROWN, J. S. "Idea Amplifiers—New Kinds of Electronic Learning Environments." Paper presented at the Claremont Reading Conference, Claremont Graduate School of Education, Calif., March 1984.

CAREY, D. M., AND M. D. GALL. "An Investigation of Factors That Affect Elementary School Teachers' Educational Use of Computers." Paper submitted to the 1986 National Education Computer Conference, San Diego, Calif.

HUNTER, BEVERLY. "What is Fundamental in an Information Age? A Focus on Curriculum," *ACM Topics on Educational Computing Policy Alternatives*, Jan. 1985.

NAIMAN, A. "Serving Inquiring Minds." *Personal Computing* (May 1985), p. 35.

ROBERTS, N. "Logo Tools for Teaching Algebra." NSF Grant No. MDR-8400328. Lesley College, Graduate School of Education, Cambridge, Mass., 1985-87.

School of the Future. Brochure. Tobin School, 197 Vassal Lane, Cambridge, Mass. 02138.

Tinker, R. "Tools for Problem Solving." NSF Grant No. MDR 8550373. Technical Education Research Center, Cambridge, Mass., 1986-88.

TWO
IMPLEMENTING
COMPUTERS
IN THE CLASSROOM

One of the more exciting events during an elementary or middle school classroom year is the day the computer arrives. A teacher can include the students in this excitement when it comes time to unpack and set up the machine. The teacher, however, should first do this outside of class, either in a course, at home, or with the help of a colleague. Setting up a computer system with students requires as much planning as any other classroom activity. The model the teacher presents to the class at this time includes:

1. the importance of first *reading instructions;*
2. demonstrating *care* in handling all the equipment;
3. *involving* both *girls* and boys equally at all stages;
4. opportunities for discussing *behavior* relating to electrically powered machines; and
5. opportunities for *joint decision making* and cooperation in finding the optimal computer setup for the largest number of students.

Reading instructions is a process that is destined to be important in the computer environment, at least until computers can communicate in English. Teachers have a perfect opportunity to model this over and over again for their students because *even teachers* need to read the instructions every time they encounter something new. Moreover, computers provide excellent opportunities for teachers to demonstrate that projects can be simplified by reading instructions first.

Impressing students with the importance of *carefully handling* all the components of a computer system right from the beginning makes school life much easier the rest of the year. Computer hardware and software are expensive, and if broken the school is not likely to replace them quickly. Rather than having to make rules later about when and when not to touch computer equipment, teachers should demonstrate and discuss how to handle each piece, including disks, the very first day. Students should be taught to handle computer parts in just the same way they are taught to open new books.

Activities that can easily be seen as male, such as carrying in the "big" boxes, uncrating the equipment, and setting up the electrical connections, must be *equally split between boys and girls.* This very first introduction of computers is critical to the way the machines are viewed by the students. A female teacher alone does not seem to be enough of a model to ensure equal use by both sexes. Girls must feel an ownership of the machines from the very first day, and this feeling must be nurtured continually all during the school years.

This first introduction of computers into the classroom provides a natural opportunity to discuss *safe behavior around electricity.* It also provides an opportunity to briefly introduce the role of electricity in computing and thus how computers work. The parts of the computer can be pointed out before everything is plugged in and while it is still easy for the teacher to hold up each part.

Computer environments *encourage cooperation* along several dimensions. Because a student's work is readily seen on the screen by others, it is common for students to impulsively offer suggestions to each other as they work. Students often have to share computer equipment because of resource limitations and therefore must learn to work together. Finally, the norms of what a fourth-grader should know about using a word processor or programming in Logo are not yet clearly defined; therefore, mutual help is more acceptable to all classroom members. It is not unusual for one student to know more about a particular piece of software than everyone else, including the teacher. Help, therefore, is eagerly sought and given. Decisions made on the first day can thus begin to establish a cooperative environment around the computer.

PHYSICAL CONFIGURATION OF HARDWARE

Computers are not always located in a self-contained classroom. The question of where to locate computers in a school building has three possible answers:

1. in a laboratory setting, housing a number of machines adequate to service a full class, usually ranging between fifteen and thirty stations;
2. in individual classrooms, with the distribution of hardware in some way predetermined; and
3. in some combination of the above, outfitting only minilaboratories when sufficient equipment is not available.

Each of these configurations has its pros and cons. Let's take a look at some of them.

The Laboratory Approach

The main benefit of setting up a computer laboratory in a school building is to get the greatest use, in terms of hours per school day, of a scarce resource. Labs require staffing by a person who either has special training in computers or has built up expertise as a result of spending time in the lab. The school then has a person who is responsible for being familiar with software and knowing how to run and maintain the hardware. This ensures that maximum time is spent by the students *using* the computer when in the computer lab. This time-on-the-machine can be increased even more by having regular classroom teachers give the pre- and postcomputer lesson in the classroom. Furthermore, computers can be available at additional times such as before and after school and during recess, since only one adult need be present (and sometimes not even that). The lab can have open periods and be used by everyone as a general school resource, similar to the library.

Another benefit from the laboratory setup is that, given enough equipment, students can work individually with a computer. Some teachers feel this to be the optimal arrangement from the perspective of maximum student learning and enthusiasm for work. Labs usually have enough machines to allow students to work, at most, in pairs.

A laboratory arrangement provides the greatest amount of time flexibility for the range of student needs in elementary and middle schools. For example, one school has found that about thirty minutes at the computer is optimal for kindergarten children, while older students often need a good hour to make progress on their projects. Three-quarters of an hour seems appropriate for the in-between ages.

Laboratories can become a focus for larger school projects, providing an opportunity for children of different ages and varying computer backgrounds to work together. One such project is a schoolwide newspaper. Another is a computer lab newsletter to announce the arrival of new software and hardware and sessions to introduce people to their use. A laboratory setup provides a place to hold courses for teachers and parents as well as special minicourses for students. The laboratory, of course, becomes headquarters for the Computer Club, as well as other school clubs that can make use of the computers. Other special projects a lab can sponsor are such things as a "girls only" time if equal access is a problem. The laboratory is an ideal place for cross-age as well as peer tutoring. Housing shared resources like computer journals, manuals, and summary sheets on different pieces of software is also ideal in a laboratory.

The disadvantages of the laboratory configuration are twofold. First, the computer teacher and the classroom teacher are usually two different people. Second, there are software purchasing implications not often considered in advance. The disadvantage of having a separate computer teacher is that it allows classroom teachers to remain uninvolved in the use of computers if they so choose. Many regard the time their students spend in the computer lab as a free period. Using computers thus may have little effect on the way classroom teachers think about teaching. It is much more difficult for computers to be meaningfully *integrated* into the curriculum. Less confident teachers tend to favor the laboratory setup.

Software implications of the lab setting center around the assumption that all students are working on the same projects when in the laboratory as a class. Some current software requires that the disk remain in the disk drive while the software is being used. This means that multiple copies of each software package must be purchased. For a tool package that has a great deal of use, this is fine. For a piece of software that might get used for just one class period, this can be an unreasonable expense. One solution is to network all the computers in the laboratory to one hard disk drive. If there is a version of the software that runs on a hard disk, it is usually more expensive than the floppy disk version, but less expensive than several floppy disk copies. Some software companies grant site licenses, allowing a school to make one copy of a piece of software for all computers housed in one room, or sell multiple disks at a reduced price. If a school chooses not to buy multiple copies and instead uses different software packages during one period, chaos can develop in the lab as everyone has different questions and concerns!

The Classroom Approach

The advantages of having computers in classrooms to some extent parallel the disadvantages of the laboratory setup. It is far easier for the classroom teacher to *integrate* computer activities into the curriculum, particularly if the classroom is organized around learning centers. Computer activities can become one center and initially pose very little threat to a new computer-using teacher. The computer can slowly be used more as everyone becomes familiar with it. Moreover, the computer is available for use by both the students and the teacher whenever it is appropriate, as opposed to the need to plan far in advance to reserve another room. In the classroom setting the computer can be a teacher's tool as well. The teacher can use it for student record keeping and word processing and perhaps take it home to work with on his or her own time. Again, this allows the less-confident teacher private time to learn and also to get "hooked" on the computer as it makes his or her administrative work easier.

Placing computers in the classroom assumes that all teachers use computers. This is not necessarily true. Some computers are undoubtedly kept in closets, which is a disadvantage to this approach. Because there is not necessarily a computer expert in every school building, teacher training may be much more a thing of chance or depend on the enthusiasm and donated time of one person.

A second disadvantage of spreading computers throughout a building is the need to establish a central place from which software and other resources can be borrowed. Thus the need to reserve software in advance requires some degree of long-range planning. Another problem is the shortage of printers. It is unlikely that each computer or classroom has a printer. Not having hard copy when it is needed is very frustrating to computer users.

Finally, most classrooms have only a few computers. According to Becker, this results in less use per hour for the equipment. However, if classrooms do have as many computers per student as do labs (about one for every two students), most of the above disadvantages to computers in classrooms disappear.

Recommendations

Given very scarce equipment (less than fifteen computers per average-size building), it seems best to start with computers on carts and put them only in the rooms of the teachers requesting them. As the number of computers in a building increases, a laboratory should be developed in order to provide opportunities for:

1. all students to use a computer at the same time when that is appropriate;
2. holding minicourses for teachers and school volunteers; and
3. maintaining a central place that can remain open and be staffed by only one adult. (Placing the room off the library allows supervision by the librarian, if he or she is willing.

However, as hardware resources build, machines should be installed permanently in individual classrooms, depending on requests by teachers and considerations of a balanced spread throughout the school. Some computers should be kept on carts for adding resources to a classroom for certain projects, borrowing during vacations, and using in such places as the teachers' room, offices, or auditorium or gym for special events. Most computer coordinators across the country agree that whichever configuration a school starts with, lab or classrooms, the school changes its mind and does the opposite after a few years. A combination seems the best approach until the time when everyone in the school has his or her own machine.

SOFTWARE EVALUATION

The curriculum primarily determines software needs and the next several chapters discuss this topic in depth. However, given a variety of software programs that appear to meet the curriculum goals, how do we choose one? Several elements of software evaluation need to be considered; among them are:

- the goals of the curriculum and the learning environment created by the software;
- the essentialness of the computer to the teaching-learning environment;
- the kinds of motivation provided by the software;
- the flexibility of the program in terms of the extent of use in the classroom;
- practical issues such as the time needed to learn to use the program; and
- the technical quality of the programming.

Matching Pedagogy to Goals

The fundamental questions to ask about any piece of educational software are: What are the program's goals? and, How are these goals achieved? One aspect of how goals are achieved involves the learning format of the software. Does it use a drill-and-practice model? Is it a simulation? Or is it completely open-ended? Does the approach match the goals? A discovery-oriented approach is probably not the best format for teaching spelling or touch typing. In contrast, a drill-and-practice program is not the optimum format for teaching the scientific method. Mechanical skills such as touch typing require a different teaching approach than an abstract process like the scientific method.

The implementation of any particular software approach carries with it a view of how learning happens and places the learner in a particular role. For example, let's consider two simulations: *Oregon Trail,* one of the classic computer simulations for elementary school use; and *Geography Search,* a newer simulation. Both simulate events in a historic era. However, in the original *Oregon Trail* a major part of the students' time is spent at the computer trying to shoot animals and hostile people, while in *Geography Search* most of it is spent away from the computer analyzing data and planning strategies with classmates. *Oregon* is usually played in one sitting without any ancillary materials, while *Geography Search* is played over several weeks with accompanying booklets for essential information on topics such as navigation and weather.

Different student roles are also found in programs that provide tutorial help. In many tutorials, if students make errors they are given a review or explanation automatically; they have no control over the help given. A different approach is found in a public domain program called *Fractions*. Included as one of the choices for each question is a HELP option. When the HELP option is chosen, the students can ask for a further explanation. Some programs provide a HELP option at all times. In this approach, the students control the timing and amount of help they receive; thus their role as learners is quite different from what it is in programs that completely control all aspects of help.

The issue of control and the role of the learner is not limited to asking for help. It can extend through many aspects of a program's design. In most approaches to practicing alphabetizing, for example, the students are given words by the computer. Compare this to a program called *Word Quest* in which students must use their own words, even incorrectly spelled words. At first glance this may seem like a ridiculous idea—accepting misspelled words. The reason relates to the role of the learner. This game is designed so that students have to set the rules and limits. Actually, for alphabetizing practice, any set of letters suffices. Students can learn a lot about alphabetizing from creating their own letter sequences. If students decide that they want to limit each other to real words, they then must also police the correctness of the words. This in itself is a worthwhile exercise. Both programs provide practice in alphabetizing, but in each the role of the student and the way the goal is achieved is different.

Both students and teachers should have as much program control as possible. This is particularly important with heterogeneous classes that include exceptional learners all along the continuum. An additional control consideration is, Does the computer do things—make decisions—that might be better left to the user? *Balance* is a program that uses an animated pan balance as a graphic model for equality in an algebraic equation. When asked for help by a student, however, the program jumps in and solves the whole equation step by step. The student passively watches the process and never gets a chance to interact.

Below is a list of areas that a user might control. It includes simple technical issues as well as deeper issues of learning style and content. The evaluator should ask if the user can:

- skip instructions at the start;
- turn sound on or off; and
- quit the program at any time and start later at the point at which the user left off.

In terms of the user's ability to move easily through and around the program, the evaluator should ask:

- Can the level and/or number of problems be specified?
- If there are several parts to the program, can users control where they are in the program? Can the program be entered from several places?
- Once begun, can users control the pace of the program or the amount of time taken to work through it?
- Can users access different sections of the program—instructions, current score, other information, or included tools?
- Can users determine when to get help?

Looking at the content of a program, the evaluator should ask if students or teachers can:

- put in their own content; and
- invent or include their own problems.

The Role of the Computer

The second major evaluation area is summed up by the question, Does the computer provide a unique teaching or learning environment? As long as the computer is a scarce resource, it should be devoted to things that cannot be accomplished as well by other means.

Let's look at both a positive and a negative example. *Darts* is a fraction game that provides a lesson using the power of a computer (see Figure 2-1). In one version of *Darts*, the user is presented with a number line from 0 to 1. Three balloons are randomly placed on the line. The user types in a fractional number representing the position of the balloon on the number line. An animated "dart" specified by the user's input is then "thrown" at the position on the number line. If the fraction is correct, the dart hits a balloon and the balloon pops. If the fraction does not correspond to a balloon's position, the dart simply hits the number line. In either case the fractional value of the dart is displayed. If the student misses, the dart gives a graphic representation of the relative "size" of the guess, thus providing visual feedback for the next try. This feedback shows the student the effect of changing his or her answer in various ways such as, "If you increase the bottom number of a fraction, does its value get bigger or smaller?" Such a dynamic experimental environment under the user's control is very hard to provide in any other way.

In contrast let's take a game called *Fraction Concentration*. Here students must match fractional and decimal values hidden on the back side of "cards" on the computer screen, as in a traditional concentration game.

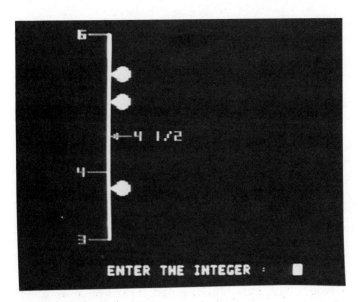

FIGURE 2-1. Darts.

The display of the cards is implemented very artfully on the machine. The question is, Why can't the teacher simply make up a pack of fraction and decimal cards and let students play concentration with them? Playing with real cards would free up the computer so that more students could use the excellent tutorial that precedes the game.

Motivation

Motivation is a third area to consider when judging a piece of software. Motivation can be differentiated into two broad categories: *internal motivation* (which derives from within the learning content of the program itself) and *external motivation* (which is external to the content of the program). The most extreme examples of external motivation are found in some drill-and-practice programs. After a certain number of correct answers the user gets to play a game, often a shoot-down-the-alien-spacecraft type. Here the actual content of the program, such as doing addition or matching synonyms, is not particularly enticing, and thus the motivation is simply an add-on.

At the other end of the spectrum are programs in which the motivation is directly tied to the content. Often these are programs that present the user with interesting problems to solve. The motivation comes from trying to devise a way to solve the problem. Let's look at three examples, each of which moves closer to internal motivation. In *Explorer Metros,* students are "transported" to an alien space colony. As they travel they meet obstacles such as a canyon to cross. Each obstacle presents a problem in metric measurement such as:

> It begins to rain and the water is filling up the canyon at the rate of 3 meters a minute. It takes 10 minutes to get across. What should you do?

Here is the first level of intrinsic motivation. The activity is tied more or less directly to the content. Contrast this to a program called *Math Mansion* in which students are trying to move through a mysterious castle. To move from room to room they must solve multiplication problems. In this program multiplication problems could be replaced with *any* content (synonyms, spelling words, or algebra equations) and the program would remain the same.

The second level of intrinsic motivation is one in which there is a direct connection between the nature of the activity and the content. *Green Globs* presents the student with a coordinate grid and thirteen green globs (points on the grid) randomly distributed (see Figure 2-2). The challenge is to type in equations that, when graphed, draw a line through (and pop) as many of the globs as possible. Here the content of the game itself is tied to the subject matter, whereas in *Explorer Metros* the context of space exploration is used only as an environment in which to teach metrics.

FIGURE 2-2. *Green Globs,* $y = \frac{1}{2}x + \frac{7}{6}$.

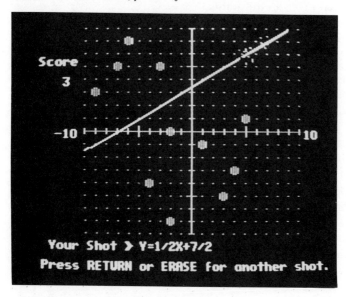

The third level of intrinsic motivation is one in which the learning content *is* the activity. An example is a game called *Suspect Sentences.* In this activity a student takes a paragraph by a well-known author and inserts her or his own sentence. The challenge is to write the sentence in the author's style so that no one can tell which is the added sentence. Once a player has inserted the sentence, it is up to a classmate to identify the suspect sentence. Here the activity is directly tied to the content with nothing added for motivation.

The ultimate example of internal motivation is a tool program, such as a spreadsheet or a database, in which the user has a problem that he or she wishes to solve and is using the software as a problem-solving aid.

The three categories above provide a perspective on the pedagogical aspects of a program. The last three areas revolve around implementation issues.

Flexibility

An important consideration about any piece of software is its range of use. How many different ways can the program be used with how many different students?

- Are the prerequisite skills such that only a relatively small group can use it? The prerequisite skills may be general (reading level of textual material), in a particular content area (knowing how to reduce fractions), or in using the computer (need to know how to use an editing system or how to use control key combinations).
- Is the program appropriate for the intended audience? For example, is the graphic reinforcement demeaning to older students?
- Can the teacher or the student change parameters in the program to tailor it to specific needs? This can be in terms of: content (Can students put in their own problems?), level of difficulty (Can an equation-graphing program go all the way from straight line graphs to sine curves?), and nature of available feedback (Can a teacher decide what hints to provide or how many tries a student gets before help is given?)
- Can the program grow with the student? If students master one part of a program can they go on to a more complex level or do they stay at the same level and grow bored?
- How long will the program be used in a classroom? Is it basically a program to be used once and then put aside, or will it continue to engage the students?

The most flexible programs are tool programs such as word processors, databases, and spreadsheets that can be used in a variety of disciplines. One characteristic of these tool programs is that they are content-free. The user puts in her or his own content. This gives the program a great deal of flexibility.

All this focus on flexibility does not mean that a one-shot program that teaches one thing in a unique way may not be worthwhile. It may be just what is needed. However, with the breadth of classroom content and limited software budgets, the issue of flexibility is an important one to consider.

Practicality Issues

Here are a few pragmatic questions to ask when selecting classroom software:

- Is the program compatible with the particular hardware setup? Does the program require color monitors in order to work effectively? Are printers, joysticks, a second disk drive, or other peripherals needed to use the program effectively? Is the amount of memory available appropriate for the program? Some programs such as *AppleWorks* "work" with limited memory, but not very well.
- How much time does it take a teacher to learn to use the program and integrate it into the curriculum?
- How much time does it take for students to learn to use the program?
- How much computer time does it take to use the program effectively? There are some excellent problem-solving games that engage students in things like exploring and understanding foreign cultures or solving problems by a complex process of logical deduction. The problem is that some programs take so much individual computer time that they may not be practical for most classrooms as of now.

Technical Considerations

Finally there are some technical program issues to consider. A few years ago every evaluation form asked if the software was free of programming bugs (errors). Today it is unusual to find a program with bugs. Here is a list of technical program considerations that are generally not a problem, but are worth keeping in mind:

- clear directions, when appropriate—which may be skipped;
- easy-to-follow steps for using the program;
- accurate content: no spelling or punctuation errors, no factual or mathematical errors, and no inappropriate terminology;
- no socially biased material that reinforces sex, race, age, or other stereotypes;
- short waiting times for the computer to perform activities, such as drawing graphics;
- protection against inadvertent or inappropriate responses—for example, accidental key presses that disrupt the functioning of the program; and
- easy correction of incorrectly entered information.

Software Evaluation Summary

As a summary to the points just raised, here is a list of questions to keep in mind when evaluating software:

1. What are the curriculum goals and the software goals and do they match?
2. What is the nature of the learning environment created by the software and is it acceptable?
3. Can the student or teacher control the major elements of the software (if appropriate)?
4. Does the software contribute to the learning process?
5. Is the motivation for using the software academically sound?
6. Is the software multidimensional enough to justify its purchase?
7. Are the necessary hardware and peripherals available to run the software?
8. Is the software free of programming errors?

For evaluating software, the National Council of Teachers of Mathematics suggests going through a new program three times: first as an average student, second as a student who does not know the material very well and is having trouble, and third as an advanced student who is inventive and who might be eager to extend the ideas presented in the program. If the simulation of all these students fares well, the software is most likely appropriate (Heck).

MANAGEMENT ISSUES

Beside computers and software, with what other areas should the teacher be concerned? Making everything run smoothly, or the management of the new environment, is one. Teaching with computers in a classroom presents the same management issues that exist for a teacher in a noncomputer environment. Becker's second national survey suggests that all experienced teachers handle a particular situation similarly, while all inexperienced teachers handled the same situation differently. Such management decisions depend on the amount of teaching experience, not on the amount of computer experience.

The Physical Placement of Hardware

Some recommendations as to the placement of hardware in a lab can be made. One suggested arrangement is to put the computers in a horseshoe or against the back and side walls so that the teacher can view all the monitors at the same time. This also provides a large space in the center for physical activities like "playing turtle" or using a robot such as Big Trak. This space is also useful for bringing the whole class together for a discussion or for viewing a blackboard or large monitor for software demonstrations. The horseshoe arrangement also creates corners to permit noncomputer small-group activities when the computer activity is better with only one student per machine and there are not enough machines.

Thought must be given to keeping electrical cords out of the way. Power strips can be run along the wall if computers are against the wall or under tables if in the horseshoe configuration. Computers should be placed so that light from windows does not glare on the screens and away from chalkboards to avoid excess dust.

When considering placement in a classroom, computers should be positioned out of the way so that the sound that sometimes accompanies software does not disturb the class. Again, screens should be placed in a way that allows the teacher to observe readily the work being done. Some space is needed around machines to accommodate small-group work. To reduce noise, the printer might be put in a closet or cabinet. Finally, there should be enough power outlets nearby. A computer system usually requires separate outlets for the monitor, computer, and printer.

Establishing Procedures for Computer Use

To promote joint decision making and cooperation in the use of computers, establishing clearcut rules is an excellent opportunity for the teacher and class to interact. The teacher's general management style strongly influences these rules and regulations. However, some areas are particularly relevant to computers and should be included in any rules and regulations that are developed. These include:

1.   Disturbing the class as little as possible when computers are being used by only some students. The same classroom rules that apply to movement in general should apply to computer use by individuals.

2.   Providing equal time for all students. One teacher has the class use the computer in alphabetical order, allowing each child twenty minutes of individual use a week. Rotation is begun in the morning. Each child taps the next person on the list as he or she finishes his or her twenty minutes. If someone is absent, that time is accumulated and redistributed at the end of the week. Teachers must be careful not to deny computer use to slow workers. However, when the computer becomes a true classroom resource, this is no longer a concern.

3.   Enforcing separate rules that apply to academic versus free-time use. There has been no conclusive evidence that computer games are useful or harmful activities. However, children need guidance on the use of their time during the school day. Computer games should not be outlawed, just controlled. If a teacher allows

twenty minutes of free in-school computer use each week, that might very likely not include games.

4. Setting clear priorities for computer use such as assignments first, programming second, free-choice academic software next, and games last. This set of priorities might also apply to recess and after-school use.

5. Changing the rules when more computers appear, such as when a child brings a computer from home. Should that child be able to use his or her own computer whenever he or she wishes? Probably not, but this is an interesting issue to discuss with the class.

Another area that needs to be taken into account when establishing procedural rules is individual differences among students. The two areas most affecting classroom computer use are general computer literacy and typing skills. There are still children who have never seen a computer and children who have grown up with several in their homes. For elementary students in self-contained rooms this is less of an issue and can be handled in a low-keyed way. These gaps can be closed by the teacher or a more knowledgeable student spending a few extra minutes with those beginning students each time a new skill is needed. Today it is the exceptional class that needs to spend a whole introductory unit on computers. There is no evidence to suggest elementary students have any problems learning to use a computer.

For middle school students the only differences might occur because of the preadolescent personality. At this age students who have no previous computer experience might become embarrassed and therefore more resistant to help. Out of shyness about asking questions, they might pretend not to be interested in the activity. This is probably truer of girls than boys, for girls at this age tend to turn away from things seen as male such as mathematics and science. The same strategy is recommended for these students as for the younger students, except perhaps a more carefully planned subtle intervention.

The second area in which individual differences are more striking in the computer environment than in other classroom activities is typing skills. Some schools remedy this by developing units to introduce these skills at an early age, spending as much as thirty classroom hours teaching keyboarding. Other schools ignore the whole issue and allow the students to pick up the skill at their own pace. Some schools take a middle stance and do some coaching, such as pointing out that the two halves of the keyboard can be more efficiently covered using two hands. Again, some interesting studies of early elementary students suggest that they are capable of acquiring excellent keyboarding skills. It is our belief that this is really a nonissue and does not deserve very much attention. Typing on a computer keyboard is much easier than on a conventional typewriter. Given the proper motivation, all students cope quite well with the task.

PLANNING AND EVALUATION

It makes good sense to want to know if you have accomplished what you set out to do. One of the major benefits of being concerned about evaluation is that it focuses on desired outcomes right from the beginning of planning a project. Planning and evaluation can be considered from two perspectives: that of the classroom teacher and that of the school, school system, or district. Let's first look at how a classroom teacher might think about planning and evaluating computer use in the classroom.

First, the desired outcomes must be stated. This is not as straightforward as it may seem. There are most likely short-term outcomes, intermediate outcomes, and long-term outcomes. It is easiest to decide first on long-term goals. For the classroom teacher a useful time line might be three years. One goal may be sufficient. For example:

> In three years computers will be used to improve and support learning to some extent in every subject taught in the self- contained classroom.

To be implementable, this long-term goal needs to be broken into immediate and then interim goals. It is useful to start by stating the current condition. This statement might be:

> Computers are currently used for drill-and-practice in mathematics, spelling, and social studies; simulations are used with one unit in social studies and one unit in science.

Next, first-year goals are stated:

> Use of databases will be included in one social studies unit; microcomputer-based laboratory tools will be included in two science units.

Second-year goals might include the following:

> The use of databases will be extended to all social studies and science units where appropriate; the microcomputer-based laboratory will be integrated into all appropriate science units; mathematics materials that use spreadsheets will be developed; and some programs in the music curriculum and graphic or drawing programs in art will be tried out.

Third-year goals might include:

> Integrating word processing into all classroom writing along with writing aids such as spelling checks and prewriting planners.

Word processing may be left for last because it requires more equipment to be effectively integrated into the self-contained classroom.

Having clearly stated the goals, the planner must decide how to measure outcomes. Some questions should be considered in order to decide what data are necessary to determine if goals are met.

1. From whom are the data being collected?
2. In what form does the final report need to be?
3. Who can collect data?
4. How much time and effort should be given to the evaluation process?

For the self-contained classroom, the data may be collected just for the use of the classroom teacher. However, the principal might be interested or request the results, as well as other teachers in the building or system, or even higher-level administrators. The formality of the final report is determined by who receives it. Let's lay out some data-collecting guidelines supposing a report is needed for the highest level administrator, or even the school committee or its equivalent. It is then easy to select just parts of the grand plan if a less formal report suffices.

Setting up a matrix, as shown in Table 2-1, helps focus in on what data is needed and who can supply it.

TABLE 2-1. Data Collection Matrix.

SOURCES OF DATA	KEY FEATURES Integrate Computers into				
	SOCIAL STUDIES	SCIENCE	MATHEMATICS	LANGUAGE ARTS	ART AND MUSIC
Classroom Teacher	anecdotal records		spreadsheets	pre/post computer compositions	notes
Students	check list	interviews	tests and logs	student papers	student work
Other Building Teachers					interviews
Principal			interviews		
Parents			questionnaire		

Once it is determined who can provide the information wanted for the evaluation, instruments and guidelines are developed. For example, the teacher might decide to keep informal anecdotal records daily and then write them up more thoroughly once a week. After taking notes for a few weeks, the teacher might find a checklist to be more useful. Such a list, completed each day for each student, might include:

1. Amount of interaction with other students while at computer:
   high----------medium----------low
2. Quality of work:
   high-----------usual-------------low
3. Interest in science (or other subject):
   high-----------medium----------low
4. Participation in class discussion:
   high-----------medium------------low

Looking at how effective spreadsheets are in improving mathematical learning, the teacher might keep only hard copies of each day's work. After several months, these hard copies might confirm or deny a trend towards greater use of spreadsheets in general problem-solving tasks. In language arts, several evaluative measures can be applied to student compositions. Such elements as fluency (word count), complex sentences (number of complex phrases, prepositions, conjunctions), paragraph transitions (rating good, fair, poor), and number of spelling and grammar mistakes can be recorded. In addition, determining the reading level of students' writing by using a computerized reading level program can be an effective way to measure changes in students' writing skills. For art and music, the key is student interest in the subject. The students can each be rated on a scale of 1 to 10 with 1 indicating boredom and 10 indicating total absorption. The ratings can be given before computer use begins, and then weekly or after each lesson.

For each item in the matrix in Table 2-1, the data-collection documents need to be created before the study begins. The different kinds of tools that might be useful include:

- tests
- questionnaires
- rating scales
- logs
- checklists
- interviews
- observations
- anecdotal records
- sociograms
- inventories

and anything else that gives the teacher a grasp on what is happening in the classroom.

It is important to recognize how difficult it is to teach and evaluate at the same time. Student teachers, graduate student assistants, or trained observers can greatly help the classroom teacher with evaluation tasks. Team teaching is another mechanism that can facilitate the evaluation process.

The data are then collected over the period of time specified, which should be long enough for change to occur but not so long that too much classroom time has been wasted on ineffective strategies. Let's say the time frame for the classroom teacher should be in the range of four to ten months. For a school building the time frame can be longer because students can be tracked over several years if they remain in the same school and program.

Once the data are collected, they need to be tabulated, analyzed, and summarized. Do not let this become an overwhelming task. If the information is not used in a timely fashion, the conclusions will become irrelevant. The usual tools such as statistics, graphs, and narratives can be implemented to report the conclusions. The major contribution of the data-collection and summary report are the recommendations made. These can go all the way from recommending additional data gathering, to more widespread implementation of computers, to discontinuing computers use with particular subjects or grade levels.

If the planning and evaluation concerns a school system computer program, it likely involves one or several schoolwide committees. Let's look at an approach to planning and evaluation taken by one school system (Kirtman). A large committee, composed of teachers, administrators, parents, school committee members, and community resource people, was divided into five subcommittees:

1. staff development
2. curriculum
3. community school partnerships
4. organization and management
5. hardware

Each subcommittee identified one or two *key results* and set a date for reaching them. The committee then listed *indicators of success*, also with dates. Next, the current condition related to the key result was stated; and finally, intermediate improvements were identified, with dates as well. The implementation of this plan occurred over three years after it was accepted by the superintendent and funded by the school committee.

As an example of a Key Result Plan, the staff development subcommittee submitted the following:

TABLE 2-2.   Key Result: A Staff Training Program in Computer Use in Effect (date)

CURRENT CONDITIONS	INTERMEDIATE IMPROVEMENTS	INDICATORS OF SUCCESS
There is no consistent program for computer training in the schools	A coordinator of computers and principals have established a consistent method for assessing current computer competencies. (date)	All schools have a computer-training program in operation that raises teachers' and administrators' competency in technology to an established level. (date)
Computer training is on a voluntary basis.	The assessment of staff and administrator's competencies is complete. (date)	
Competency levels in technology vary throughout the system.	A coordinator of computers, principals, and coordinators have established required computer competencies. (date)	
	Each principal submits plan to raise staff competencies to desired level. (date) Staff development in computers is compulsory. (date)	
	A plan is established to raise administrators, including coordinators, to required competency level. (date)	
	A plan to utilize external resources to facilitate plan is established. (date)	
	The coordinator of computers has submitted a budget that will provide for the necessary remaining staff training. (date)	

Such a Key Result Plan was written by each committee. Time frames for the varying results ranged from one to three years. As soon as the plan was accepted by the superintendent of schools and funded by the school committee, an advisory committee was set up to implement the plan and check for intermediate results and indicators of success. The "indicators of success" were extremely useful in helping the committee organize its goals and establish criteria for evaluating them. The only unanswered question is, Will the advisory committee have enough clout to implement the plan?

Perhaps, if there are enough people in the school system who understand the important elements involved in educational innovation.

Now that a variety of administrative issues generated by integrating computers into the classroom have been addressed, let's move on to the core of the subject: integrating computers into the academic areas of the elementary and middle school.

REFERENCES

BECKER, H.J. "The Second National U.S. School Uses of Microcomputers Survey." Paper presented at the World Conference on Computers in Education, Norfolk, Va, 1985.

HECK WILLIAM, JERRY JOHNSON, ROBERT KANSKY, DICK DENNIS. *Guidelines for Evaluating Computerized Instructional Materials*. Reston, Va: NCTM, 1984.

KIRTMAN, L.J. *Key Results Management*. Boston: Management Resource Group.

THREE
COMPUTERS AND
THE SOCIAL STUDIES

Two things can be said about social studies that generally bring agreement among educators: (1) The purpose of social studies in U.S. schools is to educate the future citizens of a democratic society; and (2) The majority of school-age children rank social studies as their least favorite subject (Shaughnessy and Haladyna). At any time within the last fifty years these statements have probably been valid. Let's accept the goal of social studies education as preparing the next generation to function in a democratic society and speculate on how to entice students into enjoying this pursuit.

A task force of the National Council for the Social Studies (NCSS) identified three goals to facilitate attaining this primary objective of democratic education. These goals are the acquisition of:

> **knowledge**—"facts, concepts, and generalizations that help students understand human affairs and the human condition";
> **democratic values and beliefs**—"values constitute the standards or criteria against which individual behavior or group behavior are judged. Beliefs represent commitments to these values";
> **skills**—"the ability to do something proficiently in repeated performances." (NCSS, pp. 251-52)

There is a diversity of opinions among educators with regard to each of these goals.

What body of knowledge provides students with the needed under-standings of the human condition? The NCSS suggests an expanding curriculum that begins with a study of self in the kindergarten and goes on to the family, the neighborhood, the local community, the country, and the regions of the world by the eighth grade. The knowledge base selected focuses on the traditional disciplines of history and geography, along with global studies and what might be characterized as social psychology (an understanding of people, cultures, and environments).

Controversy centers around two questions related to this knowledge base:

1. Should the precollege social studies curriculum be divided into the different discipline areas such as history, economics, and psychology as in the academic world?
2. Should social studies instruction focus on a particular predefined content, or should the process of acquiring knowledge be stressed?

Technology can support either a disciplined or an integrated approach to social studies content. However, a focus on the *process of inquiry* as it relates to acquiring knowledge is far more important than selecting particular content to teach. Technological advances are increasing the amount and value of information generally. Students need strategies for finding and interpreting information.

Considering values and beliefs as the responsibility of the social studies teacher, the task force identified two areas of importance: rights, freedoms, and responsibilities of the individual; and beliefs concerning societal conditions and governmental responsibilities (NCSS, p. 257). The issue raised by educators centers around choosing an indoctrination or an inquiry and critical-thinking teaching approach. Shermis and Barth point out that for fifty years social educators have been recommending in-doctrination. Students who study society's serious social and economic problems will, as adult citizens, be prepared to make decisions concerning these problems. The selection of certain problems, the presentation of a body of information, and the promotion of a set of values constitute the hidden agenda that should turn students into citizens who will ensure the continuation of democratic values.

However, the NCSS finds that, "youth who are most supportive of democratic principles are those who practice investigation of issues in an open-supportive environment in the classroom"(p. 257). This finding suggests an inquiry and critical-thinking approach. Technology can be used to support either style of teaching, but an inquiry approach, as illustrated in the examples throughout this chapter, leads to greater long-term objectivity.

The third goal identified by the task force is skill development. The particular skills pertinent to the social studies disciplines include acquiring information, organizing and using information, and understanding interpersonal relationships. Since the technological advances of the last twenty years relate primarily to the storing and processing of information, these skills can now *only* be taught effectively with the aid of computers and related technologies. Some exceptional software is now available for increasing students' interpersonal skills.

INTEGRATING COMPUTERS INTO THE SOCIAL STUDIES CURRICULUM

Using Commercial Software

Different types of software support different teaching styles and approaches to organizing a curriculum. Three software categories that apply to the social studies are: *tutorials, simulations,* and *tools. Tutorials* range from simple drill-and-practice of facts to sophisticated instructional programs. *Simulations* create environments that support the asking of *what if* questions. Simulations are often presented as games; the class is divided into teams and the simulation ends when there is a winning team. *Tools* are more open-ended programs that allow the user greater flexibility in shaping the end product. Tools may be used by a range of age groups for many purposes. Often the same tool package used at home or in the office is appropriate for the classroom. These characteristics of tool software contribute to making tools the current most powerful software available.

Tutorials. Tutorials offer the least diversity among these categories because they focus on content, not on process. Tutorials most closely reflect the philosophy that there is an identifiable body of knowledge that is appropriate to teach. Most teachers, if asked, can identify some set of knowledge that all students should know before going on to high school. In this case, a tutorial covering that knowledge is an excellent teaching aid. A well-designed tutorial is interesting to the user, ensures the acquisition of the particular knowledge, and frees the teacher for more creative projects. While no currently available social studies tutorial is exemplary, it is well within the technology to develop such materials. The cost and the small market are among the reasons for the lack of such software.

Currently on the market is a host of specifically focused programs, mostly at the drill-and-practice level, that can meet individual students' needs at specific times. Some children like sitting at a computer and mastering the location of each state in the United States and its capital. This type of activity provides a sense of security for children because it is a well-defined task that can ensure academic success. Further, states and capitals is a knowledge area that might be defined as important for every child to know—something akin to arithmetic facts. For whatever reason, tutorial programs can be useful and appropriate in the social studies curriculum. However, there are not enough currently on the market that justify the cost, or even classroom space, of a computer.

Simulations. Simulations are the most abundant kind of software in the social studies. Simulations also hold more promise as teaching aids than tutorials because they are far more flexible. One of the earliest social studies simulations, the *Sell Series (Sell Apples, Sell Plants, Sell Lemonade,* and *Sell Bicycles),* is still an example of worthwhile educational material. The objective of the *Sell* simulations is to introduce elementary and middle school children to economic concepts such as best price, cost, profit, and the impact of advertising. The series increases in complexity as additional economic concepts are introduced, and each simulation game builds on the previous one. The series requires only one computer per class and can be played over several sessions, providing the teacher with the ability for flexible scheduling. The initial software, produced by MECC (see Resource Section), allowed the teacher access to the program listing so that parameters could be changed, preventing the game from being too deterministic after multiple plays. More recent versions have *locked* listings because of the disk-copying problem, making changes impossible.

Another series of simulations, now considered classic, is the *Search Series,* published by McGraw-Hill. There are six simulation games designed for middle school use. Several games may be integrated into social studies, especially *Geography Search, Community Search,* and *Archaeology Search.* The simulations create reasonably accurate environments and, in addition, emphasize the importance of team work. In *Community Search,* for example, the class is divided into four groups, each playing the role of a prehistoric community searching for a new homeland. The simulation can be run over the course of several weeks in conjunction with the study of a similar time period. The simulations have also been used effectively to build cooperation and group work within the classroom. Information needed for decision making is displayed just briefly on the screen. This strategy quickly illustrates the team's need to divide the task of gathering and sharing information. Academic skills, such as note taking and organizing information, are strengthened during game play. Since these simulations draw upon skills other than purely academic ones, they can be very useful for involving scholastically weaker students.

One of the newest and technologically most advanced simulations is *The Other Side,* published by Tom Snyder Productions, Inc. "*The Other Side* is a simulation game that creates a tense world of limited resources in which two nations work together toward a common goal while each must separately maintain its own economy" (Tom Snyder Productions, Inc., p. 4). The goal is for each team to work on building a bridge, brick by brick, to connect the two theoretical countries. Several different events can prematurely end the game, such as one country running out of resources or being blown up.

The game is technologically advanced in that each of the two teams uses its own computer, and the two computers are connected either with wires or, over a greater distance, by a modem. The decision of one team therefore impacts the options of the other team, making each play of the simulation unique. Because each team is composed of three to four players, it is not as simple to use in the classroom as a simulation that involves an entire class at once. It can, however, be an excellent enrichment activity or an activity for an unstructured time block. It may also be played with one computer. The most powerful educational aspect of the game is the postgame review. If a social studies unit includes objectives such as understanding conflict, trust, honesty, the subtleties of politics, or the impact of limited resources, this game gives students first-hand involvement with these abstract notions. Moreover, the game may be played over and over again to test different theories and strategies, each game being quite different from previous ones.

Computer Tools

Computer tools, the third type of social studies software, include general tools such as word processing and database application packages as well as special-purpose tools such as survey takers. Word processing as an aid to writing is discussed in Chapter 4. Writing is a dominant part of the social studies curriculum as well.

Word processing.   Word processing can be used in several different ways during the social studies class. At a simple level, the teacher might use a computer and large screen to introduce a new unit of study. If, for example, the next unit is local town government, the teacher can brainstorm with the students to reveal their assumptions about the functions of local government. As the students volunteer ideas, these are recorded on the computer, using a word-processing package. The following list might be generated by a middle school class:

> collect garbage
> run schools
> run elections
> set tax rate
> pay mayor and selectmen
> provide water to people in the town
> repair sidewalks
> repair roads

provide electricity
provide police and fire personnel
plow snow
provide gas
pay teachers
give building permits
hire town workers
decide on town rules and regulations
run library

The list might then be printed out for each child to study or printed on Thermofax paper and duplicated for the class. During the next lesson, the list can be organized into categories such as:

Provide general services
    collect garbage
    repair sidewalks
    repair roads
    provide electricity
    provide police and fire personnel
    plow snow
    provide gas
    hire town workers
Provide educational services
    run schools
    pay teachers
    run library
Determine town rules and regulations
    run elections
    give building permits
    set tax rate

Questions are then formed for each category such as, Who decides which services the town shall provide? Does the town provide gas and electricity? How does the town provide water? What are our town's rules and regulations and why do we need them?

Work committees are formed, the membership of each is added to the information saved by the computer. Printed copies of the categories, questions raised, and work committees are then distributed to the students. This record is readily available when changes need to be made. Should an important segment of town activities be missed during the initial brainstorming session, the teacher can load in this file at any time and review the list with the class, immediately generating a revised version with additional questions and guidelines. This eliminates the lost or unreadable notes fairly common to middle school children.

Word processing can then be used to organize each committee's report. Working together at the computer, the committee generates a detailed outline for their report. Each committee member chooses a part of the outline to research and write up. As reports are written, duplicate copies of the report disk are made, allowing each person to revise or comment on the work of his or her peers until a final report is agreed upon. This process of facilitating joint authoring, in fact, duplicates writing practices in the adult world.

Database software.   Database packages are another general-purpose tool that people are finding increasingly useful as they discover more and more applications. This is also true in the classroom. Growing experience with computerized databases makes educators appreciate the tremendous flexibility of this tool. Currently, databases may be divided into three categories:

- self-created databases
- databases that are purchased on disk and may or may not be changed
- commercially available databases that are "on-line" and cannot be changed

To get a feeling for what databases are all about, let's first look at a self-created one. The best way to appreciate computerized record keeping is to use it for something that makes a personal task easier. For example, creating a database to record ongoing expenditures such as business expenses, charitable contributions, and home office expenses, quickly illustrates the power of databases to eliminate the April tax panic. Storing tax-deductible expenses on a database is almost the same as dropping into file folders the motley collection of paper that makes up a person's expense record. The same categories are useful for the database as for the file folders. In addition to organizing charity and business expenses, a database can also handle all the other kinds of information needed at tax time. For example, the record for tax-deductible expenses might include:

Category: [same as file folder]
Purpose of expenditure:
Date:
Amount:
Check number:
Slip number:
Review?:

When report time comes, the computer can separate out those expenditures you were not sure about deducting for a second review, sort your expenditures by the categories needed for the income tax report, total each category, and provide a record of expenditures for future reference. The database can be searched for the record of any of these items. If you forget whether you made a contribution to your favorite charity this year, you can get the information from the database within seconds.

Doing a task such as an expenditure database gives the teacher some preclass experience that he or she can refer to when introducing the tool to students.

The first class introduction of databases should focus on a well-understood and interesting topic such as student characteristics or school athletic records. When beginning to create a database, the teacher should discuss the following questions:

Why do we want to keep information on this topic?

What information might we like to get from the database?

How flexible does the database software need to be? Might we want to add information at a later time? Do we want to obtain computed information? Are reports needed in a certain form?

A class database can provide information about class members that can be useful when planning for a party, working on joint assignments, selecting birthday gifts, or planning weekend activities. As students talk about the kind of information they want, they see the need for a different record for each student. The class then determines what specific information about each student it might like to know. The students decide on the following topics (or fields):

Name _____

Address _____

Telephone number _____

Birthday _____

Favorite food(s) _____
_____

Favorite kind of music _____
_____

Favorite sport(s) _____
_____

Favorite kinds of books _____
_____

```
Traveled to _____

_____

Close friends and relatives living in other
places _____

_____

Hobbies _____

_____

Other favorite activities _____

_____
```

Each student then fills out one record.

After all records are complete, the database can be used to select food for the next party, send happy birthday wishes, make vacation plans by searching for people with relatives in a particular city, and create after-school hobby clubs. As we shall see, establishing a database focusing on personal information can serve as a catalyst for important discussions on ethical issues created by technology.

Using databases to study folktales.   Starting with a subject that everyone understands allows the class to focus on the new concept of electronic data. Once the idea of databases is understood, the teacher can then move on to using the tool with less familiar material. One resource appropriate for use in social studies is folktales. Nelli suggests that folktales can make students aware of how people deal with the unknown; folktales also enable students to see the universality of emotions such as love, fear, and joy. Folktales are studied by anthropologists for cultural characteristics such as high need for achievement. What role might databases play in tapping this resource?

Such a project might start with the teacher reading orally four or five folktales to the class to get a feeling for the kind of information these stories provide. The next step is to try to determine the contents of each record. This requires selecting a set of topics or fields around which to organize the information. A class brainstorming session is useful for accomplishing this. One such attempt included creating a record for each folktale containing the following topics or fields:

```
Name of story _____
Author or editor _____
Country or region _____
Main characteristics of country or region __

_____

Main character _____
```

Character description _____

_____

Other characters _____
Lessons taught _____

_____

Beliefs expressed _____

_____

Explanation of unknown _____
How basic needs are provided _____

_____

Kind of society _____
Information about humans _____

_____

Economic conditions _____
Role of magic _____

After the categories have been set up on the computer, the students enter information from the stories read together and then from a few additional stories read individually. One aspect of folktales that facilitates the involvement of the whole class is that they are generally short and easy to read. After a reasonable number of records has been created, say twenty, the students can try sorting and searching the database to see if it helps them learn about the people under study. The students might sort the database by country or region to see if they have a wide enough distribution of folktales. If they find only one folktale from Australia, for example, the class can decide to drop that country from their study. If the class is interested in how all-pervasive fear is, they can search the database for every occurrence of that word.

At this point the class can decide whether:

using a database is more effort than it is worth;
some categories or fields are useless and should be eliminated;
some categories need more space;
some additional categories should be added;
for some fields a yes or no answer makes sorting easier and so should be indicated on that field.

In the database the class decides to eliminate the categories "country description," "how basic needs are provided," and "economic conditions" because most of the folktales did not provide this information. A new topic or field, "emotions shown," is added. In addition, some fields are lengthened while others are shortened. The class then continues to add to the database. Such a collection of information is unlikely ever to be finished, so the class might agree on some goal in terms either of number of stories to read or number of weeks to spend. Goal setting such as this can lead to interesting discussions such as, What number of folktales needs to be included to make drawing conclusions from the data justifiable? (a common scientific quandary).

This folktale database used in this example includes ten stories from Africa, ten from Ireland, nine from the Antilles (the Caribbean), and nine from Greece. The first question asked relates to the importance of magic. Figure 3-1 indicates that magic was incorporated into seven of the ten Irish folktales but only four Greek ones, two African ones, and two from the Antilles. Why might this be? Do we need to read additional Irish folktales to see if magic persists? Do Irish people today incorporate magic into their writings? If we looked at folktales from the Eastern Hemisphere, would we find magic to be an important element? Ireland is described in this set of folktales as a feudal society, while the other folktales seem to come primarily from agricultural societies or monarchies. Does this provide any clues about the importance of magic?

FIGURE 3-1. *AppleWorks* report on "Kind of Society" and "Role of Magic."

```
Report: folk.two
Selection: Kind of Society is not blank
   or      Role of Magic is not blank
Country or Region      Kind of Society          Role of Magic
--------------------   ----------------------   ----------------------------
Kenya, Africa          agricultural             yes, facilitated story
Nairobi, Africa        agricultural
Kenya                  agricultural
Kikuyu, Africa         believes in taboos
Kenya, Africa                                   yes, all-important
Ireland                                         yes, used for revenge
Ireland                monarchy                 yes, small role
Ireland                feudal
Ireland                feudal
Ireland                feudal                   yes, all important
Ireland                feudal                   yes, all important
Ireland                feudal                   yes, aids heroin
Ireland                feudal                   yes, people underwater
Ireland                feudal
Ireland                feudal                   yes, whole story depende
Antilles               monarchy                 yes, in life length
Antilles                                        yes, wishes granted
Antilles               monarchy
Antilles               monarchy
Antilles               monarchy
Greece                                          yes-very important
Greece                 monarchy
Greece                 monarchy                 yes, important
Greece                 monarchy                 yes, magic bird
Greece                 agricultural
Greece                 monarchy
Greece                 city                     yes, magic demons
```

Another search revealed that none of the Greek folktales has animals as its main character because Greece did not appear in the search to find all records that contain "animal" (see Figure 3-2). What might this suggest about the Greeks? Do most Greek people live in cities rather than in the country? Does farming as a way of life have less value in Greece than in Africa, where seven of the ten folktales have animals as characters?

Looking at the "emotions shown" category, and separating out the following groups of emotions, Figure 3-3 was generated.

What might be said about the universality of emotions from the information given in Figure 3-3? Anger, fear, and panic seem to show up in all the regions in the database. The same can be said of love and kindness, even though the numbers are not as high. But what might be said about happiness, which does not appear in any of the Antilles folktales read, or unhappiness, which does not appear in any of the Irish folktales? What about hunger, which appears only in African folktales? Might folktales draw attention to a persistent regional problem?

Further insights into characteristics of regions of the world might be drawn from the way folktale collections are made. For this study four collections were used. Two were collections of individual countries, Ireland and Greece, while the other two were from geographic regions, the Antilles and Africa. Might this suggest something about the kinds of identities people form and the strength of these identities? Why does this happen? Might it have anything to do with the occurrence of a country's boundaries being close to a cultural group's traditional living space? Could this information help students understand a cause of conflict?

The value of database programs in the social studies. Why are databases useful tools in the social studies? How do they improve the academic quality of the classroom, facilitate teaching, and increase students' interest

FIGURE 3-2. *AppleWorks* search for "Animals."

```
Report: folk.two
Selection: Main Character contains ANIMAL
    or     Other Characters contains ANIMAL
Country or Region        Main Character                    Other Characters
-----------------        --------------------------------  ------------------
Africa                   animal, Fisi, a hyena             animal, Lioness
Nairobi, Africa          animals, chickens, hawks          human-like
Africa                   animal, Tortoise                  animal, Lizard
Kenya                    animal, Hare                      Widow
Africa                   animal, Fisi, the hyena           animals
Kenya, Africa            woman                             animals, lizards
Kenya, Africa            animal, spider
Ireland                  Jack                              animals
Ireland                  animal, pooka(ass)                scullery boy
Antilles                 animals-rabbit, tiger             animal, fox
Antilles                 God                               animal, rabbit
```

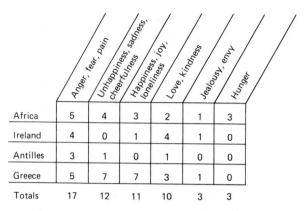

	Anger, fear, pain	Unhappiness, sadness, cheerfulness	Happiness, joy, loneliness	Love, kindness	Jealousy, envy	Hunger
Africa	5	4	3	2	1	3
Ireland	4	0	1	4	1	0
Antilles	3	1	0	1	0	0
Greece	5	7	7	3	1	0
Totals	17	12	11	10	3	3

FIGURE 3-3. "Emotions" mentioned in folktales.

and enthusiasm in this subject area? Teachers who have tried this tool have observed that databases:

1. are a catalyst for more in-depth discussions;
2. help students organize large amounts of information;
3. support an inquiry approach to teaching, giving students firsthand experience with the scientific process of developing hypotheses, collecting data, drawing conclusions, and rejecting, restating, or confirming their hypotheses;
4. vividly demonstrate that there are rarely single, simple answers to real world problems; and
5. give students firsthand experience with organizing and using information, thus making them more intelligent consumers of other people's data.

Referring again to the folktales database, how might the activity of creating that database with a class lead to *more meaningful social studies discussions?* Let's look at a class using folktales for cultural insights without creating a database. The class reads together or is assigned a number of folktales from the region currently being studied. The teacher then leads a discussion or asks the class to write essays on what they have learned about the beliefs and culture of the region. Newsprint or blackboard charts are developed to organize the data collected. These charts are temporary and difficult to change.

What, then, is different about a discussion based on information organized with the aid of a computer? For one thing, the number of stories from which conclusions are drawn is more obvious, making the validity of the conclusions based on that particular number of stories an important consideration. The class immediately struggles with a difficult but real social science problem: the validity of generalizations. Because it is possible to access a reasonable percentage of written folktales from a particular region and easy to add information to a computerized database, students can develop confidence in their ability to draw meaningful conclusions. The class, at the end of the study, can state:

- the understandings for which they have a high degree of confidence, based on the fact that there is evidence of that cultural trait in a high percentage of the folktales;
- the understandings that are on more shaky ground and for which they would need to do more research to confirm or reject; and
- those cultural traits that appear only in a small number of folktales and that the students can, with reasonable confidence, reject as representative of the region.

Thus in analyzing these folktales, the class has done original social science research using the latest social science tools.

How does using database software help the class *organize large amounts of data?* In some ways, a very disciplined researcher using file cards can as effectively record large amounts of data. The value of having the data on a computer comes when the researcher is ready to organize the data into meaningful information. Hand shuffling through file cards each time students wish to know how many times a particular incident occurs is a dull, time-consuming task. Searching and sorting electronically through a database, even one with a large number of records, takes but a few seconds. This encourages asking unlimited questions about the data, stimulating far more original thinking than a hand sort.

Databases *support an inquiry approach* to teaching the social studies for several reasons. Perhaps the most important is the flexibility of a good software package. For example, when a group first thinks about a problem, they usually do not have an exact sense of the information they need. The hypotheses developed in the inquiry approach to teaching require continuous modification. The whole inquiry cycle of hypotheses generation, data collection, testing hypotheses based on data, and drawing conclusions is iterative and constantly modified. Without flexible tools this modification process is tedious and certainly not one approached with a sense of joy by elementary and middle school children. However, a well-designed database software package makes certain aspects of this modification process simple. When students wish to add or delete a category, they can do it instantaneously. However, if a new category is added, there are still no shortcuts to collecting and entering the data for that category. But as the inquiry cycle proceeds and the validity or nonvalidity of hypotheses becomes clearer, there *is* an excitement generated about this process that makes it seem worthwhile to go back to the source of data for a second or third look.

The often-repeated idea that there are no *simple, single answers to real problems* is difficult to get across to students at this age. Most of them are not interested in transferring the learning from one social studies unit to the next. Their ability to synthesize is limited. These limits are due both to the way social studies is traditionally taught and to the students' level of cognitive development. Over the last fifty or so years learning theorists have said over and over that students need to be active participants in the learning process in order to become high-level, sophisticated thinkers.

During the folktales study one of the students noticed that God was mentioned only twice in the nineteen European folktales read. Remembering back to her study of the Middle Ages and the explanation given for why people at that time devoted their whole lives to building massive cathedrals, she suggested that perhaps folktales were used to explain things and fill needs not dealt with adequately by religion. For a sixth-grader to notice this was quite impressive. When the class began discussing how they might pursue this idea, they soon became aware of the complexity of the issue. The class concluded that to discuss this hypothesis further they would want to study at least one religion in depth. Since this was clearly a large project not previously scheduled into the year's social studies curriculum, the teacher suggested they keep this question in mind as they each study their own religion and perhaps try to interest their religious leaders in discussing it. Almost every question raised while working with the database could not be answered absolutely. This did not bother the class at all; rather, it kept them reading folktales and thinking about the issues long after the unit ended.

Giving students a *firsthand experience organizing and using a database* is probably more important for their adult life than their current needs. First, commercial databases are still expensive to use, often narrowly focused, still difficult for the lay person to access, and often boring to use unless the person is highly motivated. However, current trends suggest that in ten years or so, such databases will be readily accessible to large numbers of people at a reasonable cost. However, only by thinking about the information needed and structuring the database by selecting the fields, determining their length, and deciding how many records to complete do students understand how people-dependent the whole process is. Further, the experience of collecting and inputting data makes students realize how easy it is to enter erroneous information. The creation and use of a database in the classroom should give students a basis for evaluating the databases they might use as adults.

Concerns for the teacher.   There are areas of concern for the teacher who is considering using databases. The first several uses require a great deal of time and energy. The teacher must first select the software, then build up a minimum level of expertise in using it. As mentioned earlier, the easiest way to do this is to create a database for personal use. On a catch-as-catch-can basis this also takes time. Using a database effectively in an inquiry-oriented classroom requires a confident, enthusiastic teacher who has instituted well-established classroom management techniques. The inquiry approach to social studies, which databases so beautifully support, is a far more sophisticated teaching strategy than taking a textbook and proceeding chapter by chapter through the year.

It is, however, quite possible to use databases in a mundane way. A teacher might, for example, build a database of the U. S. presidents, their years in office, the states from which they come, their first ladies, and their parties. Such questions as, Which state produced the most presidents? and Who did not have a wife as first lady? can readily be asked, if a teacher is trapped at the knowledge level of teaching. In some ways databases make it easier to fall into this trap. It is still the teacher's role and responsibility to raise the level of class discussions and thinking. For example, in referring to a database on presidents and their parties, a class could look for possible connections between party-in-power, economic conditions, political conditions, population density, and party platforms. Using databases by no means ensures that this will happen. Using computers in the classroom clearly puts more demands on the teacher—*at first*. The *rewards*, however, do come in the form of improved student performance and more authentic academic classroom activities.

Choosing database software.   As a classroom teacher, how do you know which database software package to use with your class? The answer probably is whichever one your school has purchased. Suppose the decision is left to you, however. How do you choose? Some general guidelines can serve to start off the search. Trying out a few different packages until you find one with which you are comfortable is probably the best advice. *AppleWorks* was the package used for the folktale database and is popular with schools using Apple computers. Some software packages such as *Friendly Filer* and *Bank Street Filer* have been developed with students in mind. It is more practical to select a software package that students can use for several years. General guidelines for choosing a database package include:

1. *Ease of use:* How many different keystrokes is it necessary to master for minimal use? How clear is the manual? How clear are the menus and are they all easy to access?

2. *Flexibility:* Does the user have control over the length and number of fields within each record? Can data from different disks be combined into one database? Is it easy to add, change, and delete fields and records?

3. *Sorting and searching:* Can this be done by using either numbers or letters? If you ask the database to sort based on country size, does a country with 324,521 square miles come out larger than one with 1,205,000 square miles because 3 is larger than 1 and a 0 needs to be added to the left of the 3 for the sort to work correctly?

4. *Computational ability:* Can some simple arithmetic, like totaling one field from all the records, be done? Can an average be found?

5. *Printing:* Are the instructions for producing printed copy reasonable to follow? Are reports with different configurations easy to specify?

6. *Graphic capabilities:* Can information be requested in the form of graphs for easy visual comparisons?

As the teacher becomes familiar with using databases, he or she will find additional requirements based on his or her own teaching style and type of classroom.

Published database software.   Creating databases with students is the first step toward developing the concept of electronically stored information. However, students cannot be expected to have the time or devotion to create databases as aids to all their topics of study. As is common in the adult world, students need to also use databases created by others. Scholastic and HRM Software are the first school publishing houses to market, on disk, databases for use in the precollege setting. Scholastic is currently offering four different databases on the topics of: United States history, United States government, physical science, and life science. These are excellent resources for middle and high school students. The particular strength of these materials is that the teacher and students can add to or change the information on the disks. These packages require the use of another database package called *PFS:File* (Software Publishing Company). HRM Software is offering *Social Studies Fact Finder,* which includes a Starter Pack that introduces students to *PFS:File,* a States Pack that includes information about the fifty states, and a Working American Pack with profiles of twentieth-century Americans at work.

A new development in the area of databases is called CD-ROM (standing for *C*ompact *D*isk–*R*ead *O*nly *M*emory, because information may only be read off the disk not recorded on it). A CD-ROM looks exactly like an audio compact disk. Grolier Electronic Publishing has stored on such a disk their entire *Academic American Encyclopedia* containing over 30,000 articles. This information takes up less than half of the disk, which has the capacity to store 550 million bits of information. An equivalent amount of information would fill 1,500 floppy diskettes.

The encyclopedia can be searched by any word or combination of words; the search software is extremely easy to use and is provided on a floppy disk (see Figure 3–4). Accessing information on the CD-ROM requires a special disk drive that attaches to an ordinary personal computer. The whole package, including the special disk drive, interface card and cable for the computer, disk containing the encyclopedia, and search

FIGURE 3-4. A computer, CD-ROM drive, and a menu from Grolier's *Electronic Encyclopedia.*

software, can be purchased for around $1,000. Once the hardware has been purchased, the cost of each additional information disk is around $200.

Imagine the classroom implications of this technology. From a shelf storage perspective, every classroom could theoretically contain all the written knowledge possibly needed by the student or teacher for any course for a year. The costs might prevent such a collection, but the ease of accessing information should make the budgeting for such purchases very enticing. In addition to locating information within a fraction of a second, the user can store selected information on floppy disks and then incorporate it into a document by means of an ordinary word processor. This is a technology worth watching closely. Both its commercial and educational applications have not begun to be explored.

An interesting piece of software, *Historian,* combines a database with a simulation. The goal of this software is to provide United States history students with an experience akin to that of practicing historians. The software poses nine unresolved questions in United States History such as, Why did the Spaniards avoid establishing settlements along the coast of California for two hundred years on their trips to Mexico? and Why did the United States become involved in the Vietnam War? The teacher introduces the class to the particular question. Then, working in teams, the students develop a hypothesis and enter it into the computer. The team may then choose to read, as evidence to support or reject their hypothesis, one of three original sources from the software's database. After each round at the computer the team decides to either stay with their hypothesis, request more data, or change their hypothesis. This simulation continues over several sessions, until one team convinces the class, based on the data uncovered, that their hypothesis is the most justifiable. The teacher plays a critical role in this process by facilitating a research environment and preventing teams from becoming trapped in dead-end research directions. The liveliness generated by the interaction of the teams with the computer and the teacher adds a welcome dimension to United States history classes.

Surveys.   Surveys are a favorite activity with elementary and middle school students and are often used in social studies research. *Survey Taker* (Scholastic) is a computer-based aid for collecting data that uses this technique. The software is simple enough to use with any school-age child, with different degrees of teacher help.

A fifth-grade class studying local town government decided to take a survey of the people's feelings about the quality of town services. Class members created the survey, typing into the computer the questions as they agreed upon them. The class wrote twenty questions and then decided to pilot their questionnaire with another fifth-grade class to see if the questions were clear and sensible. They had each person from the other fifth-grade class come in and answer the questions on the computer. Once the pilot was completed, the results of the survey were immediately available because all questions had been answered directly on the computer. The pilot suggested that there were too many questions. Most of the students got bored toward the end and said some of the questions were repetitious. Based on this pilot, the class rewrote some questions, cutting the total number to fifteen.

Initially the class intended to have students give the survey to some of their neighbors. They realized that this would then require someone to enter all the written answers into the computer afterwards. One student had a brainstorm. Why not give the survey during parents' night, when they were planning to demonstrate their computer activities anyway? This way each visitor could enter his or her answers into the computer directly. One student mentioned that several parents worked for the town. Would this bias the way they felt about the quality of the town's services? Fortunately, the software allows the user to separate the survey takers into two groups, as well as look at the results of the total group. The class decided to separate town employees from nonemployees.

During parents' night the class was able to get twenty-two people to answer their survey. One of the questions was:

```
Is the police force
        A. Inadequate
        B. Somewhat adequate
        C. Adequate
        D. Excellent
```

The next day in class, the computer displayed the outcome of the survey in two ways for each question: (1) a table for each answer, separated into town employees, nonemployees (town citizens), and totals (see Figure 3-5); and (2) the same data displayed as a bar graph (Figure 3-6). What was particularly exciting to the class was that their hunch about the difference of opinion between town employees and nonemployees turned out to be accurate. The survey consistently showed the town employees rating the town services higher than did the nonemployees. A second interesting disclosure was made by question 14 of the survey:

```
Which additional service would you most like the town
to provide?
        A. Town transportation
        B. Meals for shut-ins
        C. Library to loan computers
        D. Open access to town dump
        E. Organized sports activities
```

FIGURE 3-5. Table produced by *Survey Taker*.

```
TABLE   QUESTION 3

IS THE POLICE FORCE

Group 1: TOWN CITIZENS

          A    B    C    D    Total
Number    1    2    8    4     15
Percent   6   13   53   26    100

Group 2: TOWN EMPLOYEES

          A    B    C    D    Total
Number    0    0    2    5      7
Percent   0    0   28   71    100

Total of Groups 1 and 2

          A    B    C    D    Total
Number    1    2   10    9     22
Percent   4    9   45   40    100
```

```
BAR GRAPH   QUESTION 3

IS THE POLICE FORCE

100%
 95
 90
 85
 80
 75
 70                  ∂
 65                  ∂
 60                  ∂
 55                  ∂
 50          *       ∂
 45          * #     ∂
 40          * #    ∂#
 35          * #    ∂#
 30          * #    ∂#
 25          *∂#   *∂#
 20          *∂#   *∂#
 15          *∂#   *∂#
 10      *   *∂#   *∂#
  5  *   * # *∂#   *∂#
  0  * # * # *∂#   *∂#
     A   B   C   D

Group 1:  *   TOWN CITIZENS
Group 2:  ∂   TOWN EMPLOYEES
Total  :  #
```

FIGURE 3-6.   Graph produced by *Survey Taker.*

When discussing the survey before parents' night, the class had thought that either "library to loan computers" or "organized sports activities" would be the most popular choices. As Figure 3-7 shows, the almost unanimous choice was "town transportation."

The class decided to take this on as a project and spent the next few months finding out all they could about the pros and cons of providing town transportation. They interviewed commercial transportation companies, neighboring towns that had public transportation, and the town aldermen to see if they had ever discussed the issue or might in the near future. One of the parents helped the class figure out alternate funding possibilities using spreadsheet software on the class computer (see Chapter 5). Because the students had designed and conducted the survey, they felt that *they* had discovered this town need and therefore felt that they "owned" the problem. The class was solving a problem with the help of social science skills and techniques just as adults do. Best of all, perhaps, the teacher did not have to create an artificial problem-solving environment.

ETHICAL ISSUES RELATED TO TECHNOLOGY

Two ethical areas are generally mentioned in most discussions about the impact of technology on society: equal access to new technology and the

BAR GRAPH QUESTION 14

WHICH ADDITIONAL SERVICE WOULD YOU
MOST LIKE THE TOWN TO PROVIDE?

```
100%
 95
 90
 85     ⊋
 80     ⊋
 75     ⊋#
 70   *⊋#
 65   *⊋#
 60   *⊋#
 55   *⊋#
 50   *⊋#
 45   *⊋#
 40   *⊋#
 35   *⊋#
 30   *⊋#
 25   *⊋#
 20   *⊋#
 15   *⊋#
 10   *⊋#
  5   *⊋# *        *    *
  0   *⊋# * #    * # * #
       A   B   C   D   E

Group 1: *   TOWN CITIZENS
Group 2: ⊋   TOWN EMPLOYEES
Total  : #
```

FIGURE 3-7. Additional services desired of town.

misuse of electronic information. When computers first entered public schools, most people predicted they would be a male domain because of several initial observations. First, computers were usually introduced by mathematics teachers (predominantly male), very bright math students (predominantly male), or parents working in the high-technology sector (predominantly male). Second, computers were not initially an integrated part of the curriculum but rather an extra for those who had time. The main activities in the early days were game playing and programming, which clearly appealed more to boys than girls. Finally, the first home computers were generally bought for male children, even if they were younger than their female siblings.

These initial observations were generally correct; most teachers reported that boys had more interest in computers than did girls. However, because of people's sensitivity to issues of sexual stereotyping, an effort was made by both parents and teachers to correct this situation. According to a study done by Henry Becker in 1985, this trend is reversing. Becker, in his initial data analysis, reports that there is more or less equal use of computers now by both sexes. He does find, however, that unstructured (before- and after-school) time is still dominated by males, but not instructional time. Apparently the "old boy" network now begins in the computer room. This, however, might be as much due to adolescent needs as to computers.

A second concern is socioeconomic equality. The initial fear was that because of the cost of computers children from low socioeconomic groups would lose out both at home and at school. Parents of these children could not afford a computer, even if they saw its educational benefits. The schools these children attend had the most severe budgetary problems and therefore would put computers at the bottom of their priority list. In addition, what computers were available in poorer schools would un-doubtedly be used only for drill-and-practice and not for problem solving or creative thinking, thus imposing even greater handicaps on these students as they grew up.

Some interesting observations can now be made regarding these concerns. First, all schools are buying some computers. While the ratio of computers to students is higher in the more wealthy schools, many inner-city schools have received large donations from computer manufac-turers. These companies see urban schoolchildren as the future workforce and therefore as their primary future market. Similar happenings are occurring with software. The inner-city schools are often chosen as pilot and demonstration sites. The differences in resources available are probably not as extreme as many people feared.

Looking at how computers are used in schools, the differences between richer and poorer schools are not as great as initially predicted either. According to Becker's survey, all schools are primarily using their computers for instruction and teaching programming, with word process-ing and problem solving very much in the minority. The schools that are getting the least educational value out of their computers seem to be those that fall into the average range, both in resources and size.

The second major ethical question that has arisen with the spread of technology is the use and misuse of electronic information. Is information created and maintained for a computer environment subject to the same copyright laws as printed information? When is it illegal to copy a disk? Can a student copy one of his or her disks and give it to a friend or donate it to the school? Can a teacher make several copies of a word-processing program so that the whole class can use it at the same time? The answers to these last three questions seem to be clearly *no*. In spite of this, such situations arise continually. Teachers and schools must therefore take the responsibility for acting within the law.

Other questions have less clear answers. Is information that is transmit-ted from one computer to another personal property? Should stolen or vandalized information be considered subject to the same laws as stolen property? Should electronic information be protected as free speech? Should it be subject to the same protections as telephone conversations (against wiretapping) or the mails (against interception)? It will take many years and many legal actions to establish the necessary precedents to clarify these issues. In the meantime, the public is continuously being informed of unethical, if not clearly illegal, misuses of computer-based information; and the culprits are often teenage hackers. It is appropriate that the social studies curriculum should try to integrate the study of these issues.

CONCLUSION

We are now at a plateau in implementing educational technology. The revolution is over and the next steps are still very hazy. Computers are in the schools and most people agree they won't go away. They may, however, stay in the closet for a while longer or be used primarily to deliver factual knowledge to students. Social studies is one of the curriculum areas in which tools such as databases and word processing are available and inexpensive, and can add important dimensions to the teaching-learning process. It takes a long time for a novice to feel comfortable using these tools. It even takes a long time for an experienced computer user to master a new tool. Patience and conviction are the two most important elements for bringing about exciting and meaningful curriculum change. Teachers cannot minimize the effort such change requires. The authors, however, believe the effort will produce exciting pedagogical results that will make teaching far more satisfying than it has been for many years.

It is imperative to look continuously to the future. There are new technologies available that have interesting educational possibilities. Videodiscs and telecommunications perhaps have the greatest potential. Videodiscs are recordlike objects that can store very large amounts of information—both text and still and motion pictures. Think of them as a book in motion. Combined with a computer as the controlling device, videodiscs can deliver all sorts of lessons and allow for a very different dimension in research. Databases on videodiscs allow such things as art or archaeological treasures to be examined, searched, and sorted almost instantaneously. One such project is being done by a faculty member at Simmons College in Boston. She is recording, on videodisc, the contents of the tomb of the Chinese emperor who built the Great Wall. As yet, videodiscs are not cheap or plentiful enough to impact the elementary or middle school classroom.

Telecommunications amplify the power of computers by tying together many computers and computer users. From home, today's computer user can access large databases stored in distant computers and communicate with people all over the world in very different ways. These technologies are already being used in a small number of classrooms (see Chapter 6). They are still costly, relatively primitive, and therefore difficult to use. When a mass market materializes, prices will drop and use will become easier, opening up fascinating educational possibilities. The continuing development of new technologies has the effect of compressing time and space. This makes the responsibilities of teaching more complex and exciting for those who take a future-oriented perspective toward teaching social studies.

REFERENCES

BECKER, HENRY. *The Second National Survey of Instructional Uses of School Computers: A Preliminary Report.* Baltimore: Johns Hopkins University, 1985.

National Council for the Social Studies Task Force on Scope and Sequence. "In Search of a Scope and Sequence for Social Studies." *Social Education,* vol. 48, no. 4 (April 1984), 249–73.

NELLI, E. "Mirror of a People: Folktales and Social Studies." *Social Education,* vol. 49, no. 2 (February 1985), 155–58.

SHAUGHNESSY, J., AND T. HALADYNA. "Research on Student Attitudes Toward Social Studies." *Social Education,* vol. 49, no. 8 (Nov./Dec. 1985), 692–95.

SHERMIS, S., AND J. BARTH. "Indoctrination and the Study of Social Problems: A Re-Examination of the 1930s Debate in *The Social Frontier.*" *Social Education* (March 1985), pp. 190–93.

Tom Snyder Productions, Inc. *The Other Side Manual.* Cambridge, Mass.: Tom Snyder Productions, Inc., 1985.

FOUR
LANGUAGE ARTS
AND COMPUTERS

For instructional purposes, language arts is presented by most schools as a hierarchy of skills. The emphasis is first on reading, second on writing, third on listening, and last on speaking. Recent research points to the inherent dangers in this hierarchical approach. It tends to separate the language arts into four distinct aspects in a way that is artificial and counterproductive for language literacy. Such research decries the separation of the encoding (speaking and writing) and decoding (listening and reading) functions of language for the purpose of neat little curriculum packages.

Recently, a computer resource teacher described a series of activities that had evolved from a fifth-grade class's introduction to databases. This incident is a dynamic example of how the use of the computer and appropriate software can facilitate language-rich classroom experiences. Mrs. Leonard, the computer resource teacher, chose the topic of Student Profiles for the class's first independent work with databases because she knew it was a subject about which students have a great deal of readily accessible data. A brainstorming activity led to the development of a file with nine fields. Students then had an opportunity to fill out their own records. Here is Eric's complete record:

```
                    STUDENT PROFILE
NAME: ERIC
BOY OR GIRL: BOY   AGE IN YEARS: 10
COLOR OF HAIR: BROWN    COLOR OF EYES: BROWN
NUMBER OF BROTHERS: 1
NUMBER OF SISTERS: 0
FAVORITE SCHOOL SUBJECT: SCIENCE
FAVORITE TV PROGRAM: DR. WHO
FAVORITE HOBBY: READING SCIENCE FICTION BOOKS
```

Once these records were compiled, Mrs. Leonard realized that this wealth of data, familiar and understandable to the children, could be the basis for additional learning experiences. A printout of all eye colors demonstrates visually the concept of a normal curve:

```
FILE COLOR: EYE COLOR
BLUE
BLUE
BLUE
BROWN
BROWN
BROWN
BROWN
BROWN
BROWN
BROWN
BROWN
BROWN
BROWN
GREEN
GREEN
GREEN
GREEN
GREEN
HAZEL
HAZEL
```

The same data were used to teach the children the elements of a simple bar graph. With interesting, highly personal information the students learned what a normal curve is as well as the components of a bar graph. Next, the students got practice in mathematical and language skills when they were asked to refer to the data and answer questions such as, What is the eye color of the fewest children? or, Does half the class have brown eyes? (See Figure 4-1.)

The students were then taught how to interpret and present data from their personal survey sheets and from the Student Profile database. Each student wrote a summary of her or his class's eye color, siblings, and hobbies. For example, here is Ari's summary of his classmates' siblings:

> Twenty people from the fifth grade responded to this survey. There was a total of 55 siblings. Mendy and Yocheved had the most siblings at four brothers and two sisters each. Each person had an average of around three siblings. The total of brothers was one more than the sisters, the former being 28 and the latter being 27.

As she looked over each child's summaries, Mrs. Leonard realized that the summaries could be tied into a report if students were taught to write an introduction and a closing paragraph. Thus the students were able to create interesting factual reports on the Wilson School's fifth-grade class. In doing so they gained valuable practice for the content-area report writing they would be expected to do later in the year.

Two recurring issues in language arts are touched upon in this classroom example. First, the issue of skills taught in isolation versus skills taught through application is addressed. Second, the separation of reading and writing is avoided as the students develop meaningful individual and class products. The students in this fifth-grade class were engaged in activities that employed the computer and two important tools: a database (*PFS: File*) and a word processor (*Bank Street Writer*). They were involved in activities on and off the computer. The files were created and the summaries were written on the computer, while the bar graphs and the data collection on the Personal Survey Sheets were done off the computer.

FIGURE 4-1. Eye colors of students in grade 5.

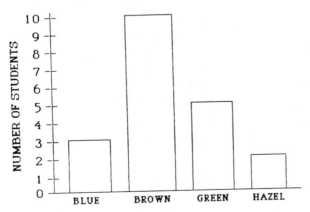

Skills were not isolated from content but were applied and extended. The children learned to store, retrieve, and sort data in their database for a variety of math and language arts activities. Finally, reading and writing were integrated as the children read the information on the screen, from their survey sheets, and from the printouts in order to compose their reports on their classmates.

READING

Reading is the component of language arts that is most emphasized in the early and middle grades. Reading is usually divided into beginning reading skills, emerging literacy, and reading instruction, or extended literacy. The two most prevalent approaches in beginning reading instruction are the *whole-language approach* (language experience approach) and the *phonetic approach,* which emphasizes sound and letter recognition. In beginning reading, the computer is used to enhance traditional readiness skills, particularly letter naming and matching, beginning phonics (sound-letter relationships), and directionality. *Juggles Rainbow* is an example of a child-oriented readiness program that makes good use of color and graphics to give children practice with "above," "below," "left," "right," and the easily confused letters *b, d, p,* and *g,*

In another program, *Instant Zoo,* the computer enhances beginning word-recognition skills by emphasizing letter substitution, matching, and correct spelling. In addition to its colorful graphics that entice young children, *Instant Zoo* has four separate activities and the option of cus-

FIGURE 4–2. *Instant Zoo,* "Scramble."

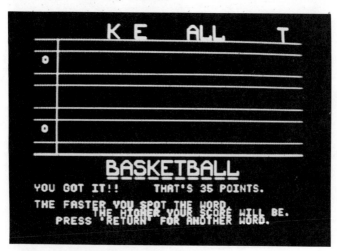

tomization of lists to help children acquire particular letter- and word-recognition abilities. In the activities "Quick Match" and "Scramble," the students are challenged to spell words correctly and to unscramble letters to form words that are a part of their developing sight vocabulary.

Another use of the computer in early reading is the IBM *Writing to Read* program, which stresses the children's learning of the forty-two English phonemes (sounds), the ability to write what they say and the subsequent ability to read what they or their peers have written. The program takes place in a total *Writing to Read* center that, in a carefully prescribed manner, incorporates computers equipped with voice output, cassettes and work journals, typewriters, a listening library, and games. This early reading program is composed of ten separate sequences designed to introduce words, their sounds, and their phonetic spellings. The computer provides intense multisensory introductory instruction and reinforcement of the forty-two phonemes needed to write English speech. For about fifteen minutes a day the children work in pairs at the computer, where they hear voiced words, see associated pictures and words, and type words that focus on particular sounds. Additional writing, reading, and listening takes place at the other centers in the room.

The long-range outcomes of such a program have yet to be explored, although the short-term effects measured by the Educational Testing Service are very impressive (ETS). Some critics question whether too much

FIGURE 4–3. Writing to Read Center.

emphasis has been placed on word-by-word reading on the computer screen, in the writing "journals," and on the listening tapes of standard children's literature (Ohanian). Also, given the limited funds available for hardware and software, is the computer being used appropriately and is its full potential being captured?

The word-processing capability of a computer and the opportunity for composing at the computer can have a profound effect on the Language Experience Approach for both the students and the teacher. If used well it gives children a firsthand experience with the interactive nature of expressive (speaking and writing) and receptive (reading and listening) language. In this approach the teacher uses the student's or group's own words or oral compositions, which are written down as the materials of instruction for reading, writing, speaking, and listening. In any classroom where a language experience story is treated as a rich literacy event, the teacher can use the computer to enhance what Edelsky calls a psycho-sociolinguistic process. There is also an immediate connection between writing and reading and "sense of a book," with a hard copy available for each child as a personal record of the story created together.

With simple word-processing programs like *Magic Slate* and *Kidwriter,* children can create their own stories. Children can create a simple group book about "Our Favorite Foods," for example, with individuals filling in their own name and favorite food in an entry that says:

_____'s favorite food is _____

or write an early story in invented spelling like this one by a first grader:

My stumeck fel's like it is goeen 2'0 mills an awrr in Srcul.

Of particular usefulness are the edit and replace functions of word processors, which seem to encourage more language experimentation and word play by the children as they create their language experience stories.

A program like *Storymaker* allows the student to do both text and graphics for a story. A teacher can even choose to start with a series of pictures, on or off the computer. The students then come up with a title and a description of the individual events for a story. If several small groups respond to the same set of pictures, children's language-learning experience is enriched not only by their own creation but by comparing them to other stories from the same raw data. The length of stories, the richness of language (particularly synonyms), the use of dialogue, and improved sense of audience all seem to be positive results of using the microcomputer with the Language Experience Approach. What is missing from the literature and what is needed to allow the language experience approach to yield vast improvements in reading and writing instruction is

FIGURE 4-4. *Storymaker.*

for the teacher to use the word processor for the development of follow-up activities to the stories created by individuals or groups of children. The opportunity for the teacher to add comments, directions, or thought questions directly onto the computer instead of the old red pencil method can be a positive follow-up to any young author's work. In such sequences the reading-writing interrelationship is clearly and personally reinforced for the individual.

Reading Comprehension

Throughout any well-balanced language arts program, one major strand focuses on comprehension. At the middle grades comprehension becomes crucial as students are expected to do more self-selection of texts, more reading for a purpose, and more independent reading for a variety of content area classes and projects.

Vocabulary. Vocabulary skills are an important component of comprehension for a student to become an independent reader. Too often vocabulary development programs in existing elementary and middle school classrooms consist of children memorizing unrelated lists of words, doing repetitive dictionary exercises, and filling up endless workbook pages with synonyms, antonyms, and homonyms. Although numerous computer programs of a drill-and-practice nature foster these activities, the computer's abilities have led to a new emphasis on vocabulary development. First, conceptual development is enhanced as the young student is exposed to the technical vocabulary of the computer itself. Students should be helped to learn, and encouraged to use, such words as "menu," "network," and "hardware." This focus on accurate and specific nomenclature teaches the student early on that a given area of content has its own vocabulary. Children are eager to demonstrate their expertise by accurately communicating with "sophisticated" words.

A second way in which the computer can extend vocabulary and language awareness is through the cloze procedure, enhanced by such software as *M-ss-ng L-nks* or *Cloze Plus*. Students must focus on linguistic cues at both the semantic (word) and syntactic (grammar) levels. Students manipulate vocabulary and rely heavily on prior decoding experiences (listening and reading) in order to produce an accurately encoded (written) product.

Using the capacity of the computer for word processing exemplifies a third aspect of vocabulary development that is unique to the technology. As students locate, replace, and move text, they are experimenting with language in a way that is much more realistic than any isolated drill on synonyms or parts of speech. Students become more aware of their own vocabulary needs and language limitations and therefore are more receptive to interventions by the teacher or their peers. An example of this follows in the first and second draft of a descriptive paragraph written by a learning-disabled fifth-grader.

1st Draft

```
My favorite ice cream is chocolate. I like it because it tast
good. I like it in a dish and sometimes is a cone. I buy it in
a icecream store and sometimes at a store.
```

2nd Draft

```
My favorite ice cream is chocolate. I like it because it
tastes good. I like it in a dish and sometimes in a cone. I
buy it in an icecream store and sometimes at a supermarket.
```

Figure 4-5. *M-ss-ng L-nks.*

Cloze providing every other word:

    Now ------ had ----- almost --- the ------ that --- be ----- in --- York ----: the ------
    of ------ trains --- the ------ their ---- wheels ----, ...

Cloze providing every other letter:

    N-w -u-k-r -a- h-a-d -l-o-t -l t-e -o-n-s -h-t -a- b- h-a-d -n -e- Y-r- C-t- t-e -u-b-e
    -f -u-w-y -r-i-s -n- t-e -h-e-k -h-i- i-o- w-e-l- m-k-; . . .

Comprehension games. Another aspect of comprehension fostered by the use of the computer is the opportunity to manipulate ideas so as to develop interpretive and critical thinking and to reinforce main ideas and important details. The advantage of programs such as *Galaxy Search* (predicting outcomes) or *Troll's Tale* (making inferences and applying information to solving a problem) is that the student's involvement in the application of these comprehension skills is the motivation to attain the desired goal.

FIGURE 4–6. *Galaxy Search.*

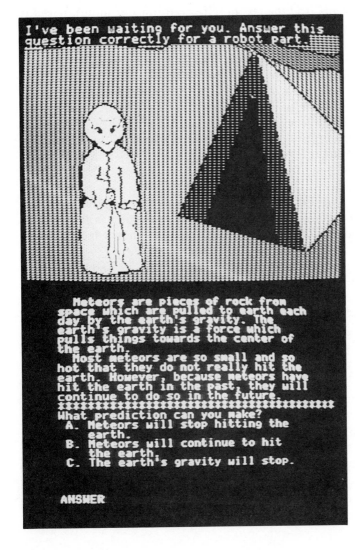

The student can see clear-cut consequences of their judgments as they go along with *Galaxy Search*'s outer-space fantasy or recapture a treasure in *Troll's Tale*. The teacher's role with such comprehension games is to challenge the students by having them discuss and analyze their strategies for solving these fantasy-oriented problems; and to see the usefulness of such strategies for future reading and writing, both on and off the computer.

Another powerful use of the computer for reading comprehension is exemplified by the program *Gapper* (Figure 4-7). This program is made up of a five-part game procedure on one disk and text entry and editing practice on another. In this program, students' comprehension is enhanced because they read a text three times. Following a series of prereading questions, the students *read* the text (a self-paced timed reading), *reread* it if necessary to answer the questions for postreading, and *read* it again as a *Cloze* passage with certain words randomly deleted. In this last procedure, students use their memory as well as their knowledge of semantic and syntactic clues to earn points by correctly filling in the blanks. Finally, in *Star Text* students are asked to fill in words from the passage they have been working on, which is now presented as a series of asterisks and punctuation marks. Such exercises give students practice in developing strategies of prediction, as well as an increased sensitivity to the sounds, vocabulary, and grammar of their language, and a sense of power and control over both text and their own learning.

Flow charts.   A third aspect of the computer that can enhance comprehension and make significant contributions to reading is *flow charts*. The flow chart idea, from programming, requires knowledge of a par-

Figure 4-7. *Gapper.*

Pre- and postreading questions (several samples):

Q1: Who was "The Cat"?
Q2: What was "The Cat's" real name?
Q3: Who was Armand?

Cloze selection:

IN ALL THE HISTORY OF SPYING, ONE -- THE MOST BEAUTIFUL AND SUCCESS
FUL SPIES --- A FRENCH WOMAN NICKNAMED "THE CAT."
WHEN --- GERMANS OCCUPIED FRANCE AT THE BEGINNING OF --- SECOND
WORLD WAR, THE CAT SET UP A --- RING WITH A POLISH GENERAL NAMED
ARMAND. ---- COOPERATED WITH THE FRENCH RESISTANCE MOVEMENT ---
GERMANS.

---

ticular topic and the ability to identify a main idea and its supporting ideas. In addition, the ability to sequence ideas or statements and to determine cause and effect is strengthened. Flow charts can help students analyze a book and its plot or plan a report or class presentation. By relating the computer skill to reading and writing, students foster two aspects of literacy simultaneously. Flow charting often requires the students to make decisions (branching), and this in turn gives them essential practice in questioning and critical thinking.

A flow chart relies on symbols and typographical aids to indicate relationships and choices (see Figure 4-8). A story such as the following can be charted to enhance comprehension:

Henry selects a ball to buy in a toy store. He approaches the cashier. The cashier tells him how much money he needs. He gives her the money to pay for the ball. He receives his change. He leaves the store.

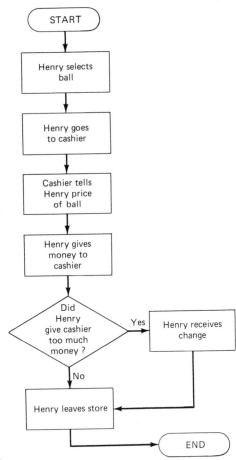

FIGURE 4-8. Flow chart of a story (Wepner).

Colony on the Moon

Abigail hops along in the moon's lighter gravity down the hall to her room. When she gets there she discovers that the door is missing and the room is pitch dark.

The choices are:

She can go into the room:

She can run away:

After Abigail walks into the room the leader of the moon rock spiders (natives of the moon) locks the entrance. One of the spider soldiers pounces on her and wraps her up in his web.

Abigail tries to find someone but she can't. As she turns a corner a spider pounces on her.

The choices are:

Try to get free from the web:

She can scream for help:

She can run away

She can fight the spider:

A security guard hears and comes racing in. He stuns the spiders and unwraps Abigail. He throws the spiders out of the colony and they never return.

Abigail trys to struggle free and grabs a log from the fireplace and chases the rock-spiders out of the colony on the moon and seals the entrance.

Abigail runs as fast as she can to the security chief's office. She tells him about the spiders and he orders his men out to find the spiders and throw them out of the colony.

Abigail fights the spider. She hurts one of his legs, so he runs out of the colony, and the others follow him.

Figure 4-9. Sample of a branching story using *Story Tree*.

With a flow chart, students can demonstrate their understanding of texts of varying lengths and complexity. A commercial piece of software like *Story Tree* uses the flow-charting format to encourage students to develop interesting and logical stories of their own. An example of such a story, "Colony on the Moon," was written by a fourth- and sixth-grade pair of student-authors in a summer language arts enrichment course (see Figure 4–9).

The capacity of the computer to present branching stories contributes to the development of comprehension skills as well as to the natural integration of reading and writing. "Participia" stories like those in *Story Maker* or *Microzine* enhance the student's awareness of story structure, the importance of sequence, and the consequence of actions. As students make choices among actions or directions in a story, they are getting firsthand experience in detecting important details and using these to draw conclusions or make inferences.

These valuable comprehension skills are best practiced when a student can alternate between the reader and writer mode, as in *Suspect Sentences* (Figure 4–10). In this program the student can choose to either enter or detect forgeries placed in professionally written passages from a variety of genres—mystery, sports, humor, the classics, or adventure and romance. For example, a student who liked sports took a passage for "Baseball Fever" and added one sentence of his own (underlined). He then asked a friend who also liked sports to be a detective and find the *forged* sentence.

FIGURE 4–10. *Suspect sentences.*

> Ezra was almost ten years old, and he liked baseball more than anything else in the world. He listened to baseball games on the radio, and he watched baseball games on television. When he read books, they were books about baseball. He read the sports page every day looking for stories on baseball. When he talked, he talked a lot about baseball. At night when he slept, he often dreamed about baseball.

The friend was successful and therefore earned credit toward a "Degree in Detecting Suspect Sentences."

Research skills.   Research skills that are traditionally taught in the middle grades can also be greatly enhanced with the use of the microcomputer. The first step in good research is posing questions related to the topic of investigation and finding answers to those questions. Software such as "Planner" in *Quill* is designed to encourage students to use such basic research skills. Having organized information, a student can then proceed to writing a report or participating in a discussion. An example of this is a sixth-grade project that began with a survey on the class's favorite restaurants. Some of the questions asked about each person's favorite restaurant on the "Planner" were:

What is the restaurant's name?
Where is it located?
What type of food does it serve?
How would you describe its atmosphere?
What is the average cost per meal?
Who likes to go there—parents, kids, both?
What specialties does it serve?

The students were taught how to draw up a table representing the similarities and differences in their choices, and they also learned how to create a database. They discovered some similarities in their choices; six restaurants were oriental and five were fast-food places. As a culminating activity, each student wrote a description and drew a picture of his or her favorite restaurant to entice someone else to try it. The following is one example of such a description.

The Andover Jade is my favorite Chinese restaurant. The service is great and the food is excellent. I personally like the shrimp and chicken wings. The crab rangoon, spare ribs, and gold fingers are also good. On the whole I would recommend the Andover Jade to anybody who likes Chinese food. I would rate the service as A minus and the food an A++++.

The final product was an illustrated guide, "Ou Dinerons-Nous Ce Soir?", which the students then proudly distributed throughout their school.

Reading Text from the Screen

In the foregoing examples comprehension skills are practiced or enhanced through the use of particular software that capitalizes on the unique capabilities of the computer. A final area to be considered when looking at reading and the computer is the recent proliferation of software packages offering a variety of forms of text on the screen. These range from a computerized magazine for students like *Microzine,* to content area materials like *Reading in the Content Areas,* and finally to Newbury award-winning books like *The Witch of Blackbird Pond* or *A Cricket in Times Square,* which are packaged with disks filled with accompanying comprehension questions and puzzles. What are the implications and the prudence behind such developments in language arts software? Will this software really replace well-established classroom and community libraries? Do these materials make good use of the computer? While it is important to continue to expose students to texts they can sign out, take home, and keep at their desks, teachers should take advantage of the special capabilities of the computer to do some things differently in the classroom.

Literature about Computers

There is a body of literature being written about computers for children and young adults. The teacher should encourage students to read books like Betsy Byars's fantasy *The Computer Nut,* or information books like Isaac Asimov's *How Did We Find Out About Computers?,* or Karen Jacobson's *A New True Book: Computers.* These books add to students' knowledge and interest about the current technological era. Students enjoy using them as sources for book talks or book reports since they can weave in their own experiences. Additionally, they like to use contemporary dictionaries like Melvin Berger's *Computer Talk* as models for their own illustrated dictionaries of "computerese."

In summary, programs and tools that enhance true literacy and build on the students' cultural and social values of reading and writing produce learning that makes the most prudent use of microcomputers in the schools.

WRITING

As the acceptance of microcomputers in the classrooms broadens, the availability of software designed for writing instruction increases steadily. However, for the most part, this software mirrors the same reliance on and replication of skills and narrow academic tasks as that found in traditional writing curricula. Most such materials are designed as supplements to existing curricula and therefore emphasize only what is easily quantifiable in terms of student response.

FIGURE 4-11. *Word Invasion.*

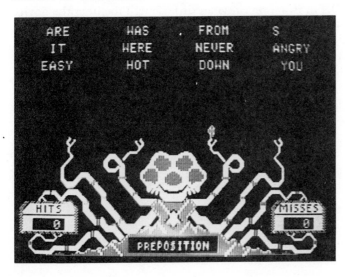

There is much student appeal in using the computer generally, in self-paced activities, and in software that incorporates a gamelike format. Teachers find appeal in lists that can be individualized, records that can be kept, and the ability for students to work independently. Software programs that focus on the mechanics of writing, such as the parts of speech in *Word Invasion* (see page 75) or in *Word Viper*, or spelling skills as in *Spelling Wiz* or *Magic Spells*, address these areas.

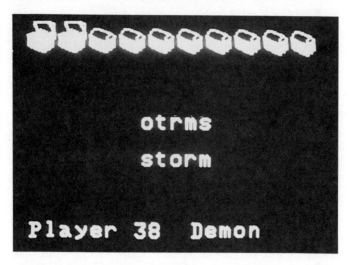

FIGURE 4-12. In *Magic Spells*, the student unscrambles a series of winter words; in this figure, "storm."

Poor spelling and incorrect sentence structure can prevent writers from reaching their readers and lead to a breakdown of communication. However, practicing such skills in isolation provides little benefit to either the novice or more experienced writers. Students need many opportunities to practice and to expand their language proficiency. The best way to provide such opportunities is to encourage students to write often and for a variety of purposes. It is only by emphasizing context and making meaningful corrections that students' written expression shows any qualitative development. The potential impact of the computer on writing instruction can be considered in three areas.

1. the role of the computer and the software;
2. the process approach to writing; and
3. new roles for the teacher and the students.

World-Processing Programs

The tool that has the greatest impact on literacy is the word processor. The proliferation of word-processing programs aimed at all levels of writing skill and computer expertise, as well as the number of related spelling checkers, electronic dictionaries, and text editors, makes clear the message that computers have impacted on the process and products of written expression. Word-processing packages for elementary students vary greatly in complexity of format and edit commands, guidance on prewriting, and use of graphics. However, the availability of such tools has led to a generation of young writers who write more willingly and who produce longer pieces with more enjoyment than their predecessors. Additionally, word processors are credited with taking the pain out of recopying or rewriting by allowing deleting and inserting without ruining the look of the printed page. All writers can now produce work that looks published.

Although the writing process—prewriting, composing, and revising—is the same for novice or expert, there are differences that impact on the nature of the tool needed by each. All word-processing programs allow three related activities: the ability to create and edit text; the ability to format and print text; and the ability to store and retrieve files or works in progress. The way these functions happen determines the suitability of a program for a particular population.

The characteristics of a tool such as a word processor must be considered carefully in light of the needs and background of the potential writer. Especially important attributes with regard to novice writers are:

1. Displays upper- and lower-case letters
2. Automatically moves a whole word to the following line instead of splitting it inappropriately
3. Screen display that uses large print with space between each line
4. Words on screen that are static rather than scrolled across the page
5. Editing commands which are few in number and easy to remember
6. Editing commands available on screen
7. Mnemonic devices related to some commands
8. Programs that can be copied
9. Warning system available when deleting
10. Password protection possible (Piazza and Dawson, pp. 10, 11)

A particularly clear list of features of word-processing software and the needs of beginning, intermediate, and advanced students was developed by Collins and Sommers (Table 4-1). Two pieces of word processing software for beginning writers that meet most of these criteria are *Kidwriter* and *Magic Slate* (see Figures 4-13 and 4-14.) Three that serve the needs of intermediate writers are *Bank Street Writer*, *Magic Slate*, and *Apple Writer*.

Word-processing software provides the step-by-step assistance the writer needs for planning, writing, revising, and producing a final product. With the development and improvement of word-processing tools, each age group and level of ability can derive benefits from its use. Several

TABLE 4-1. Selecting word-processing software (Collins and Sommers).

WORD PROCESSING FEATURES FOR STUDENTS			
FEATURE	BEGINNER STUDENTS	INTERMEDIATE STUDENTS	ADVANCED STUDENTS
upper and lower case	1	1	1
upper/lower case display	1	1	1
single key capitalization	1	1	1
80-column display	3	2	1
word wrap	1	2	2
cursor movement			
multiple options[1]	3	2	1
rapid scrolling	3	2	1
ease of use	1	2	2
inserting phrases	1	1	1
deleting phrases	1	1	1
moving phrases	1	1	1
search and replace			
multiple options	1	1	1
ease of use	1	1	2
italics/boldface/underline	3	2	1
sub and superscripts	5	3	1
screen display			
"what you see you get"	2	2	2
print to screen	1	1	1
flexible formats[2]	3	2	1
long file length	4	3	1
file linking	4	2	1
safe file handling	1	2	2
easy file loading/saving	1	2	2
logical command structure	1	2	2
simple command structure	1	2	3

EVALUATION SCALE		
NECESSARY	DESIRABLE	UNNECESSARY
1	3	5

Notes:
[1] The ability to move the cursor in a variety of ways.
[2] The ability to change the line spacing or margins within a document or within a page of a document.

classroom instructions lend themselves to word-processing use (see Chapter 3). A resource center, however, with adequate hardware and software and opportunities for extended time on-task (at least twenty minutes) is essential for any real writing to be accomplished.

Current research suggests that writing is a process of dual discovery. Writers are not aware of their ideas until they articulate them either in speaking or writing, and they are not aware of the extent of their com-

FIGURE 4-13. *Kidwriter.*

munication skills until these are revealed in their own writing. The writing process stimulates a writer's initial thinking and keeps it going throughout the composing process. Good prose is generated *only after a number of drafts.* In using the word processor for the prewriting stage, students can get their initial ideas down on paper almost as quickly as they can produce them. Students can then take the hard copy and reorder the

FIGURE 4-14. *Magic Slate.*

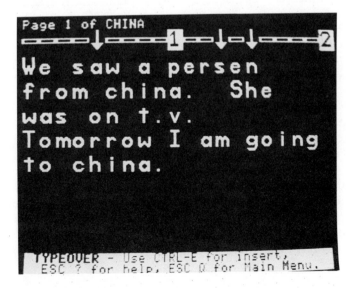

ideas, link them in a meaningful way, or get reactions from teachers and peers before they begin additional composing. Software packages such as *Writing a Narrative* provide clear prewriting prompts to help students with descriptive writing. For example, a student deciding to write about a cabin and a country road using "Idea Storming" has the following organized information to start an expository piece.

Idea Storming Tree

Names selected: COUNTRY ROAD and CABIN

Action words for COUNTRY ROAD:

NARROW
DUSTY
TREE-LINED
SCARY
SOLITARY

Sensory words to describe how your COUNTRY ROAD appears:

NARROW	DRY	NOISELESS
TREE-LINED	ROUGH	WHISTLING
SHADY	PEBBLY	SWISHING
TRANQUIL	SMOOTH	RAMBLING
WINDING	DAMP	CREEKING

Sensory words to describe how your CABIN appears:

SMALL	ROUGH	QUIET
ROUGH-HEWN	SMOOTH	STILL
LOG	SPLINTERY	NOISY
LONELY	ODD	LOUD

Words you might use to order your story:

THEN	LATER	LAST
BEFORE	NEXT	
WHEN	FINALLY	
AFTER	FIRST	

This prewriting data gives students the content about which to write. Students appear to jump in and get started with their compositions more readily with word processors because they know that any minor as well as major change in paragraphing, spelling, or punctuation can be made quickly and easily. Moreover, working from a legible printed copy rather than a messy, crossed out, cluttered draft is an important incentive. The easily produced multiple drafts contribute to another aspect of the revision process—peer review and teacher conferencing. Because of the professional look of each draft and the ease with which suggested changes can be made, students are more willing to share their drafts for critical analysis and to try suggested changes. Without the pain of recopying, a student can go back to a composition and use devices like spelling checkers or thesaurus programs to rework the piece so that it clearly communicates the message to the intended audience.

The real change in the classroom writing program is that teachers are working together, and instruction comes from evolving texts rather than from prescribed scope-and-sequence charts or language arts textbooks. Daiute sees the teacher as a guide who directs a variety of simultaneous activities from prewriting to revising to publishing; as a consultant who gives advice on content and grammar, spelling, and vocabulary; and as a technician who has mastered the hardware and software.

Students find themselves in new roles as collaborators and evaluators of others' writing. These roles improve the students' personal writing and reading. Students using the computer for writing show a marked improvement in the use of mechanics and in fluency; they also show more interest in reading what others have written. Students seem more sensitive to the variety of ways in which writing can influence their lives or help them influence others.

The major concern about the impact of computers on writing instruction is the teachers' belief that more writing is better writing. Certainly the word-processing software makes it easier to keep track of prewriting ideas, easier to transcribe writing, and easier to evaluate it; but as Knapp says, "No matter how powerful the word-processing tool is, it can't teach a student how to write. That job still belongs to the classroom teacher" (p. 219).

Two areas of concern have arisen regarding the use of word processors and their impact on elementary and middle school students' writing competency. One is a technical logistics issue and the other is a pedagogical one. As Knapp points out, students are often introduced to both new writing strategy lessons and new word-processing commands or functions at the same time. Such lack of coordination or knowledge of prerequisite skills confuse many youngsters and may also cause most of the surface-level (spelling, punctuation, inserting and deleting words) revisions of text by elementary and middle school writers.

A second and perhaps more important concern is the lack of qualitative improvement or real writing growth even by those students who make numerous revisions of their written pieces (Daiute). Real revision is a process of rethinking and reformulating one's ideas and message with the reader's needs in mind. In order for novice writers to do such revision, they need more than a word processor with its various functions and prompts; they need the questioning, conferencing, and support of a teacher trained in the process approach to writing.

In a recent doctoral study Kaplan demonstrated this point clearly as he found that a group of fifth-graders using a conference process approach (CPA) with word-processing technology (WPT) for five weeks produced far more qualitative (holistically scored) and lengthier compositions than did those students of the same age in the three treatment groups (CPA with paper and pencil, and traditional writing approach with and without WPT).

What is clear is that inexperienced writers do not improve with the use of word processors alone. It is the combination of the use of word-processing tools and an adult knowledgeable about the writing process that makes a difference in the written products of elementary and middle school writers. A more open, collaborative atmosphere in which conferencing with the teacher and peers is part of the writing process seems essential in order for the rapidly expanding realm of word-processing technology to have a profound and lasting effect on the products of the next generation of school-aged writers.

SPEAKING AND LISTENING

In most current literature on language arts and computers the predominant focus is on writing, with reading coming in a distant second, and with speaking and listening only occasionally and briefly mentioned. However, children often work in a collaborative situation to maximize the use of computers. When students are working together, there is far more to be attended to than social studies skills. There is a rich opportunity for communications skills to develop as students make suggestions and question the meaning of one another's work. More attention to the nature of the discussion occurring at the computer, and to the teacher's role in encouraging discussion, is necessary.

In the elementary grades speaking and listening expand the children's use of syntax and vocabulary. Children who dread reading orally in their basal reading group are spontaneously reading one another's texts on the monitor. In a very natural way children are experimenting with the oral production of text to test its audience appeal and understanding. They are also gaining experience as fluent oral readers who understand the use of punctuation to enhance meaning. The connection between what the voice can do and what one attempts with the conventions of writing is more apparent as a result of these collaborative writing and talking experiences around the microcomputer.

A recent analysis of students' messages written with "Mailbag," a component of *Quill,* in which students had complete choice of subject and audience, showed much evidence of "speech written down." The children felt comfortable using expressive language in the way with which they were most familiar: speech. A teacher can thus provide direct instruction on the conventions of quotation marks and the value of dialogue in writing not only for students to use in their "Mailbag" messages but also to make a situation or a purpose clearer in other writing events.

The interconnections among the language arts are also reinforced when children are engaged in any of the well-designed simulations available for the elementary and middle grades. Reading skills are enhanced on the screen and in the user's guide, and writing skills are enhanced with the necessity for note taking, plotting of details, and record keeping. However, teachers often fail to realize the value of the speaking and listening skills that are enhanced by pairs or groups of students motivated and captivated by programs such as *Geography Search* (see Chapter 3). Teachers should follow up with appropriate listening and speaking practices that are being fostered naturally by the computer. Students need more opportunities to transfer and apply these important language arts skills.

NEXT STEPS: INTEGRATING COMPUTERS AND LANGUAGE ARTS

The introduction of the microcomputer into the classroom has enhanced the occurrence of dynamic contextual situations for reading and writing. The display of text on the screen, the access to multiple clean copies, and the collaboration and editing that occur spontaneously are all related to this new, more natural integration of reading and writing in the classroom. Many of the literacy events fostered by using the computer appear to be extensions of children's social interactions and real-life communication needs. A particular middle school classroom was recently using the computer for three different writing functions.

- for community-related social reasons like printing notices or bulletins;
- to demonstrate academic competence through research reports and book reviews; and
- for personal writing such as letters and cards.

The impact of the computer and its accompanying software has been to create a classroom atmosphere where the students are beginning to assume control over their literacy.

The Computer Chronicles enables students to use an interactive writing tool to create news stories, reviews, editorials, and sports articles. The stories written by student reporters at each participating school are made available to the other schools using the "Network Maildisk" system; at each site a newspaper can be created from a pool of both local and distant stories. A functional writing environment that fosters reading (one's own and other school articles), writing (news stories of various kinds), and editing (of one's own drafts and articles from other schools) is easily created with such a tool.

In addition to the language arts competencies that are sharpened by such a program, social skills are learned and an awareness of other places and cultures is developed that is clearly another aspect of the larger communication environment. Children are not only improving their writing skills by editing their own and others' works, but are participating in consensus gathering as they work together on editorial boards. This computer program also helps educate children about other cultures; for example, Tuinudak Eskimo children are connected by wire service to American students in San Diego. Imagine a child who lives near the Bering Sea hearing about someone swimming in the ocean in the wintertime or the California children's fascination with an Eskimo child's story of how her father hunted and killed a mink that had bitten him.

Another integrated software package that fosters a functional writing environment is *Newsroom*. This software provides all the tools necessary for students to produce a professional-looking classroom newspaper. Students can take on different roles (editor, photographer, layout person, reporter) and responsibilities for the production of the paper using the six options: "Banner Room," "Photo Lab," "Copy Desk," "Layout Room," "Press Room," and "Wire Service." Thus the computer not only motivates students but takes advantage of a great range of student abilities. *Newsroom* fosters decision making collaboration by groups of students, necessitates a fair balance of reading and writing, and enhances communication skills beyond the classroom walls if the "Wire Service" option is used. A teacher of special-needs adolescents found these students more willing to edit and rewrite short news or sports stories, something they had done previously only with reluctance. These students were also more attuned to the who, what, where, when, and how of their own stories and questioned others if such details were missing. These students began to grasp the connection between main idea and title when developing headings for their own stories. The more graphically or pictorially oriented students can make their contribution working on "Banner Room" or on "Photo Lab." Again, the aspect of collaboration and the thrill of a professional-looking product reinforces the students' hard work because they are involved in a true "literacy event."

Other media production such as a flyer or a brochure is also possible with *Newsroom*. With a program called *Print Shop*, students can produce professional-looking greeting cards, signs, stationery, and banners. Again, various literacy events can be connected with these tools; a play can be announced with a sign or a flyer, students can create their own personalized stationery, or social writing skills can be reinforced with greeting cards, thank-you notes, get-well cards, or invitations. Recently in a computer club program third-, fourth-, and fifth-graders used the greeting card format in *Print Shop* to make covers for a branching sequential story they had written using *Storymaker*. These children not only collaboratively wrote a story but became involved in deciding how to capture readers with the title and illustration on the cover of their "book." One creative twosome even brought in colored pencils to do what their printer could not, adding a further dimension of interest and individualization to their story.

Another piece of software that supports real-life communication is *Quill*, particularly the component "Mailbag," an electronic mail system for students. Using "Mailbag" a co-correspondence model is often established in which one student, the writer, expresses opinions or feelings or asks questions, and the other student, the reader to whom these messages are directed, responds by sharing his or her own feelings or thoughts. The cycle is completed when the original writer is then placed in a reader role. The messages of a group of suburban third-graders revealed a set of self-generated, highly functional pieces of writing linked to their everyday lives. The eighty-five messages sent during one semester were analyzed by type and nature of content; they were found to be primarily friendly letters, thank-you type messages, and invitations. The topics of these messages ranged from academic concerns, sports, and sticker-trading interests to social issues such as complimenting someone or inviting a friend over. What can be more useful than finding a way to extend students' awareness of language as demonstrated in these spontaneous messages and true literacy events?

The computer acts as a powerful tool to help children communicate easily and effectively with others around them. Students are being exposed to a variety of texts in a way that expands their world while drawing on what they already know to ensure both understanding and appropriate literacy learning.

REFERENCES

COLLINS, J. L., AND E. A. SOMMERS. *Writing On-Line: Using Computers in the Teaching of Writing.* Upper Montclair, N.J.: Boynton/Cook, 1985.

DAIUTE, C. *Writing and Computers.* Reading, Mass.: Addison-Wesley, 1985.

EDELSKY, C. "The Content of Language Arts Software: A Criticism." *CRLA* (Spring 1984), pp. 8–11.

Educational Testing Service. *ETS Evaluation of Writing to Read.* IBM Executive Summary, ETS. Princeton, N.J., July, 1984.

KAPLAN, H. *Computers and Composition: Improving Students' Written Performance.* Unpublished doctoral dissertation, University of Massachusetts, Amherst, 1986.

KNAPP, L. R. *The Word Processor and the Writing Teacher.* Englewood Cliffs, N.J.: Prentice-Hall, Inc., 1986.

OHANIAN, S. "Hot New Item or Same Old Stew?" *Classroom Computer Learning* (March 1984), pp. 30–33.

PIAZZA, C. L., AND J. C. DAWSON. "Choosing a Word Processor for Writing Instruction. *CRLA* (Summer/Fall 1984), pp. 10–12.

WEPNER, S. B. "Computer Flowchart: Road Maps to Reading Skills" *Computers, Reading and Language Arts,* Vol. 1, No. 2, (Fall, 1983), pp. 14–17.

FIVE
COMPUTERS
IN MATHEMATICS

Computers are natural tools for doing mathematics. Understanding and responding to their influence on content and methodology is one of the critical problems facing mathematics educators today. These tools have the potential to shift the focus of mathematics education from manipulative skills to the development of concepts, relationships, structures, and problem-solving skills (NCTM).

There are continuing problems in teaching mathematics. Students often learn by rote and cannot transfer their knowledge to even slightly different problem situations. They view the world of mathematics as one in which there is only one right answer for any given problem and only one right way to find that answer. The "magic" comes not from the ability to *think through* a solution but from the ability to find and apply a specific formula to manipulate the information given.

The work students are given reinforces their understanding of what mathematics is all about. Students literally spend hundreds of hours learning to manipulate numbers and symbols. The problems in which students apply their knowledge usually are those that are contrived, simplistic, and boring. With the growing availability of technology, mathematics education does not have to continue to be so narrowly defined, and students can become involved in significant ways at very early ages.

TEACHING AND LEARNING MATHEMATICS

How do people think about mathematics? How does mathematical understanding develop? What combination of experience and intellect results in "mathematical ability"? Keep these key ideas in mind when integrating the use of technology into the learning and teaching of mathematics.

Concrete to Abstract Representations

Learners look for meaning, regularity, and order in the environment in which they learn. Their learning depends on linking new information with previous knowledge in order to interpret familiar situations and to reason about new ones. Consequently, how new knowledge is presented becomes very important.

New knowledge needs to be developed from concrete to abstract representations (Resnick), for a person to organize and connect it to past experiences. For example, students in upper elementary grades may be introduced to concepts in logic through the use of the concrete material, such as in *Attribute Blocks*. These materials consist of thirty-two blocks, each block having three attributes: color (red, blue, yellow, or green), size (large or small), and shape (diamond, triangle, square, or circle). Students can explore a variety of activities focused on relationships among these attributes. These involve making trains of blocks, placing blocks in matrices, and playing "ring" games using the blocks and card labels.

As an example of the "Two-Ring Game," two "rings," or sets, are arranged using colored strings to identify their boundaries and show their intersection. There are twenty cards, each labeled with one attribute. The first player chooses two cards such as red, circle, large, not green, or not square, and places one face down at each ring:

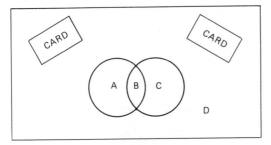

The second player selects one "test block" at a time, and the first places the chosen block in one of the four possible regions (A, B, C, or D), based on the hidden labels. The second tries to guess the exact labels, selecting the fewest number of test blocks.

Two computer programs, *Gertrude's Secrets* and *Gertrude's Puzzles*, provide a "pictorial" version of the *Attribute Blocks* world. The pieces in

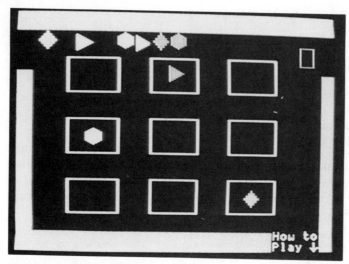

FIGURE 5-1. *Gertrude's Puzzles.*

the computer version have the attributes of color, size, and shape as well but are not identical to those in *Attribute Blocks*. Students may again participate in activities that involve making trains, completing matrices, or playing "ring" games. Informally, teachers who have used both the concrete materials and the pictorial computer programs have found that students are more engaged in both activities than when each is used alone.

In a second example, concepts important to coordinate graphing can be developed pictorially through the use of the computer programs *Bumble Games* (ages 4–10) and *Bumble Plot* (ages 8–13). *Bumble Games* provides a set of developmentally sequenced games. These games start with a number line, proceed to grid representations that first involve boxes, then crossed

FIGURE 5-2. *Bumble Games, "Tic Tac Toe".*

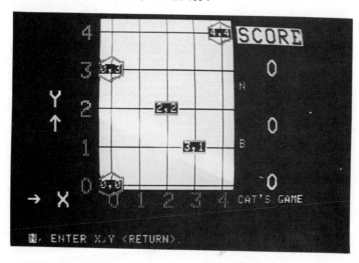

lines, and end with the traditional *x-y* coordinate grid. All numbers used to designate locations are positive so that students deal only with the first quadrant of the coordinate grid.

Bumble Plot proceeds through a set of games developmentally sequenced in a fashion similar to *Bumble Games*. However, both positive and negative numbers are used in designating locations, and students finish by working within the four quadrants of the traditional coordinate grid.

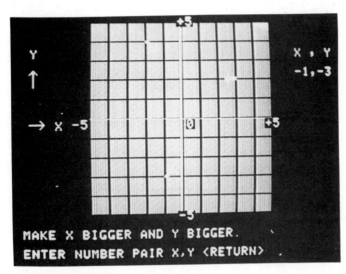

FIGURE 5-3. *Bumble Plot,* "Hidden Treasures".

Multiple Embodiments

Each concept to be learned should be "clothed" in a number of different embodiments (Dienes and Golding). Every concept must be presented in as many different ways as possible to aid in learning the abstraction. One example of a computer application in which multiple embodiments can be identified involves the use of two software packages, *Number Quest* and *Word Quest*. These programs can be used to develop search strategies. *Number Quest* consists of five programs, each of which is designed to challenge students to find a number or set of numbers randomly selected by the program. The first three programs deal with numbers in a line. "One Thousand" involves students in identifying a number between 1 and 1000. "Fractions" focuses on finding a number in fraction form between 0 and 1 (with a denominator no larger than 16). "Decimals" involves identifying a three-digit decimal between 0 and 1.

As an example, consider the program "Fractions." When run, the student is told that a fraction between 0 and 1 must be identified. The fraction has a denominator of 16 or less. Visually, the game uses number lines. In the first trial, a number line is presented showing the range of choice:

0 == 1

(The dashed lines (---) indicate that the number is somewhere along this line):

Trial 1: 1/2 (*student's guess*)

In the second and remaining trials, two number lines are presented. The first shows what is left, the second shows the current upper and lower bound. (Note: student guess is entered *after* the two number lines are shown.)
In Trial 2, the range is 0–1/2. The guess is 1/4.

0 ============================ ———————————— 1

Trial 2: 1/4 (*student's guess*)

0 == 1/2

In Trial 3, the range is 1/4–1/2. The guess is 3/8.

0 ———————————— ------------- ———————————— 1

Trial 3: 3/8 (*student's guess*)

1/4 == 1/2

In Trial 4, the range is 1/4–3/8. The guess is 5/16.

0 ———————————— -------- ———————————————— 1

Trial 4: 5/16 (*student's guess*)

1/4 === 3/8

In Trial 5, the range is 1/4–5/16. At this point, the student recalls that the denominator will not be larger than 16. The correct number is still not found, so the student needs to reanalyze what is known about fractions. In this case, the guess is 2/7.

0 ———————————— --- ———————————————— 1

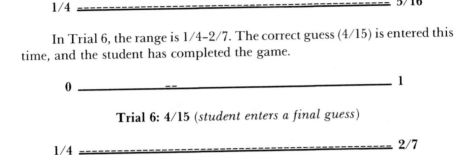

Trial 5: 2/7 (*student's guess*)

1/4 == 5/16

In Trial 6, the range is 1/4–2/7. The correct guess (4/15) is entered this time, and the student has completed the game.

0 ————————— == ———————————— 1

Trial 6: 4/15 (*student enters a final guess*)

1/4 == 2/7

The remaining two programs involve two- and three-dimensional figures. In "Numbers in a Plane," students enter points in the form of number pairs (50, 76 or 3, 29). In "Numbers in Space," a point in three-dimensional space must be located (23, 8, 76 or 25, 50, 88).

The second software package, *Word Quest,* has two programs available: "What's the Word" and "Word Chain." In the first program, one player chooses a secret word. The other players try to guess the word by doing alphabetical searches. In "Word Chain," one or more students challenge themselves or each other to find words that fit into an ever-narrowing alphabetical gap.

Each of the other programs presents the same type of problem: developing a search strategy. While a variety of search strategies are possible, some are more efficient than others. It is possible to develop one common strategy—the *binary search*—that can be applied in the use of each of the programs. This search strategy involves always cutting the search space in half and is the maximally efficient strategy to use in these programs. Such a strategy guarantees that half the search space is eliminated during each round. Educationally, the programs provide students opportunities to work with search problems in different contexts and to extend strategies to new domains (*multiple embodiments*).

A second example of a computer application that integrates multiple embodiments is an algebra tool currently being developed to help students express simple functional relationships (Roberts). In this program, students can use one of four ways to state a relationship involving marbles: English words, marble bags, symbolic notation, or numbers. Suppose a student "picks a number." This is a real number, in this case 12, and can be represented by the two digits 1 and 2. It is an unknown number to the computer (or the student). This unknown can be represented by a marble bag containing an unknown number of marbles, or the standard algebraic representation of x. The computer screen can display all four representations as shown on page 92.

Words	Marble Bags	Symbolic Notation	Number
Pick a number:	🎒	x	12
Multiplies by 2 and:	🎒 🎒	$2x$	24
Adds three marbles:	🎒 🎒 . . .	$2x + 3$	27

Using this tool, students may choose any one of these representations, thus having several different methods for building an understanding of the algebra concepts involved.

Another crucial component to mathematics learning is the role of language. Research on the effects of discussion among children while at work shows significant improvement in learning rate and retention by those who are able to verbalize their discoveries with one another (Dienes). In addition, small-group and class discussions are necessary in order to generalize the concepts to be learned.

USING COMPUTERS IN THE TEACHING OF MATHEMATICS AND THE PROCESS OF MATHEMATICAL INQUIRY

The use of computers can contribute in powerful ways to overall mathematical goals, but their use must be considered within the framework of the entire mathematics curriculum. The computer may be used as an interactive source of information. It may also be used in a context that engages the learner in generalizing, searching, observing, experimenting, deducing, or remembering (Hatfield). Any decisions for use must be preceded by careful consideration about the purpose and content of the mathematics being taught and the reason for computer use.

Augmenting Existing Content and Methods

One way to think about computer use is to view it as augmenting existing content and methods of teaching. In this role, the computer helps deliver the knowledge and skills that are currently taught in the mathematics curriculum.

For example, the concept of factoring—underlying work with fractions and, later, work with quadratic equations—is an important topic starting in the elementary grades. Introduction of the concept should involve students in concrete activities. For example, a student is given twelve wooden cubes and asked to arrange these cubes in different-sized rectangles:

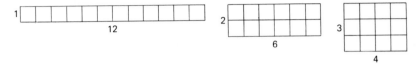

The dimensions of each rectangle are interpreted as "factor pairs" of 12: 1 × 12, 2 × 6, and 3 × 4. Next students become involved in listing all the factors of a number (in the range 1-50). Eventually, in the elementary grades, this concept is applied in working with fractions when students learn to reduce fractions to lowest terms.

Because of the computation demands, students seldom engage in exploring large numbers to see which have only a few factors, which have many factors, and which are prime. This may often lead to the naive theory that "big" numbers always have more factors than do "small" numbers. Students do not develop a "number sense" about how many factors a given number may have. A simple BASIC program, included as a tool in teaching the concept of factoring, can provide opportunities for more in-depth intuitive exploration in this area. The program, shown in Figure 5-4, is designed to print out using "*"s for the total number of factors of each number in a given range of numbers. Figure 5-5 shows a sample run for the numbers 1 to 50. It is more fun to use the program to explore larger numbers, which, without the use of the computer program, necessitate extensive computations. Figure 5-6 shows a sample run for the numbers 1,000 to 1,050. The program can actually be run for a very large range such as 1,000-3,000, with the results printed on paper and the paper hung in the classroom for exploration activities.

Using the information shown in Figures 5-5 and 5-6, students can now look for patterns in these ranges and in other ranges they may wish to investigate. In both, some numbers have only two "*"s—these are prime numbers because they have only themselves and 1 as factors. Twin primes

]PR#0
]LIST

FIGURE 5-4. BASIC Program: Number of Factors.

```
10   INPUT "LOWERBOUND: ";LB
20   INPUT "UPPERBOUND: ";UB
30  R = 0
45   FOR I = LB TO UB
46    PRINT I;: HTAB 6
50    FOR J = 1 TO SQR (I)
60     IF  INT (I / J) < > I / J THEN
        100
70     IF I / J < > J THEN 90
80     PRINT "*";
85     GOTO 100
90     PRINT "**";
100    NEXT J
150    PRINT
160   NEXT I
170   END
```

```
]RUN
LOWERBOUND:  1
UPPERBOUND:  50
1      *
2      **
3      **
4      ***
5      **
6      ****
7      **
8      ****
9      ***
10     ****
11     **
12     ******
13     **
14     ****
15     ****
16     *****
17     **
18     ******
19     **
20     ******
21     ****
22     ****
23     **
24     ********
25     ***
26     ****
27     ****
28     ******
29     **
30     ********
31     **
32     ******
33     ****
34     ****
35     ****
36     *********
37     **
38     ****
39     ****
40     ********
41     **
42     ********
43     **
44     ******
45     ******
46     ****
47     **
48     **********
49     ***
50     ******
```

FIGURE 5-5. Number of Factors: 1-50.

can be found, such as 5-7, 11-13, 1,031-1,033. Some numbers have only three factors (4, 9, 25, 49). Can students determine why? Other numbers have many factors (1,008). Can students actually compute all the factors? The use of such a program encourages the development of a sense about the size of numbers and the number of factors they have.

Teasers by Tobbs: Puzzles and Problem Solving provides another

```
]RUN
LOWERBOUND: 1000
UPPERBOUND: 1050
1000 ****************
1001 ********
1002 ********
1003 ****
1004 ******
1005 *********
1006 ****
1007 ****
1008 *****************************
1009 **
1010 *********
1011 ****
1012 ************
1013 **
1014 ************
1015 ********
1016 ********
1017 ******
1018 ****
1019 **
1020 **************************
1021 **
1022 *********
1023 ********
1024 ***********
1025 ******
1026 *****************
1027 ****
1028 ******
1029 *********
1030 *********
1031 **
1032 ******************
1033 **
1034 ********
1035 *************
1036 ************
1037 ****
1038 *********
1039 **
1040 *********************
1041 ****
1042 ****
1043 ****
1044 *********************
1045 *********
1046 ****
1047 ****
1048 *********
1049 **
1050 ************************
```

FIGURE 5-6. Number of Factors: 1000–1050.

example of augmenting existing content and methods of teaching. This program can give students experience in developing mental arithmetic and problem-solving skills involving addition and multiplication. "Tobbs" is a character who jumps around addition and multiplication grids, landing on any locations that are missing number entries. When Tobbs lands, the students enter the missing number that belongs in that location.

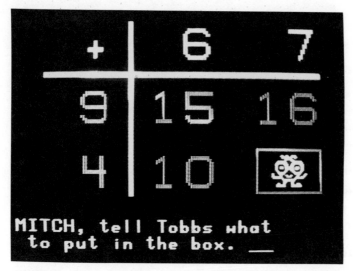

FIGURE 5-7. *Teasers by Tobbs*, level 2 addition puzzle.

In the program, there are six levels of difficulty for each operation. At the lower levels, students perform computations in the standard form:

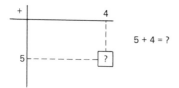

At the higher levels, students have to work backward in solving problems:

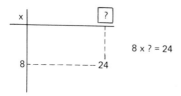

At the sixth level, multiple solutions for puzzles are possible.

A third example of augmenting existing content and methods of teaching is the program *Power Drill*. This program involves students in estimating the results of arithmetic operations and in mental arithmetic. *Power Drill* permits exploration of patterns in numbers and in their operations. Four options for operations are possible:

1. Altogether (*addition—find the sum*)
2. What's the Difference? (*subtraction—find the minuend*)
3. Easy Times, Hard Times (*multiplication—find the product*)
4. The Great Divide (*division—find the dividend*)

Three different ranges of numbers may be designated: 100–999; 1,000–9,999, and 10,000–99,999. The choice of range determines the complexity of the problem. Once the range is selected, all numbers in problems are within this range. As an example, suppose "What's the Difference?" is chosen, with a range of 1,000–9,999. A sample problem is:

$$9,500 - ? = 3,714$$

Entering 6,000 as a first estimate:

$9,500 - 6,000 = 3,500$ ← *results of the estimate are shown. The answer is* <u>lower</u> *than the desired results*

Now 5,500 is entered:

$9,500 - 5,500 = 4,000$ ← *The answer is* <u>higher</u>
$9,500 -\ \ \ ?\ \ \ = 3,714$
$9,500 - 6,000 = 3,500$

A further estimate of 5,700 is entered:

$9,500 - 5,700 = 3,800$ ←
$9,500 -\ \ \ ?\ \ \ = 3,714$
$9,500 - 6,000 = 3,500$

Some further refinement with 5,750:

$9,500 - 5,750 = 3,750$ ←
$9,500 -\ \ \ ?\ \ \ = 3,714$
$9,500 - 6,000 = 3,500$

And then the final entry of 5,759:

$$9,500 - 5,759 = 3,714$$

The principal purpose of this program is to develop and practice skills of estimation as they relate to the four operations of addition, subtraction, multiplication, and division. To actually estimate, students must be encouraged to respond quickly, should not be permitted to use paper and pencil, and should be reminded that the purpose of this program is not precision but sensible estimating.

In addition to the examples shown above, it is possible to identify series of related computer activities that may be used to augment existing content and methods of teaching. For example, two pieces of software, *King's Rule* and *Guess My Rule,* focus on pattern finding involving numbers; each can be used independently to foster problem-solving skills at various grade levels. These programs may also be combined as part of a developmental sequence of planned activities to be used at one grade level to introduce and extend the concept of a *function*—a concept particularly important in algebra.

Functions are used to describe mathematical relationships. Distance traveled depends on (is a function of) how fast and for how long someone is traveling. Profit is a function of how much money is earned from the sale of a product and how much money is spent on costs to produce and advertise the product. The chirping of a cricket is a function of how hot the day is. A grade earned in a course is a function of a student's performance on various evaluation measures.

Students can be exposed to work with functions in a variety of ways. One way is to have students explore the idea of *function machines*. These are machines in which the input is a number and the output is another number that results from applying a rule to the input number.

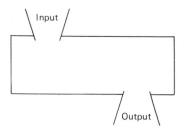

A machine might be a "plus 2" machine. Every time a number is input, the output is that number plus 2. It might be a "times 4" machine: input numbers are multiplied by 4 and the result is output. More complicated rules are also possible such as input-number times 2 plus 5, input number times itself minus 3. Once students gain experience with function machines, they can explore sequences of numbers to identify number patterns that can be described in functional terms. Two pieces of software, *King's Rule* and *Guess My Rule* provide opportunities for additional work in this area.

King's Rule is designed to build skills in recognizing number patterns and relationships and in critical thinking and problem solving.

There are six levels of difficulty. At each level, three numbers are shown. These numbers correspond to a secret rule. Students generate hypotheses about the rule and then test these hypotheses by entering their own sets of three numbers. When a set is entered, the computer checks it against the rule and lets the students know if, yes, it conforms or, no, it does not. When students are confident they know the rule, they may take a quiz that tests their conclusions.

As an example, consider Level 2, The Guard's Room. The teacher's manual states that the rules involve constant multiplication or division by 1-5 inclusive. The starting number for the sequence is in the range 1-9. A possible number sequence is:

36   12   4

If the relationship is displayed in descending order (as done here), the operation is division. If in ascending order, it is multiplication. Students can then begin to test hypotheses in the form of their own number sequences:

1st	2nd	3rd	yes/no
45	15	5	yes
21	7	4	no

When ready, students take the quiz which consists of five different number sequences that are presented by the computer. For each, students must indicate whether it meets the rule by typing yes or no. If the quiz is completed with no errors, students have identified the rule.

The majority of the rules used in this program are function rules such as: the third number is the sum of the first two, the second and third numbers are multiples of the first, the third number is 10 minus the sum of the first 2 numbers. In some instances, a function is not involved, such as all numbers end in 9 or all numbers are multiples of 100. The levels become increasingly complex and present students with some excellent challenges. As introductory work in identifying and stating relationships, this program provides informal experiences that can be very valuable.

Guess My Rule is designed to give students opportunities to work with number patterns and relationships, functions, graphing, and problem solving. If used as part of a sequence of activities, it comes after *King's Rule*. In this program, students collect information in order to guess an unknown rule. Unlike *King's Rule*, in which a rule involves students using sequences of three numbers, in *Guess My Rule* students give the computer one number at a time. For each number entered (the x value), a rule is applied to the number and the result (the y value) is displayed either in a table or as part of an ordered pair (*x, y* as values) shown as a point on a graph. The goal for students is to look for numerical and graphical patterns and to write functions as equations that define the relationships behind those patterns. The program capitalizes on the manipulative potential of the computer and, by using both tables and graphs, permits multiple representations of the information.

Guess My Rule provides an introductory tutorial, lets students play the game, or lets students make their own rules. In playing the game, students select a level from "Pre-Algebra," "Algebra 1," "Algebra 2," "Mixed Area," or "Mystery Problems." Once a level is selected, students can choose how the rule is presented: they may select a rule, the computer may pick a rule randomly, or the computer may select rules in order.

As an example, suppose the "Pre-Algebra" level is chosen. The students are presented with a screen that looks like this:

X	Y	GUESSES

```
Press the first letter of an option
PLOT  GUESS  INPUT  DECIMAL
```

Choosing INPUT lets students enter values for *x* one at a time. After each entry, the corresponding value for *y* is determined and printed. If students have selected several values for *x*, the following might be their table:

X	Y	GUESSES
5	8.0	
2	5.0	
9	12.0	
1	4.0	
3	6.0	
4	7.0	

At this point, or any earlier point, students can choose to plot their number pairs. A coordinate grid is shown, scaled by the program. However, students can change the scale of the graph if they wish. A graph of the number pairs is drawn.

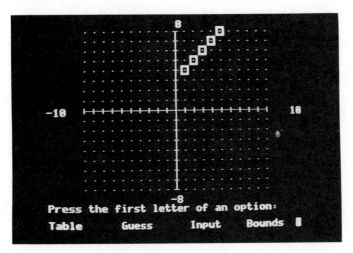

FIGURE 5-8. *Guess My Rule.*

In either representation (table or graph), students can guess the rule $y = x + 3$. In the graphics mode, the computer draws the graph of the entered rule. If it is correct, it is superimposed on the earlier plotted line. If the rule is incorrect, the line for the entered rule is plotted so that the student can compare the two lines.

In the table mode, the guess of a rule is shown with the resulting y values and the originally entered x values:

X	Y	G1
5	8.0	8.0
2	5.0	5.0
9	12.0	12.0
1	4.0	4.0
3	6.0	6.0
4	7.0	7.0

If the values associated with the GUESS match those values already shown for y, the rule has been determined. If not, students can compare the tables of data.

In using this program, some important strategies emerge. Students, with time, begin to enter values systematically, such as 0, 1, 2, 3, 4, and examine the results in order to determine patterns of differences in the table. For example, consider the two tables below:

Table A				Table B	
x	y			x	y
0	3			0	1
1	5			1	2
2	7			2	5
3	9			3	10
4	11			4	17

The difference pattern in the y-values in Table A is constant: the difference between 3 and 5 is 2; between 5 and 7 is 2; between 7 and 9 is 2; and between 9 and 11 is 2 (rule: $2x + 3$). The difference pattern in the y-values in Table B is not constant: the difference between 1 and 2 is 1; between 2 and 5 is 3; between 5 and 10 is 5; and between 10 and 17 is 7 (rule: $x^2 + 1$). In the study of an area in mathematics known as finite differences, these difference patterns indicate the types of rules being used. In addition to looking for difference patterns, students explore the graphical representations and note where the line is relative to the graph axes. Each of these programs can be used independently. However, when used together, they augment, as part of a developmental sequence of activities, the introduction and exploration of the concept of function.

Reconceiving Existing Content and Methods

Another way to think about computer use is to view it as helping mathematics educators reconceive existing content and methods of teaching. In this role, the computer becomes a tool that can carry out a variety of tasks that allow students to focus on knowing and doing mathematics and not on mastering algorithmic procedures. Without the hundreds of hours needed to develop paper-and-pencil skills, the student and teacher are free to investigate mathematics in a more substantial way than was previously possible.

Several kinds of software can be used to emphasize problem solving and enhance mathematics education. Microworlds provide investigative environments for students to explore problems by experimenting, making observations, developing hypotheses, and generalizing. General tool programs, such as a word problem calculator program, a geometry construction program, spreadsheet programs, or graphing programs, help students solve particular categories of problems. Finally, programming permits students to write their own tools for solving problems.

Microworlds provide self-contained computer environments designed to put students in control of their own explorations in a specific problem area. Microworlds may be presented as games or as open-ended problem domains. Each microworld has its own specific set of commands that students use to manipulate the environment. Because of their flexibility, microworlds can be used to encourage hypothesis testing and generalization. In mathematics, microworlds are generally designed to permit students to investigate a major conceptual or content area and to develop problem-solving skills in environments that are sufficiently complex to be challenging and intriguing.

Guess My Rule is an example of a microworld in a game format. While flexible in its use, it is presented through a series of menus that clarify options and tasks for students as they proceed through the program. *The Factory*, as another example, provides a problem-solving microworld that emphasizes visual reasoning and exposes students, on an intuitive level, to preliminary concepts found in transformational geometry. The program puts students in the role of factory workers. They make "products" using machines that punch, rotate, and paint stripes on a raw material in the shape of a square. The punch machine punches one, two, or three circles or squares at one time; the rotate machine rotates a raw material 45, 90, 135, or 180 degrees; and the stripe machine paints thin, medium, or thick stripes on a raw material.

There are three parts to the program. In the first part, "Test a Machine," students may try each of the machines to see what effect they have on a raw material. The second part, "Build a Factory," has students involved in setting up an assembly line of as many as eight machines in order to make a product using the raw material. "Make a Product," the third and most challenging part, gives students a complete product, and they must build the assembly line of machines that produced that product.

Once students are familiar with the program, they are challenged by a variety of problems that focus on generalizing from their experiences. Students can be asked to determine if using the same machines in a different order produces an identical product. If they punch and then stripe or stripe and then punch, are the results the same? What happens if they rotate, stripe, and then punch or punch, stripe, and then rotate? Can students make the same product using different numbers of machines? What products take three machines? four machines? five machines? How many different products can be made using three machines? four machines? five machines?

A third example, *The Super Factory*, is designed to let students work with a raw material that is in the shape of a cube. Again, this program has three parts. The first, "Research," allows students to explore the program options; the second, "Design," provides opportunities for making products; and the third, "Challenge," gives completed products that students must duplicate. The program provides students opportunities to become familiar with the properties of a three-dimensional object, a cube, and involves them in extensive visualization and problem solving.

Gertrude's Secrets and *Gertrude's Puzzles* are examples of microworlds presented as open-ended problem domains. In these domains, students are given very little direction and no menus for options and tasks. A similar program is *Rocky's Boots*, which introduces students to the logic of constructing computer circuits. Part of the flexibility and challenge of all three programs is the need to determine what each piece of software does before using it to explore the given problem domain.

Unlike microworlds, **computer tools** do not define problems for student exploration. Rather, students define problems and then select the computer tools that facilitate their exploration of the problem. In mathematics, these tools are designed to perform time-consuming, manipulative tasks such as computation, compass and straightedge constructions, formula evaluation, and graph construction that may discourage or limit student investigations. Tools also can be used to enhance learning by permitting new and different investigations that previously were not possible because of the unreasonable amount of manipulative work needed to accomplish the "what if" questioning that characterizes true experimentation.

The *Semantic Calculator (SemCalc)* is a computer program that may be used as a calculator-like tool for solving word or story problems. In such problems, two questions are of concern: How many? (a number) and What? (a referent—the units to which the number refers). *SemCalc* is designed to help the user pay attention to manipulating numbers *and* their referents. Consider the following problem:

> A killer whale needs to eat a lot of fish—about 250 pounds per day. The average fish a killer whale eats weighs about 7 pounds. About how many fish does a killer whale have to catch and eat each day to keep from being hungry? (EDC)

The program, when run, displays something like a notepad on the screen. The pad has two columns: the first is labeled HOW MANY? and the second WHAT? The students enter all the quantities that are pertinent to a given problem. In this case, the pad might look like this:

```
         HOW MANY?        WHAT?
  A      250              POUNDS/DAY
  B      7                POUNDS/FISH
  C
```

Suppose students wish to divide the two quantities (A ÷ B). The program responds with

```
THE UNITS OF THE ANSWER ARE
         FISH
         ————
         DAY
```

and gives students the option of starting over or proceeding. If the students are satisfied that these are the units needed, they proceed and the program responds with

```
250 POUNDS/DAY / 7 POUNDS/FISH =
       31.7142857  FISH
                   ────
                   DAY
```

and adds this quantity and referent to the pad as item C. If the students decided to multiply the two quantities (A × B), the program responds with

```
THE UNITS OF THE ANSWER ARE
       POUNDS POUNDS
       ─────────────
       DAY FISH
```

Note that it is up to the *students* to recognize that they need to rethink their strategy because these units are not the ones that answer the question of how many fish need to be caught each day. However, if the students choose to continue, the program responds with:

```
250 POUNDS/DAY * 7 POUNDS/FISH =
     1750   POUNDS POUNDS
            ─────────────
            DAY FISH
```

The goal of the program is to get students to pay attention to the referents of numbers and how these referents influence the kinds of computations that can be done. While it is useful in helping students solve the more traditional textbook word or story problems, its power encourages extensions to more realistic multistep problems that involve the statement and computation of several quantities. For example,

> In 1968, a male killer whale named Hyak was captured and taken to the Vancouver Aquarium. He was 11 feet long and weighed 1,000 pounds. By 1974, Hyak had grown to a length of 17 feet and weighed 4,500 pounds. What was Hyak's average growth rate (in feet per year) during these years? (EDC)

Students can be encouraged to look for real-world applications or to create their own word problems focused on things they are currently studying in other areas such as science or social studies.

The Geometric Supposer: Triangles is a program that lets students explore triangles by carrying out a variety of constructions on triangles that, in the past, have always been done using a straightedge and compass.

The program is a tool for the geometer. Students can construct any kind of triangle, can draw line segments, medians, altitudes, and perpendicular lines. They can bisect angles and inscribe or circumscribe circles. Finally, students can measure lengths, angles, areas, and distances and can determine arithmetic combinations of these measures.

As a teaching tool, *The Geometric Supposer: Triangles* can be used in a problem-oriented teaching environment that seeks to place students in the role of mathematicians and permits them to develop their own conjectures. (Indeed, one student using this program actually discovered a new mathematics theorem.) As an example, consider the following problem: "Find the measures of each of the three angles inside a triangle. What do you believe to be true about the sum of all three of the angles?" To explore this problem, students either select a triangle or create their own:

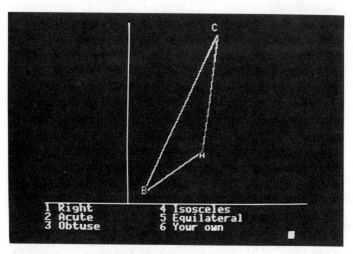

FIGURE 5-9. *The Geometric Supposer: Triangles.*

They then can choose the option to measure each of the angles and determine the sum of these measures (see Figure 5-10 on page 107).

Once completed for one triangle, students can begin to gather more data using other kinds of triangles. After some exploration, they can make a conjecture about what they believe to be true about the sum of the angles in triangles.

The Geometric Supposer: Triangles is one of a series of programs, all designed to have students investigate geometry in order to make conjectures. While this program and another, *The Geometric Supposer: Quadrilaterals,* are most appropriate for high school classes, several middle school classes have worked with it to explore geometric ideas that are not part of the standard curriculum. In addition to these two programs, a third program, *The Presupposer,* is designed to provide a foundation for geometry in the elementary grades. These three programs have the potential to

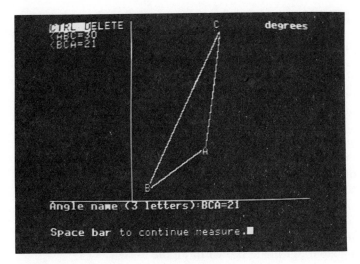

FIGURE 5-10. *The Geometric Supposer,* measuring angles.

significantly revolutionize how the content of geometry is presented and the role of the student in the learning of mathematics.

Collecting, organizing, displaying, and analyzing data are increasingly important skills. Several software tools are available to help students with the graphical display of data. Three programs that simplify the process and help students make professional-looking graphs are *Exploring Tables and Graphs* (Levels 1 [ages 7–10] and 2 [ages 10 and up]), *DataPlot* (ages 12 and up), and *PFS-Graph* (ages 10 and up), which can be used with a companion database package, *PFS-File.*

While each of these programs has different characteristics, they all require that data to be graphed be entered in table format. For example, an interesting investigation involves the use of M & M plain or peanut candies. The problem, given one type of M & M candies, is to determine if it is possible to predict the number and color distribution of the candies in an individual bag. Using M & M peanut candies, pairs of students can each be given a bag of candy (*note:* bags should be the same weight) to determine by counting how many of each color there are in the bag. This data can be displayed as a table:

BAG 1

COLOR	NUMBER OF CANDIES
ORANGE	12
YELLOW	6
BROWN	7
GREEN	9

Using the graphing capability, students enter this data in a table provided by the program. Since the software is designed to create bar, picture, pie, or line graphs, the first task for students after entering their data in a table is to select the type of graph. A crucial question must be answered. Which graph is an appropriate choice to display the data? All graphs cannot be used to communicate all kinds of information. A bar graph is appropriate for showing comparisons of most kinds. A picture graph uses pictures (or symbols) to show amounts and, like bar graphs, is useful in making data comparisons, especially when great accuracy is not needed. A pie graph is used when a whole and its parts must be known—the whole population of the school, the whole set of team scores, the number and colors of candy in a whole bag of peanut M & Ms. A line graph connects points of data and is used to display trends—increases or decreases in the stock market, temperature, or population.

In this example, a bar or picture graph may be used. As a sample, the results of choosing a bar graph are shown in Figure 5-11.

The M & Ms investigation, with its goal of prediction, necessitates that students examine several sets of data (the results from several bags of

FIGURE 5-11. Data from M & Ms Investigation as a bar graph.

COLORS	NUMBER IN BAG 1
1> ORANGE	1> 12
2> YELLOW	2> 6
3> BROWN	3> 7
4> GREEN	4> 9

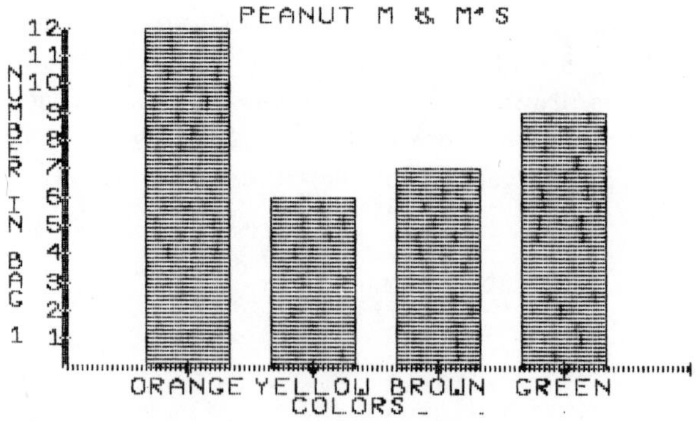

peanut M & Ms). Both *Exploring Tables and Graphs* and *PFS-Graph* permit entry of multiple tables of data and display of multiple sets of data on a single graph. Given these options, students can explore a variety of questions using graphs. Figure 5-12 shows some of the possibilities.

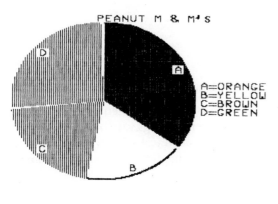

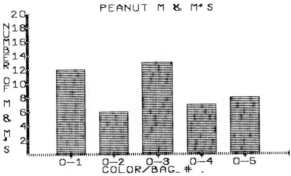

FIGURE 5-12. M & Ms Investigation.

Another consideration when designing a bar or line graph is scaling. For example, suppose students keep track of barometer readings for several days (*note:* barometric pressure is an indication of weather; when the pressure falls, it indicates bad weather). Students can find readings reported daily in the newspaper or can make their own barometers. Figure 5-13 shows a table of the data. A line graph is an appropriate graph for displaying this kind of data.

Graphing software automatically sets the scales for a graph. The user can change this if needed or desired. Given the data on barometric readings,

```
           DATE            ! BAROMETER READING
=====================!====================
  1> SEPT 29             !  1>  30.17
  2> SEPT 30             !  2>  30.2
  3> OCT  1              !  3>  30.01
  4> OCT  2              !  4>  29.75
  5> OCT  3              !  5>  29.76
  6> OCT  4              !  6>  29.99
  7> OCT  5              !  7>  30.28
  8> OCT  6              !  8>  30.47
  9> OCT  7              !  9>  30.5
 10> OCT  8              ! 10>  30.25
 11> OCT  9              ! 11>  30.24
 12> OCT 10              ! 12>  30.37
 13> OCT 11              ! 13>  30.19
 14> OCT 12              ! 14>  30.19
 15> OCT 13              ! 15>  30.18
```

FIGURE 5-13. Barometer Readings as a Table.

the line graph shown in Figure 5-14 has been made, letting the software set the scale from 0 to 32.5. Since barometer readings vary only slightly in a range, this graph appears to be almost a straight line. If the scale is adjusted to reflect a significantly limited range from 29.5 to 30.5, changes

FIGURE 5-14. Barometer Readings with Automatic Scaling.

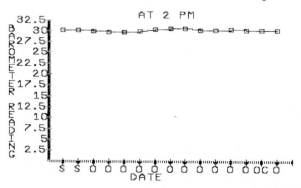

in the barometric pressure are dramatic (see Figure 5-15), and students can now comment on the kinds of weather that must have occurred over the period of time under consideration.

FIGURE 5-15. Barometer Readings with Adjusted Scaling.

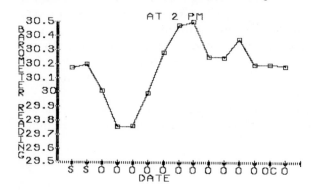

Changes in scale can be used not only to clarify data but to create a "message." In particular, experimenting with scale changes can help students explore how graphs may be used to provide misleading information. Suppose 100 students were surveyed about their preference for Coke or Pepsi; fifty-two liked Coke and forty-eight preferred Pepsi. Figure 5–16 shows three different graphs of the same information. Which graph should Coke use if it wants to argue its benefits? What is misleading about this graph?

FIGURE 5–16. Survey Results: Coke or Pepsi? with automatic and adjusted scaling.

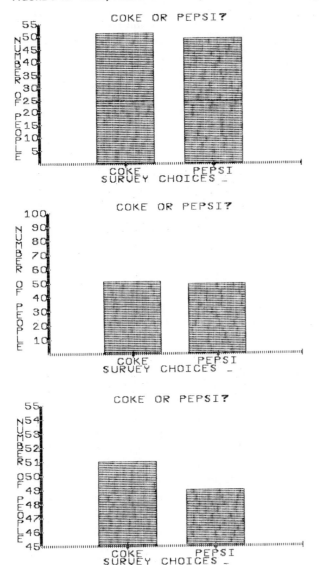

Once data have been gathered, graphing software provides a variety of opportunities for "what if" experimenting that encourage a more extensive understanding of the power of data display in conveying information. Beyond this, the quality of the presentations (as opposed to "handmade" graphs) is truly exciting for students. Educationally, two issues need consideration when thinking about the use of graphing software:

1. Graphing programs should be introduced as part of a sequence of activities that is developed to teach students about bar, picture, line, and pie graphs. A crucial question is how much precomputer experience must students have in constructing their own graphs. Graphing software may be viewed as "magic" by those students who do not possess conceptual understanding. Yet, given such a powerful tool, should we move quickly from "student-created" to "machine-created" graphs?

2. Graphing programs have their own idiosyncrasies. For example, labeling of the displays has limitations (see Figure 5-14). Labels may be limited in the number of characters, or table labels may be shortened on the graph, causing unintended confusion. Teachers need to experiment with the software in order to be aware of limitations.

Graphing software provides opportunities to engage students in significant data-representation problems. Such software may be combined with database software or spreadsheet programs to provide powerful tools for data analysis.

Spreadsheets are tools designed in the format of a matrix consisting of rows and columns. A *cell* in a spreadsheet is a location at which a given row and column intersect. Generally a spreadsheet consists of rows designated by numbers and columns designated by letters. A cell is identified by its row and column name—for example, A5 (column A, row 5), E12 (column E, row 12).

A cell can contain one of three things: a label, a value, or a formula. A *label* is a word or words that can be entered to clarify data shown on the spreadsheet (similar to a label on a graph). A *value* is a numerical constant such as "243" or "−5.93." A *formula* is an expression that contains one or more variables (which are cell names), numbers, and mathematical functions, such as $((C4 + D9) / F12) * 6$.

Spreadsheets are versatile tools for teaching. Teachers can use the spreadsheet to provide frameworks for investigating problems. For example, spreadsheets can be designed as function machines and can be used as part of the sequential development of function concepts mentioned earlier in this chapter. A variety of frameworks can be created like those shown in Figures 5-17 and 5-18. The student loads the predesigned framework (template)—in this case MACHINE 1 for Figure 5-17 or MACHINE 2 for Figure 5-18—and enters a number in the cell to the right of the label INPUT. The remaining cells' values are built from the value entered in this

```
]PR#0-                          COLUMN A COLUMN B
     ROW        1                  NUMBER
     ROW        2                 SEQUENCE
     ROW        3
     ROW        4        INPUT         0
     ROW        5
     ROW        6        RESULT        3
     ROW        7
     ROW        8                      6
     ROW        9
     ROW       10                      9
     ROW       11
     ROW       12                     12
     ROW       13
     ROW       14                     15


 _                      COLUMN A COLUMN B
     ROW        1                  NUMBER
     ROW        2                 SEQUENCE
     ROW        3
     ROW        4        INPUT        -8
     ROW        5
     ROW        6        RESULT       -5
     ROW        7
     ROW        8                     -2
     ROW        9
     ROW       10                      1
     ROW       11
     ROW       12                      4
     ROW       13
     ROW       14                      7


 _                      COLUMN A COLUMN B
     ROW        1                  NUMBER
     ROW        2                 SEQUENCE
     ROW        3
     ROW        4        INPUT       107
     ROW        5
     ROW        6        RESULT      110
     ROW        7
     ROW        8                    113
     ROW        9
     ROW       10                    116
     ROW       11
     ROW       12                    119
     ROW       13
     ROW       14                    122
```

FIGURE 5-17. Machine 1: Plus 3.

cell. The purpose is to have the student identify whether the machine is a "plus" machine, a "times" machine, a "minus" machine, or a "divide" machine. The examples shown in Figure 5-17 and 5-18 demonstrate several trials using a "plus 3" machine and a "times 4" machine respectively.

Students and teachers can design spreadsheets together. For example, continuing with an earlier investigation involving peanut M & Ms, what if students wanted to compute the averages for each color and for the total number of M & Ms found in a bag of candy? A spreadsheet can be set up so that each pair of students enters its individual data under the correct title

		COLUMN A	COLUMN B
ROW	1		NUMBER
ROW	2		SEQUENCE
ROW	3		
ROW	4	INPUT	0
ROW	5		
ROW	6	RESULT	0
ROW	7		
ROW	8		0
ROW	9		
ROW	10		0
ROW	11		
ROW	12		0
ROW	13		
ROW	14		0

		COLUMN A	COLUMN B
ROW	1		NUMBER
ROW	2		SEQUENCE
ROW	3		
ROW	4	INPUT	-8
ROW	5		
ROW	6	RESULT	-32
ROW	7		
ROW	8		-128
ROW	9		
ROW	10		-512
ROW	11		
ROW	12		-2048
ROW	13		
ROW	14		-8192

		COLUMN A	COLUMN B
ROW	1		NUMBER
ROW	2		SEQUENCE
ROW	3		
ROW	4	INPUT	107
ROW	5		
ROW	6	RESULT	428
ROW	7		
ROW	8		1712
ROW	9		
ROW	10		6848
ROW	11		
ROW	12		27392
ROW	13		
ROW	14		109568

FIGURE 5-18. Machine 2: Times 4.

(see Figure 5-19). The row marked TOTAL and the column marked AVERAGE are formulas that the students or teacher enter in order to summarize the data.

Spreadsheets offer great potential for helping students explore mathematical relationships without the tedium of extensive computation. A

FIGURE 5-19. Peanut M & Ms: Five Bags.

	BAG 1	BAG 2	BAG 3	BAG 4	BAG 5	AVERAGE
ORANGE	12	6	13	7	8	9.2
YELLOW	6	11	5	12	9	8.6
BROWN	7	6	8	5	8	6.8
GREEN	9	9	7	7	7	7.8
TOTAL	34	32	33	31	32	32.4

variety of applications extend beyond the traditional curriculum and engage students meaningfully in exploring mathematics.

Programming with languages such as Logo or BASIC enhances mathematics instruction in a variety of ways. "Teaching" a computer to do a task requires very explicit instructions. Students who engage in making a computer solve a problem must have a clear understanding of the steps needed to solve the problem. When a program does not work, students must refine and correct their own thinking as they "debug" the program. Programming also permits students to investigate outcomes that require a great deal of computational work. Having the computer assume the burden of the computation allows students to make observations, explore patterns, and generalize without being interrupted or defeated by tedious computation.

Logo is an excellent language to use with elementary and middle school students. Because of its graphics capabilities, Logo can be used to provide fresh opportunities for work in geometry.

One activity centers around an exploration of regular polygons (closed figures having sides of equal length). What different regular polygons can be created using Logo? To investigate this problem, students need to gather data. The easiest place to start is to have students, working in pairs, create a square. Once that is done, they can record their commands on a strip of paper and post it on a bulletin board. Following this, students can now be challenged to continue investigating polygons with differing numbers of sides—three-sided, four-sided, five-sided, six-sided, seven-sided, and more. Each time one is created, the commands used are recorded on a strip of paper and posted on the bulletin board. The data on the bulletin board becomes the vehicle for making generalizations about procedures that can be designed for making polygons.

For example, students who have used the REPEAT command may observe that with the square, the number of sides and the amount of turn were always the same:

```
REPEAT 4[FD 40  RT 90] or
REPEAT 4[FD 90  LT 90] or
REPEAT 4[BK 56  RT 90] or
REPEAT 4[BK 100 LT 90]
```

Similar observations can be made about the procedures for other polygons. Specifically, students can consider which numbers are important and which numbers can be changed. It is then possible to generalize a MASTER PROCEDURE for each polygon. For example, for the square: REPEAT 4[FD or BK—RT or LT 90].

Depending on students' experience with Logo, many extensions are possible that combine further work with geometry in this programming environment. Students can explore the TOTAL TURTLE TRIP theorem and discover the relationship between the number of sides, the amount of turn, and the total turn of 360 degrees to make one "trip" around (REPEAT 5[FD 40 RT 360/5] or REPEAT 8 [FD 30 RT 360/8]). Students may write procedures that create "growing polygons" in which they draw a triangle, then draw a square surrounding the triangle, then draw a pentagon surrounding the square, then draw a hexagon surrounding a pentagon, and so on. Eventually, they discover how a circle may be made in Logo. Students may be ready to use variables. Referring to their earlier development of a MASTER PROCEDURE for a square, the syntax needed for using a variable can be introduced:

```
TO SQUARE:SIDE
   REPEAT 4[FD:SIDE RT 90]
END
```

A variety of other areas lend themselves to programming activities with either Logo or BASIC. The design and use of *simulations* is one area in which mathematics can be easily applied. Students may design programs that simulate the tossing of two dice or the flipping of a coin. They can simulate a variety of other probability experiments using the computer. Beyond this, with the increasing use of simulations, students have greater opportunities to explore concepts associated with model building.

Simulations, as models of real-world environments, are based on the statement of functional relationships between variables. In *Lemonade,* a now-classic computer economic simulation for the elementary grades, one relationship involves profit: profit is related to the price charged for a glass of lemonade, the number of glasses of lemonade sold, and the costs to produce and advertise the lemonade. In *Island Survivors,* a computer simulation focused on investigating concepts in ecosystems, one relationship involves the size of the population of land or pond animals: population density is related to the time of year, a given animal's food resources, and whether a given animal's population is depleted because it serves as a food resource to other species.

The relationships that govern models are stated as mathematical equations. Students can interact with already-developed computer simulations to try to determine the relationships that govern the model presented. They also can explore programming simple models of their own.

One such programming activity provides an introduction to simulating population-growth models. Students are involved in two explorations that focus on a few of the variables that affect population levels. The experiments are about imaginary animals called tribbles (named after the fuzzy creatures that are presented in one of the "Star Trek" episodes).

The first experiment involves students in an exploration of population growth. Students begin with 50 tribbles as the starting population.

Each pair of tribbles produces a litter of one tribble every month, and single tribbles cannot reproduce. Thus, if the total population is 25 tribbles in a given month, there are 12 pairs of tribbles and each pair has a litter of one tribble. The single tribble has no litter that month.

For this experiment, students need a data sheet as shown in Figure 5-20. Students must determine what happens to the population of tribbles after ten months by filling in the missing numbers on the data sheet. Doing this activity by hand involves students in what becomes a very mechanical task. The only problems, once students understand what is happening, are maintaining accuracy in computation, and boredom.

FIGURE 5-20. The Tribble Experiment.

Assumption:

1. Each pair of tribbles produces a litter of one tribble every month.

Problem:

If the initial tribble population is established as 50 newborn tribbles, what happens to the population in 10 months?

Challenge:

TOTAL POPULATION represents the total number of tribbles at the end of every month, and BIRTHS represents the total number of births in one month. How is BIRTHS determined each month? How is TOTAL POPULATION determined each month?

Data Collection:

MONTH	BIRTHS	POPULATION
1	50	50
2		
3		
4		
5		
6		
7		
8		
9		
10		

As a follow-up, the BASIC computer program shown in Figure 5-21 can be developed by or provided to students as a check on their calculations for the 10 months (see Figure 5-21A for a run of the program). Students may also use the program to explore the model of population growth presented by the tribbles problem. For example, how many months does it take for the tribble population to exceed 100,000 if the starting

```
]LIST

100   REM   P = POPULATION OF TRIBBLES EACH MONTH
110   REM   M = NUMBER OF MONTHS TO LET PROGRAM RUN
120   REM   NB = NUMBER OF NEW BIRTHS IN A MONTH
130   INPUT "STARTING POPULATION OF TRIBBLES:";P
140   PRINT
150   INPUT "NUMBER OF MONTHS:";M
155   PRINT
160   PRINT "MONTH","BIRTHS","POP"
165   PRINT 1,P,P
170   FOR I = 2 TO M
180 NB =   INT (P / 2)
190 P = P + NB
200   PRINT I,NB,P
210   NEXT I
220   END
```

FIGURE 5-21. BASIC Program: Tribbles.


```
]RUN
STARTING POPULATION OF TRIBBLES:50

NUMBER OF MONTHS:10
```

MONTH	BIRTHS	POP
1	50	50
2	25	75
3	37	112
4	56	168
5	84	252
6	126	378
7	189	567
8	283	850
9	425	1275
10	637	1912

FIGURE 5-21A. Sample Run: Tribbles.

population is 50 tribbles? Students can predict and then use the program to test this question. As a further example, what must be the starting population of tribbles if, by the tenth month, the population is just over 100,000?

Students can also change the model of population growth presented in the program. Suppose that pairs of tribbles produce litters of 2 tribbles each month. The number of new births (line 180) would need to be multiplied by 2: 180 NB = 2 * (INT(P/2). Suppose that each pair of tribbles produces a randomly sized litter that varied between 1 and 3 tribbles. Line 180 has to be replaced with the following code:

```
180 NB = 0
182 FOR J = 1 TO INT(P/2)
184 NUM = INT ( 3 * RND(1)) + 1
186 NB = NB + NUM
188 NEXT J
```

Students quickly realize that there are other things (called *variables*) that affect a population. These include not only reproduction (as shown in the previous paragraph) but also such things as death rate, disease, and predators.

In the second experiment, death rate is introduced. Every month, 10 percent of the tribbles die. This occurs after the new births for that month (it can also occur before the new births, in which case the final population figures for each month are different). For this experiment, students need a different data sheet (see Figure 5-22) in order to determine what happens in 10 months when each pair of tribbles produces a litter of tribbles once a month.

FIGURE 5-22. The Second Tribble Experiment.

Assumptions:

1. Each pair of tribbles produces a litter of one tribble every month.
2. 10% of all tribbles die every month. (Rounding)

Problem:

If the initial tribble population is established as 50 newborn tribbles, what happens to the population in 10 months?

Challenge:

TOTAL POPULATION represents the total number of tribbles at the end of every month, BIRTHS represents the total number of births in one month, and DEATHS represents the total number of deaths in one month. How is BIRTHS determined each month? How is DEATHS determined each month. How is TOTAL POPULATION determined each month?

Data Collection:

MONTH	BIRTHS	DEATHS	POPULATION
1	50	5	45
2			
3			
4			
5			
6			
7			
8			
9			
10			

After the hand computation, students notice that now the population is not increasing as quickly as before. Again, as a follow-up, the BASIC computer program (shown in Figure 5-23) can be developed or provided for students to check their calculations for the 10 months (see Figure 5-23A

```
]LIST

100   REM   P = POPULATION OF TRIBBLES EACH MONTH
110   REM   M = NUMBER OF MONTHS TO LET PROGRAM RUN
120   REM   DR = DEATH RATE EXPRESSED AS DECIMAL
130   REM   NB = NUMBER OF NEW BIRTHS IN A MONTH
140   REM   D = NUMBER OF DEATHS IN A MONTH
150   INPUT "STARTING POPULATION OF TRIBBLES:";P
160   PRINT
170   INPUT "NUMBER OF MONTHS:";M
180   PRINT
190   INPUT "DEATH RATE AS A DECIMAL";DR
200   PRINT
210   PRINT "MTH";"    ";"BIRTHS","DEATHS","POP"
220   GOSUB 500: REM   COMPUTE D
230   PRINT 1;"       ";P,D,P - D
240 P = P - D
250   FOR I = 2 TO M
260 NB =  INT (P / 2)
270   GOSUB 500
280 P = P + NB - D
290   PRINT I;"        ";NB,D,P
300   NEXT I
310   END
500   REM   COMPUTE D
510 D = (P + NB) * DR
520   IF  INT (D) = D THEN 580
530 DECIMAL = 10 * (D -  INT (D))
540   IF DECIMAL < 5 THEN 570
550 D =  INT (D) + 1
560   GOTO 580
570 D =  INT (D)
580   RETURN
```

FIGURE 5-23. BASIC Program: Tribbles.

```
]RUN
STARTING POPULATION OF TRIBBLES:50

NUMBER OF MONTHS:10

DEATH RATE AS A DECIMAL.10
```

MTH	BIRTHS	DEATHS	POP
1	50	5	45
2	22	7	60
3	30	9	81
4	40	12	109
5	54	16	147
6	73	22	198
7	99	30	267
8	133	40	360
9	180	54	486
10	243	73	656

FIGURE 5-23A. Sample Run: Tribbles.

for a run of the program). This program can also be used to explore the model of population growth with death rate included as presented by the tribbles problem. In this case, what must the death rate be for the population of tribbles to stabilize (to remain constant without any increase or decrease)?

Introducing further variables quickly makes the model of the tribbles population more detailed. What happens if the tribbles' food supply is limited and famine results? What happens if tribbles can reproduce only during the first six months of their lives? What happens if overcrowding occurs because there are too many tribbles for the available space (population density increases)? What happens if there are changes in temperature in their environment? Adding more variables makes it more difficult to experiment by hand. It also makes the design of the computer model more complex. Discussing the variables in this light helps students develop an awareness for the complexity involved in describing any population model and the things that affect it and that it affects.

RETHINKING THE MATHEMATICS CURRICULUM

Traditional mathematics instruction at the elementary and middle school levels has stressed the development of students' skills in using mechanical procedures. These include computational skills needed in arithmetic and computational and symbol-manipulation skills needed in algebra and geometry. The use of computers (and calculators) reduces significantly the need for students to develop efficiency and proficiency in such skills. Arithmetic today requires skills in doing mental operations for quick approximations and not skills in pencil-and-paper manipulations. Calculators can be used to perform actual one-time computations, and computers can be used for repetitive computations. In algebra, computers can be used to do the numeric and symbol-manipulative procedures, thus freeing students from the countless hours necessary to master these skills. In geometry, computers can be used to complete compass and straightedge constructions or transformations, thus allowing students to explore concepts and theories derived from the results of such constructions. Clearly, the resources provided by technology indicate a different kind of mathematics learning and teaching than has been done in the past. Because of available technologies, it is now possible to change the direction of mathematics instruction and to include a range of new or previously neglected topics. (NCTM)

At a conference held by the National Council of Teachers of Mathematics (NCTM), several recommendations were made for the direction of the mathematics curriculum. At the elementary school level (K–4), focus should be on the development of basic facts in order for students to become proficient in mental arithmetic and estimation. This does *not* include devoting extensive time to skills associated with multiple-digit calculations. Work in this area should be eliminated from the curriculum. Calculators should be routinely available to students. One focus of instruction should be on providing students with the ability to decide when to rely on mental operations, when on a calculator, or when on paper-and-pencil computation. Because of the availability of technology, mathematics topics not ordinarily taught in K–4 may be considered. These include transformations, decimals, negative numbers, scientific notation, statistical concepts, and the concepts of variable or function.

At the middle school level (grades 5–8), emphasis should be on the development of number sense. Students need an intuitive feeling for number size in order to be skillful in estimation and approximation and in judging the reasonableness of results. Topics from discrete mathematics (probability, logic, graph theory, and counting), from statistics (gathering, organizing, presenting, and interpreting data), and from geometry (using visual-display capabilities for informal geometry) should be introduced. There should be an increased emphasis on problem-solving strategies that are enhanced by the availability of technology (making lists, guess and check, successive approximations, and geometric sketches).

At both the elementary and middle school levels, programming should be used to convey mathematics and computer concepts. By the end of the sixth grade, students should be able to write programs that involve looping and branching concepts. These programs should be directly related to the content of mathematics they are learning.

Not only will the content of mathematics change. The way mathematics is taught using technology suggests a new relationship among teachers, students, and subject matter. Teachers and students will become partners in the exploration of mathematical ideas. This will provide a new and different instructional environment than the one currently in place.

REFERENCES

DIENES, Z. P., AND GOLDING, E. W. *Approach to Modern Mathematics.* New York: Herder & Herder, 1971.

Education Development Center. *Dreadful Deamons of the Deep.* Teachers' Manual. Newton, Mass.: Education Development Center, 1981.

HATFIELD, L. L. "Toward Comprehensive Instructional Computing." In Hansen, V.P., and Aweng, M.J., eds., *Computers in Mathematics Education.* Reston, Va.: NCTM, 1984.

National Council of Teachers of Mathematics. *The Impact of Computing Technology on School Mathematics.* Reston, Va: NCTM, 1906 Association Drive, 1984.

RESNICK, L. B. "Mathematics and Science Learning: A New Conception." *Science,* vol. 220 (1983), 477–78.

ROBERTS, N. "Intelligent Logo Tools for Learning Algebra." NSF Grant No. MDR-8400328. Lesley College, Graduate School of Education, Cambridge, Mass., 1985–87.

SIX
COMPUTERS AND
SCIENCE INSTRUCTION

"Tell me what you remember learning in science in the elementary grades."

"What do you mean—specifically what we did during science period or just in general the topics we studied?"

"Both, but especially what science you remember learning in the lower grades."

"All I can remember is in the first few grades we did things like collect and classify plants, germinate seeds, and grow the plants under lights; study meal worms and learn that they were sensitive to light, heat, and touch; and went to two environmental camps where we studied trees, the life cycles of a marsh, and the animals that live in marshes."

"In the middle school years science focused more on the life sciences. We also studied the human body and its major systems like the heart. We learned about the effects of smoking and other drugs on such systems. We learned about the hierarchy of animal life starting with the amoeba. We dissected fish, worms, and frogs to see how systems become more and more complicated but continue to perform the same basic functions in different ways."

"Finally in the eighth grade we began *real science*, where we did experiments in laboratories and wrote them up in our lab notebooks. We studied physical science, biology, and chemistry."

This conversation, conducted with a sophomore in college, is actually more positive than the author anticipated. The amount of science remembered is reasonable, and if the conversation persisted, the student would probably have indicated fairly in-depth knowledge. The comment that *real science* began in the eighth grade when experiments were done in a laboratory is particularly revealing. Active involvement in scientific investigation in an appropriate environment is indeed much more like real science than textbook assignments or even classroom-based demonstrations and experiments.

In the fifties, trends in science education showed a concerted attempt to develop hands-on, interactive, discovery-oriented classroom materials. Following *Sputnik,* several well-funded science curriculum projects created carefully developed curricula for elementary and middle schools. These programs were commercially published, with all the support materials needed by the classroom teacher, by such companies as Rand McNally (*Science Curriculum Improvement Study,* or *SCIS*), Ginn and Company (*Science—A Process Approach,* or *SAPA*), and McGraw-Hill (*Elementary Science Study,* or *ESS*).

Over time, the impact of many of these programs disappeared as emphasis shifted from process to content (learning facts). It is only recently that there has been a resurgence of interest in designing active learning environments in which students are scientists. Part of the reason for this shift may be due to the fact that "the accumulating evidence on the science curriculum reform efforts of the past two or three decades consistently suggests that the more activity-process-based approaches to teaching science result in gains over traditional methods in a wide range of student outcome areas at all grade levels" (Bredderman, p. 513). The essence of this new direction is summed up in the introduction to Addison-Wesley's *Elementary School Science* series:

> The authors believe that children learn best through direct personal experience and frequent interaction. The Addison-Wesley Program ensures ample opportunity for children to explore their environment, to manipulate and transform objects and forces, and to observe the results of their actions. (Rockcastle, p. T-4).

THE CRISIS IN SCIENCE EDUCATION

Over the past decade an increasing number of reports have claimed that the United States education system is in crisis. Indications of this crisis are:

- Japanese and Chinese first-grade children are doing the equivalent of our sixth-grade mathematics and science.
- A grave shortage of mathematics and science teachers exists.
- The U.S. education system is unable to produce the number of engineers, scientists, and computer technicians needed for our economy to retain its technological leadership.

To increase the number of scientists and engineers, more students than ever before must elect science and mathematics courses in high school and science-related majors in college. It is the task of precollege educators to present science and mathematics as exciting, meaningful, and approachable subjects to a greater number of our students.

If doing "real science"—identifying problems, developing hypotheses, collecting data, and drawing conclusions that lead to new hypotheses—is important to students and considered to be educationally sound, why are we in today's crisis in science education? Teachers and researchers can suggest a variety of reasons why the post-*Sputnik* science curriculum materials, many in the form of "kits," did not succeed in improving the quality of science instruction and attracting a significantly larger percentage of students into science as a career. These reasons include the following:

• The introduction and implementation in the classroom of any well-conceived new curriculum materials are not a trivial matter. This is certainly true of materials such as *SCIS, SAPA,* and *ESS.* Teacher reeducation is critical for change to occur, as suggested in Chapter 1. In most schools thorough and complete teacher education is *not* provided. Those teachers with extensive science backgrounds can do a great deal of reeducation on their own, but for teachers with little or no science education, such a task is overwhelming.

• Piaget's theory about learning still influences curriculum developers; therefore hands-on experiences are considered vital. Hands-on experience, however, is not easy to create in most classrooms. One of the major problems with the science kits is the large number of pieces required for each student during each lesson. Even a teacher experienced in using these materials has a time-consuming job keeping everything in repair, making sure there are enough items for the students, and finding an accessible storage place for the kits. In addition, because the kits contain so many different things, a teacher must be reasonably skilled in classroom-management techniques to feel comfortable using the materials.

• The decline in the birth rate and the conservative tax measures adopted in many parts of the country have also affected the quality of science education. Many teachers have worried about being "RIFed" (Reduction In Force) over the last few years. Those people with appropriate skills often move out of teaching or do not choose teaching at all. The sectors of the economy recently offering the most jobs are those related to technology and are therefore open especially to people with science and mathematics backgrounds. This leaves schools with fewer and fewer qualified science teachers.

• Most science curriculums, new or old, have a strong reading component, discouraging students who can not read near grade level.

• The research on how people learn—in science or any subject—is a slowly evolving body of knowledge and is still in its early stages. Researchers are currently attempting to understand the "mental models" students use to explain their world. The idea is that as students have appropriate science-related experiences, these models slowly get closer to scientists' understandings of how things work or occur. As in every other area of teaching, it is extremely helpful, but often difficult, to know each student's level of understanding when instruction begins.

• The influence of society (and therefore the home) must not be overlooked. Traditional sex roles are still valued in most U.S. families. Girls, therefore, are not expected to be attracted to science and mathematics-based careers. Teachers, especially at the secondary and college level, do not give the same amount of support to females who might consider these areas of study.

There undoubtedly are other reasons for the current crisis in science education in the United States. These are just some of the more obvious and well-documented ones.

THE ELEMENTARY AND MIDDLE SCHOOL SCIENCE CURRICULUM TODAY

A review of a number of popular science textbook series reveals the uniformity of topics covered. The specific content, often presented in a spiral approach, includes matter, energy, the Earth, space, and life. The subtopics found across all text series involve the following content areas:

- solids, liquids, gases
- heat and temperature
- weather
- physics topics such as sound, motion, force, electricity, and light
- geological processes, rocks and minerals
- living things, their environments, and their life cycles.

In addition to the topics covered, certain processes are deemed important, including:

- observing, measuring, recording
- interpreting data, forming hypotheses, predicting
- developing laboratory techniques
- analyzing, synthesizing, and communicating results and conclusions.

Given this general agreement on what should be included in the elementary and middle school science curriculum, energy can now be directed toward finding ways to encourage student interest in science and science-based careers. There is a variety of ways in which the computer can help teachers develop enticing science-learning environments that allow students to do "real science" in an active, knowledge-rich manner.

INTEGRATING COMPUTERS INTO THE SCIENCE CURRICULUM

Computers provide powerful new ways to help students become active participants in the learning process. Fostering such a goal in science education implies using computers as scientists use them: as simulators, as laboratory tools for data gathering, as data retrieval and analysis tools, and as vehicles for communication. In addition, computers provide teachers with another pedagogical device for enriching the knowledge base of their students.

Simulations

Simulations are used as aids in decision making when the problem under study is complex and the group responsible for making decisions can be helped by first asking a series of "what if" questions. The laboratory is the traditional vehicle used by scientists to try out many possible answers for solving a given problem. Laboratories, however, work best when problems can be broken into very small parts, and when each part is more or less controllable so that the impact of varying only one element can be observed. Many situations, however, do not lend themselves to laboratory investigation. Model building and computer simulation provide alternative problem-solving environments for the scientist. A model can be thought of as a specially designed laboratory and a simulation as an experiment.

An example of using a simulation model to aid in the solution of an ongoing problem is in the area of finding and producing petroleum, which is a complicated and costly procedure. At many points along the way, critical decisions must be made by the engineers. An important tool in this decision-making process is simulation models of the oil reservoir under development. These models aid in projecting development costs, geological changes in the reservoir as it is developed, and potential profits. "Today, simulation plays an important role in the development and operation of virtually every major reservoir. The importance of reservoir simulation will continue to grow. The need to exploit reservoirs more efficiently will lead to increasingly difficult investment decisions, in which mistakes will be extremely costly. Under these circumstances, accurate prediction of reservoir performance is essential" (Watts, p. 23).

Using a simulation such as *Geology Search* provides the teacher with an opportunity for relating uses of simulation models to solving such real-world problems. In this simulation a team of students works for an oil company. Their job is to search for oil on a large continent known as Newlandia. Other companies (teams) are also searching for oil on the same continent. Through a set of readings and other activities, students learn how to conduct oil explorations. They use the computer simulation to apply the concepts they have learned in studying geology to a realistic application. As a follow-up to this simulation, students can explore the variety of issues and events that mark the history of the oil industry in the United States, paying particular attention to the energy problems of the last ten years. Using this simulation therefore also provides an opportunity to include social studies issues in the science class.

Each simulation model is a mathematical description of the situation being studied. Some person or group, of course, has to write the mathematical model; and the real learning about the problem occurs at the model-creation stage. Teachers often comment that they finally learn a subject when they have to teach it. Model building can be thought of as teaching the computer about the outside world. It is impractical to suggest that everyone who uses simulation models should build them. However, the important issues in using simulation models for decision making are most clearly understood when building models. Such questions as, How likely are behaviors observed on the computer model to be replicable in the actual problem situation? or, If I find policy choices that solve my problem on the computer, will the same policy choices solve my problem in the real world? Giving students some experiences with building mathematical models is important if they are to become intelligent consumers.

Students can create their own simulations, as was shown in Chapter 5 with the population simulations. Those programs involved students in hypothetical situations. It is also possible to have students experiment with real objects such as bouncing balls or pendulums or melting ice cubes and, from these experiences, design their own computer simulations. As an example, Figure 6-1 shows the listing for a computer program that simulates a bouncing ball.

Students can do their own experiments with bouncing balls. They can explore such variables as the size and weight of a ball when it is dropped from different heights (as measured against a classroom wall). Their exploration can focus on the number of bounces that can be counted. Students may even extend this exploration to bouncing a ball of a given size and weight from a given height on different floor surfaces—concrete, wood, or covered with a rug—and explain why the ball's bounces are different. However, even a simple action such as bouncing a ball is surprisingly complex. Not only do size and surface texture affect bouncing behavior but so do density, elasticity, and momentum of the ball, the angle at which it is thrown (if not just dropped), and even the humidity and temperature of the air.

Creating a simulation of such a phenomenon generally results in a model that is considerably simpler than the actual situation. In the simulation produced by the program given in Figure 6-1, students may experiment with three variables: initial velocity, acceleration, and elasticity. When asked for the initial throw, the student enters a number that reflects the initial velocity (or "kick") of the ball—this can be thought of as a certain number of units of distance traveled per some unit of time. Suppose 8 is entered. An initial velocity of 8 may be interpreted to mean traveling a distance of 8 feet per second.

```
]LIST

100   REM   START OFF WITH NUMBERS LIKE
110   REM   INITIAL THROW EQUAL TO 8 OR 9
120   REM   GRAVITATION EQUAL TO .8
130   REM   ELASTICITY EQUAL TO .9
140 :
150   GOSUB 1000
160   COLOR= 0
170   IF DIST < 0 OR DIST > 38 THEN 190
180   PLOT X,39 - DIST
190   COLOR= C
200 DIST = VO * T + ((A * T ^ 2) / 2)
210 VT = VO + A * T
220   IF DIST >  = 0 THEN 270
230 DIST = 0
240   IF VT >  = 0 THEN 260
250 T = 1
260 VO = VO * E
270   IF X <  = 38 THEN 300
280 INC =  - 1
290   GOTO 320
300   IF X >  = 1 THEN 320
310 INC = 1
320 X = X + INC
330   IF DIST < 01 OR DIST > 38 THEN 350
340   PLOT X,39 - DIST
350   IF DIST <  > 0 OR (X < 39 AND X > 0) THEN 380
360   GOSUB 1000
370   GOTO 390
380 T = T + 1
390   GOTO 160
400   END
1000   REM   ....
1010   GR : COLOR= 9
1020   REM   DRAW BORDER
1030   VLIN 0,39 AT 0
1040   VLIN 0,39 AT 39
1050   COLOR= 1
1060 C = 1
1070 X = 0
1080   PLOT X,39
1090 X = 0
1100   INPUT "INITIAL THROW? ";VO
1110   INPUT "GRAVITATIONAL FORCE? ";A
1120   INPUT "ELASTICITY OF BALL? ";E
1130 A =  - A
1140 T = 1
1150 INC = 1
1160 DIST = 0
1170   RETURN
```

FIGURE 6-1. Computer Program to Simulate a Bouncing Ball.

The student then enters a number for the gravitational force, which affects the acceleration of the bouncing ball. A gravitational force of 1 can be used to represent gravity on Earth. A number greater than 1 might represent gravity on Mars, while a number less than 1 gravity on Jupiter.

Acceleration is based on the force of gravity, which reduces the velocity of the ball as it moves upward. Finally, a value is entered for the elasticity of the ball against the floor surface. After the initial upward movement based on the entered velocity, elasticity affects (changes) this velocity at every new bounce. By entering values that are less than 1, equal to 1, and greater than 1, students can determine how elasticity affects velocity (for example, they can try an initial throw of 2 and a gravitational force of 1). While numbers are suggested for the values requested, ideally a student experiments with different values to understand what is meant by initial throw, gravitational force, and elasticity.

The design of this simulation requires some understanding of elementary concepts in physics. If not programmed by students themselves, the simulation can be used, following the concrete experiments described earlier, to help them develop an understanding of some of the many elements that affect the movement of a bouncing ball. Since students cannot change gravitational force in the classroom, a simulation model allows them to ask such questions as, How would this ball bounce on the Moon? on Jupiter? in a spaceship? or, What material will cause the highest bounce? Computer simulations allow scientists and students to carry out experiments for situations that are impossible to experiment with in actuality.

Simulations are also powerful pedagogic tools and many are commercially available; they are designed for a variety of classroom uses, including:

- enriching students' scientific knowledge base;
- teaching students the scientific processes used in investigations and experimentation; and
- supplementing or replacing hands-on experimentation when such activities are dangerous, costly, or impractical for precollege courses.

Let's look at examples of software that might help teachers in these three ways.

Island Survivors is a simulation designed to accompany the *Ecosystems* module in the *Voyage of the Mimi* curriculum developed to integrate the study of mathematics and science (see Chapter 8). This simulation enriches students' knowledge about ecosystems and gives them a hands-on experience that would be impossible because of time constraints. The program has two parts. In the first part, students select the species of plants and animals they want to live together in a balanced ecosystem. Two ecosystems are created: a land ecosystem and a pond ecosystem (each having four species of plants and animals).

In the second part of the program, students become involved in an adventure game. Three people are shipwrecked on an island that is inhabited by the animals and plants the students have selected. These people are not rescued for twelve months. Three activities may be chosen each month from the following: building shelter, collecting firewood, and getting food by hunting, fishing, or gathering. The food-gathering activities directly affect the populations of animals and plants on the island. The goal is to help the humans survive until a ship arrives to rescue them without destroying the balanced ecosystems of the island.

Island Survivors is a good extension of the simulated population programs described in Chapter 5. As a simulation, it can be used by students to participate in an experiment that is not possible to replicate in the laboratory because of time and complexity. The game is based on a model of an ecosystem. Students can discuss some of the factors that affect the populations of species on the island: starting population levels, the season of the year, the availability of food, and the food-gathering conducted by the humans. After several opportunities to play, students can discuss the *simplicity* of the model. What things are not considered that actually happen in an ecosystem?

Another simulation designed to extend students' knowledge base is *Sir Isaac Newton's Games*. This program contains five games that provide a hands-on environment for the study of Newton's laws of motion. In each game, students are given a marker that they must move either by kicking it or letting it coast. Friction may or may not act upon its motion. The games are designed so that "time" stops and waits for each move of a player. This encourages students to continually assess the consequences of their next move.

There are different levels in the understanding of movement. While most are taught in advanced physics courses that require advanced mathematical knowledge, it is possible to create an exploratory environment for younger students that permits an intuitive development of the concept of change in motion.

The use of a simulation can be specifically directed to the development of scientific processes such as inquiry skills. In *The Incredible Laboratory*, students act as scientists working in a laboratory to create fanciful monsters. The problem-solving methods of science, rather than a specific science concept or content area, are the purpose of this simulation. Students, selecting from a list of chemicals, make a monster with such features as a red head, furry legs, or a scaly body. Students must determine which chemical creates each of five body parts: head, body, arms, legs, and feet. Altogether, fifteen chemicals may be combined to make colorful and unusual monsters.

The Incredible Laboratory has three playing levels: novice, apprentice, and scientist. At each level, students may choose either the play mode, in which they select ingredients and try to determine the effects as a monster is made, or the challenge mode, in which they use their conclusions to compete with one another in recognizing monsters.

As novices, students use the same five chemicals (with such names as "alien oil," "sparkles," or "magic powder") in every play. Each chemical affects one feature of the monster and has the same effect each time the

FIGURE 6.2. *The Incredible Laboratory*, the machine.

program is run. As apprentices, students can choose one of two levels of difficulty. In either level, five groups of three chemicals each are used, and each group relates to a specific body part. Chemicals or combinations of chemicals have the same effects each time the program is run. The object is to identify which feature is affected by which group of chemicals. Once students are scientists, they again may choose from two levels of difficulty, each of which uses five groups of three chemicals each. However, the effects of chemicals or combinations of chemicals change each time the program is run.

This software helps students focus on data gathering, developing lists to organize information, and looking for patterns to develop hypotheses about the effects of the various chemicals. Hypothesis-testing strategies should be discussed as students attempt to *verify* or *negate* a current hypothesis. Hypothesis verification is the more common technique. Students develop a guess about the effect of one or more of the chemicals and design follow-up experiments to verify their guess. For example, at the novice level, students may determine that alien oil creates the head of the monster and go on to design several further experiments that combine it with a variety of different chemical mixes. After several experiments, students may conclude that if the head of the monster always stays the same it must be the continuing result of the presence of alien oil. However, it is possible, through verification, that the students are maintaining an incorrect hypothesis. It is possible that some other chemical has also been consistently used in the various mixes and may be responsible for the head.

In hypothesis negation, students develop a guess (hypothesis) and then design experiments to negate, or disprove, it. Continuing with the example, once students develop the hypothesis that alien oil creates the head of the monster, they may attempt to disprove it by designing several experiments that exclude the use of alien oil. The computer, however, randomly supplies the monster's features the user does not specify. If the head remains the same after several experiments involving this same set of chemicals, the student concludes that alien oil is *not* the chemical determining the head. However, if the head changes, the student concludes that the head is determined by alien oil.

IBM has just released software (coming out of years of research and development at the Educational Technology Center at the University of California at Irvine) that also attempts to give the user insight and experience with the scientific process. Twelve *Scientific Reasoning* modules have been developed for use with middle school students through adults. The thrust of the materials is general scientific literacy. The materials have been structured to work in both formal and informal educational settings. The modules "attempt to aid students in problem solving. They concentrate on issues associated with how the scientist goes about developing scientific theories and what is science all about" (Bork et al., p. 12).

The twelve modules focus on measurement, developing scientific theories, concept formation, and formal reasoning skills. One of the modules, "Families," provides an imaginary environment for students to discover Mendel's rules of genetics by mating "tribbles" and observing the characteristics of their offspring. Another module, based on the *Elementary Science Study* unit on batteries and bulbs, challenges students to light a bulb, given a bulb, battery, and wire. The difference between this computer-based unit and the original hands-on experience is that the computer prompts the student at selected intervals as necessary. The original *ESS* unit leaves prompting totally in the hands of teacher or peer. The presence of a teacher is not assumed, since these units are designed to be used in library settings.

Other simulations are available to replace hands-on laboratory experiments for students. *Operation Frog* is a computer program that permits students to investigate frog biology by simulating a frog dissection. There are two stages to the program: dissecting the frog and reconstructing the frog. To dissect the frog, students have the use of four instruments: surgical scissors, a probe, forceps, and a magnifying glass. When they begin the dissection, students are presented with a opened frog with its first layer of organs visible. (There are three layers). They also have an examination tray that contains the outlines of all the organs they can remove. To remove an organ, students use the probe, surgical scissors, and forceps. The organ is placed in the correct location on the examination tray. The magnifying glass can be used to "study" the organ; a full-screen display of the organ (in some cases, in motion) with all parts labeled is shown. In the reconstruction stage, students must put the dissected body back together. This requires knowledge not only of an organ's location but also in which layer it belongs.

As the written materials accompanying the software indicate, there are some differences between a simulation and an actual dissection of a frog. For example, a real frog has dozens of different muscles and bones that are not shown in the program. Also, the organs are colored to make them easier to find, which is not the case in an actual frog.

Such a simulation may be used as a replacement for, or a supplement to, hands-on experience—particularly if the type of laboratory experiment is expensive or difficult to manage. When possible, the teacher should combine simulated computer experiences with other strategies for acquiring knowledge such as demonstrations, some hands-on experiences, or slides and movies.

Laboratory Tools for Data Gathering

A new set of science tools is now available that may dramatically change the way science is taught and learned at all educational levels. The use of computers in the collection of physical data dates back to the beginnings of computer applications. The particular design of some personal computers, allowing easy interfacing through the game paddle or joystick connectors (ports), provides an inexpensive means to carry data gathering into science classrooms. Now referred to as microcomputer-based laboratories (MBLs), these laboratory tools combine personal computers with reasonably priced data-collecting instruments and appropriate software, putting the practice of science within reach of most classes.

Microcomputer-based laboratories have several unique characteristics. First the data gathered by the computer can be immediately displayed as a graph or table. For example, a student can see his or her heartbeat as a

FIGURE 6-3. *Experiments in Human Physiology.*

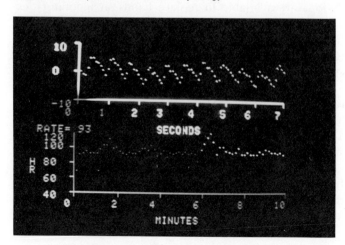

graph on a computer screen. As the student goes from exercising to resting, he or she can observe, in actual time, his or her heartbeat slowing down. This experience takes graphing from the realm of abstract science or math symbolism to a concrete representation of the concept *heartbeat*.

Second, the student is physically involved in some way in each experiment. For example, the student learning about thermal transfer can put a heat probe into a container of hot water, watch the temperature being immediately graphed on the computer screen, and then move the thermometer from the bottom of the container to the top and see the temperature graph rise. The student never has to be told the rule that heat rises. The student is physically and visually involved in ascertaining this for him or herself. Using this same probe, the student can investigate such questions as, What kind of material provides the best insulation?, which leads to energy studies. Or, What kind of cup keeps hot chocolate hot the longest?, which makes an engaging classroom challenge. Students are also very likely to design their own experiments because of the ease in doing so, the immediacy of the data collection and graphing, and the often engrossing results.

FIGURE 6-4. Students using a microcomputer-based laboratory.

Third, graphing, an all-purpose scientific means of communicating ideas and information about behavior over time and relationships between variables becomes an immediately useful tool for students. Reading and drawing graphs is a nonissue because students are physically involved in generating the graphs on topics that interest them.

This ability to learn the use of graphs quickly is explicitly illustrated when the students work with the MBL motion detector, a sonic probe similar to the rangefinder in a Polaroid camera. When middle school students were asked what a graph would look like of them walking across the room, turning around, and coming back, they almost always drew:

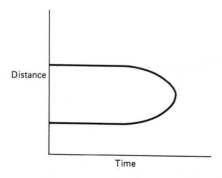

suggesting that students often think of graphs as pictures. Once students carry out this exercise with their own bodies being graphically recorded by a motion detector, they immediately realize that the following graph is the accurate representation:

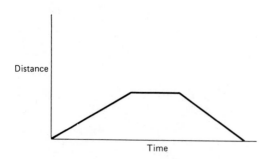

The motion detector opens up many physics-related experiments that involve acceleration and velocity over time. Students can race toy cars over

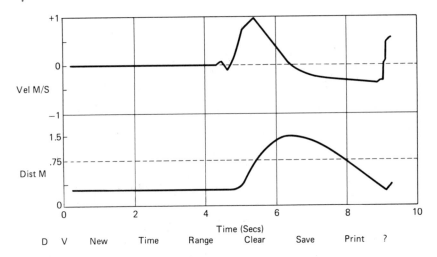

FIGURE 6-5. Graph of a toy car being pushed up an inclined plane and rolling back.

a variety of terrains, study the action of weights on springs, and become choreographers by moving their bodies to replicate on the computer graphs drawn on paper. Figure 6-5 shows a computer screen of a graph of a toy car being pushed up an inclined plane and rolling back. The top graph represents the car's velocity. The vertical axis is meters per second (*m/s*). The bottom graph represents the distance the car traveled (*m* standing for meters). The horizontal axis of both graphs is *time* (Barclay, p. 6). Reading information from these graphs, students can answer questions such as:

1. When does the car start back? (When velocity is 0 and distance is the greatest—which occurs at the same time.)
2. Why does the velocity graph go negative? (Because the car is coming back and losing meters/second.)
3. Why is velocity not the greatest when distance is the greatest? (Because the car slows down as it goes up the incline.)

An example of how gripping MBL learning experiences can be is documented by the MBL research team. The following occurred in a sixth-grade classroom:

> The girls made a velocity graph of a cart that was speeding up, and correctly demonstrated a positive slope. As they completed their worksheet questions, a teacher told them their graph was wrong. "No, it's not," replied one of the girls, "see how it gets faster, that's why the graph keeps going up." "It should be level," said the teacher. "No, it shouldn't!" insisted the girls. "Level would mean that it's going at the same speed." The teacher shrugged and walked off. "We got it right," said one of the girls, and the other nodded knowingly. (Mokros, February 1986, p. 5)

Instead of being an obstacle to overcome in science, graphing, within a very short period of time, becomes a meaningful tool. Jan Mokros, TERC's research director, has summed up this learning environment as "multimodal" because each experiment combines physical experiences (body movements), visual experiences (computer graphs), and intellectual experiences (explaining data collected). In fact, all the components of MBL—the probes, the microcomputer, and the software—can be thought of as a general-purpose science tool.

The complete collection of probes now includes temperature, light, sound, and motion detectors. These tools can be integrated into biology, chemistry, physics, Earth science, and technology. In fact, MBL is an appropriate tool for just about every grade level, including the elementary level.

The full potential of having available such powerful scientific tools as MBL is not yet understood because these tools have not had extensive classroom use. Initial studies indicate, however, that students from about grade four on are able to collect and analyze data. What is not known is how much scientific training a teacher needs to have in order to guide students in drawing reasonable hypotheses from the kind of data students are able to collect.

In addition to MBL (published by HRM Software), there are other similar tools designed for learning-disabled students. Published by D.C. Heath, *Exploring Matter* and *Exploring Heat* were also designed by TERC. These materials are visually simpler; each computer screen contains less information and is slower paced. In addition to the probes, this software contains a dictionary, quizzes, and additional graphical representation of the data collected in the form of animated molecules.

A National Science Foundation project now underway is attempting to combine MBL tools with model building and simulation (Tinker). The focus of this project is to develop middle and high school materials that will take students through a more complete scientific experience. Students will collect data, using MBL probes, and then express their theories of what the data suggest, about the world as a model. If the results of their model, simulated on the computer, match the data collected with their probes, the students have one measure of a valid model. Having developed a reasonable model, the students now have a laboratory for further experimentation.

As an example, Figure 6-6 shows a cooling curve as it might be generated with a temperature probe placed in very hot water and graphed over time.

The theory to explain this phenomenon might be expressed as a causal diagram, a first step toward building a mathematical model (see Figure 6-7).

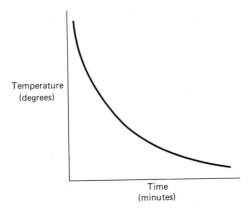

FIGURE 6-6. A cooling curve.

Figure 6-7 suggests that the higher the temperature of the water, the greater the heat loss, causing the temperature of the water to fall. As the gap between the room temperature and the water temperature closes, the water cools more slowly, producing an exponentially declining graph, as shown in Figure 6-6.

Given a working simulation model, the students can carry out other experiments to see if their theory holds. They might put a probe in ice cubes and collect data on the process of water warming to room temperature. Students can then test their computer model to see if the same theory holds for warming as for cooling. If the same theory holds, then changing a few model parameters should produce the warming curve as well. If the model cannot produce the warming curve, either the theory or the model is incorrect, thus bringing the students through the full scientific inquiry process.

FIGURE 6-7. Causal diagram of heat loss in water.

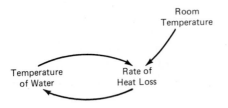

Data Retrieval and Analysis

Work in science readily lends itself to the development of classification activities that encourage the use of databases to store information. One topic encountered in the elementary and middle grades is the study of small animals. Students are intrigued by a whole range of questions that can form the basis for the development of databases.

For younger students, investigation might focus on small animals they can collect outside (Eccles). Key questions about each animal found include:

1. What is it called?
2. Does it have wings?
3. How many legs does it have?
4. How many body parts does it have?
5. What is its size in cm? (Student must measure.)
6. Does it have antennae?
7. How does it move? (e.g., crawl, swim, fly, hop, slide)
8. Where was it found? (e.g., sidewalk, pond, on flower, in air, on bush)
9. What is its color(s)?
10. What is its texture? (e.g., segmented, delicate, hard, hairy, wettish)

From this information, students can be introduced to databases by means of a simple program such as *Bank Street Filer*. The questions naturally lead to the development of the following fields: name, wings, legs, body parts, size, antenna, movement, where found, color, and texture. Three entries from students' collections show how they treated these data (Figure 6-8).

Students then can explore the data they have collected to look for common characteristics. For example, they might print a report that shows each animal's name, wings (yes or no), legs (number), movement, and texture (Figure 6-9).

Do any creatures have some characteristics in common? This should lead students to identify the beetle, bumblebee, butterfly, dragonfly, housefly, grasshopper, or mosquito. Each has wings, six legs, and flies. They are all classified as insects.

With older students, a database may focus on a single type of animal, with each record being a species. For example, most students are very interested in whales. There are several species of whales, including sperm whales, humpback whales, dolphins and porpoises, blue whales, and gray whales. A variety of databases can be developed. One such database, designed with *PFS-File*, emphasizes the classifications important for studying these animals: color and markings, distinguishing characteristics, size, food, habitat, and behavior. The students can search for unique characteristics of different groups of whales to get a sense of how animals are

```
DATA FILE: SMALL CREATURES
_____

NAME        FLY
WINGS       Y
LEGS        6
BODYPARTS   3
SIZE        1CM
ANTENNA     N
MOVEMENT    FLIES
WHERE?      KITCHEN
COLOR       BLACK
TEXTURE     HAIRY



DATA FILE: SMALL CREATURES
_____

NAME        WORM
WINGS       N
LEGS        N
BODYPARTS   1
SIZE        7CM
ANTENNA     N
MOVEMENT    CRAWLS
WHERE?      UNDER ROCK
COLOR       BROWN
TEXTURE     WETTISH



DATA FILE: SMALL CREATURES
_____

NAME        SNAIL
WINGS       N
LEGS        N
BODYPARTS   2
SIZE        1CM
ANTENNA     Y
MOVEMENT    SLIDES
WHERE?      UNDER LOG
COLOR       GREY
TEXTURE     HARD,SHINY
```

FIGURE 6-8. Student data on small animals.

identified. One class that used this database concluded their study by going on a whale watch armed with a list of unique characteristics of the whales the database suggested they could expect to see off the coast of Massachusetts (Figure 6-10 on pages 142 and 143).

In addition to student-created databases, an increasing number of commercially created databases are available for students to use. Two of these are *PFS: File/Physical Sciences Databases* and *PFS: File/Life Science Databases*. In the latter, databases are available on bird migration, animals, and animal biological systems. The manual that accompanies the software also includes directions on how students can develop their own databases on wildflowers and on drugs.

DATA FILE: SMALL CREATURES

```
------------------------------------------------
NAME            W LEGS MOVEME TEXTURE
------------------------------------------------

ANT             N 6    CRAWLS SHINY

BEETLE          Y 6     SWIMS  HARD,SHINY

BUMBLE BEE      Y 6     FLIES  FUZZY

BUTTERFLY       Y 6     FLIES  DUSTY

CATERPILLAR     N LOTS CRAWLS FUZZY

CENTIPEDE       N >100 CRAWLS SEGMENTED

DRAGONFLY       Y 6     FLIES  DELICATE

FLEA            N 6      HOPS   HARD

FLY             Y 6     FLIES  HAIRY

GRASSHOPPER     Y 6      HOPS   WEIRD

MOSQUITO        Y 6     FLIES  DELICATE

SNAIL           N N     SLIDES HARD,SHINY

SPIDER          N 8    CRAWLS HAIRY,

WORM            N N    CRAWLS WETTISH
```

FIGURE 6-9. *Bank Street Filer* on insects.

ORDER : CETADEA

SUBORDER: MYSTICETI

NAMES:

GENERAL: HUMPBACK WHALE

SCIENTIFIC: MEGAPTERA NOVAEANGLIAE

COLOR AND MARKINGS: DARK GRAY OR BLACK O
N UPPER SICE; WHITE PATCHES ON UNDERSIDE
, BELL, AND FLIPPERS

OTHER DISTINGUISHING CHARACTERISTICS:

1: BLOWHOLE

2: DORSAL FIN

3: FLIPPERS - LONG, 1/3 LENGTH BODY

4: FLUKES - PATTERNS ON ADULTS MAY BE UN
IQUE; SERVE AS MEANS OF IDENTIFICATION
5: HEAD - BUMPS ON SNOUT, CHIN AND JAW

6: RORQUAL

FIGURE 6-10. Humpback Whale database file.

FIGURE 6-10.   *(Continued)*

7: SPOUT — 10 FEET

8:

9:

SIZE IN FEET:

AT BIRTH — LOW: 13.5   HIGH: 15

MATURE F — LOW: 39   HIGH: 45

MATURE M — LOW: 36   HIGH: 44

FOOD: SCHOOLING FISH (CAPELIN, SAND EELS
, HERRING), KRILL, COPEPODS, SQUID

HABITAT OR RANGE: FOUND IN ALL OCEANS; 6
 DIFFERENT BREEDING GROUNDS IDENTIFIED;
SEPARATE POPULATIONS IN MAIN OCEANS

BEHAVIOR:

1: SLOW-MOVING

2: FREQUENTLY COMES INSHORE

3: GREGARIOUS, INQUISITIVE

4: SEEMS UNSUSPICIOUS

5: PLAYFUL AND TENDS TO PERFORM ACROBATI
CALLY
6: SONGS ARE COMPLEX COMMUNICATIONS, LAS
TING 20-30 MINUTES, WITH THEMES
7:

8:

9:

STATUS:

1: RARE AND ENDANGERED

2: FULLY PROTECTED

3: ORGINAL POPULATION OF 100,000 REDUCED
 TO 7,000
4: SOME SIGNS OF RECOVERY

5:

6:

7:

8:

9:

COMMENTS: LAST ENTRY MADE FALL, 1984

These databases can be used to formulate a series of questions that permit students to gather data and make generalizations. In particular, with some experience, higher-order questions are possible. For example, using the animals database, the students can ask:

1. Is there a relationship between body temperature and size?
2. Is there a relationship between heart rate and body temperature?
3. Is there a relationship between number of heart chambers and blood pressure?
4. Is there a relationship between heart rate and weight?

Each question requires some advanced work with search techniques. For question 4, it is necessary to search for all the animals that have a heart rate as measured by beats per minute (BPM) greater than 0 *and* a body weight greater than 0 (Figure 6-11).

Once these data are reported, it does appear that a relationship exists between heart rate and body weight. Animals with faster heart rates generally have lower weights. Also, it seems that those animals that are exceptions, having slower heart rates and lower weights, are similar: carp, perch, cod, frog, pike, trout, haddock, bullhead. With the exception of the frog, all are fish. With this data, the question Why? naturally arises. It can provide the basis for student investigation to gather further information about these animals in order to explain the observed relationships.

Data in databases naturally lend themselves to being counted. This, in turn, provides opportunities for graphical representations. Using the data on small animals, students can use graphing software to make bar graphs to display the number of creatures that have wings and the number that do not. Such graphing of data frequencies can be extended to other data as well.

Using the whales database, each whale's size at birth can be shown on a bar graph. This data can be combined with size at maturity to show

FIGURE 6-11. Database report of heart rate compared to body weight.

HEART RATE AND WEIGHT

HEART RATE—BPM (XXX)	WEIGHT IN KG. (XXXXXX.XX)	ANIMALS
782	0.01	Shrew, Musked
720	2.27	Vulture, Turkey
690	0.02	Canary
650	0.01	Hummingbird, Cuban bee
615	0.01	Hummingbird
600	0.02	Mouse, House
588	0.10	Bat, little brown
534	0.02	Mouse, White-footed
450	0.12	Hamster
401	0.38	Gull, Herring
390	0.55	Squirrel, Gray
388	0.09	Starling, Common
380	0.34	Rook

FIGURE 6-11. *(Continued)*

HEART RATE AND WEIGHT

HEART RATE-BPM (XXX)	WEIGHT IN KG. (XXXXXX.XX)	ANIMALS
378	0.36	Crow, Hooded
350	0.10	Chipmunk, Eastern
347	0.11	Kestrel, lesser
347	0.96	Falcon, Peregrin
347	0.96	Goshawk
342	0.14	European Jackdaw
340	1.05	Mink, American
320	3.86	Chicken
312	0.25	Guinea fowl
301	0.66	Buzzard
300	18.16	Porcupine
270	0.45	Guinea Pig
268	1.70	Duck, Mallard
240	6.00	Fox, Arctic
211	18.16	Turkey
170	0.27	Pigeon
150	4.09	Rabbit, Domestic
140	13.00	Beaver
130	3.30	Cat, domestic
128	0.90	Bat, Flying fox
125	24.00	Kangaroo, Red
120	9.08	Dog, Boston Terrier
120	3.63	Dog, Pekingese
120	11.35	Dog, Beagle
110	400.00	Dolphin, Bottlenose
100	22.70	Dog, Collie
100	11.80	Dog, Irish Terrier
95	7.26	Dog, Fox Terrier
92	18.16	Dog, Basset Hound
90	24.97	Dog, Pointer
80	4.54	Woodchuck (Groundhog)
80	28.00	Goat, Milch
80	9.99	Dog, Whippet
75	79.44	Sheep
75	29.50	Dog, Foxhound
70	102.00	Pig
70	69.00	Human
70	125.00	Ostrich
70	72.63	Dog, Saint Bernard
66	800.00	Giraffe, male
59	38.00	Carp
59	1.95	Perch
55	453.92	Cow
55	250.00	Manatee
48	680.88	Mule
48	22.70	Cod, Atlantic
48	0.04	Frog, leopard
47	363.14	Donkey
44	317.74	Tapir
42	19.06	Pike, Northern
40	200.00	Lion
40	226.96	Alligator, American
40	113.40	Crocodile, Saltwater
38	18.16	Trout, brown
37	453.92	Horse
35	5,900.00	Elephant, African
35	3.30	Haddock
30	4,000.00	Elephant, Indian
29	550.00	Camel
25	272.35	Shark, Hammerhead
22	1.13	Bullhead, Brown
16	181,568.00	Whale, Blue

multiple bars on the same graph in order to make comparisons of growth in a single species, as well as comparisons across species. One way to do this is to use *Data Plot* graphing software. In this case, the data must be entered as shown on the table in Figure 6-12. It is then displayed in a bar graph. In Figure 6-12, the Cs, Ms, and Fs along the horizontal axis stand for Calf (baby whale), Male, and Female. Another way to do this is to use a database that has companion graphing software. An example is *PFS-File* and *PFS-Graph*. In this case, the numbers entered in the database are used by *PFS-Graph* to make appropriate tables for three different graphs: one each for child, male adult, and female adult. This data can then be displayed on a single graph with distinguishing bars for each classification.

Telecommunications

One final computer-related technology that has the potential to cause meaningful change in science, as well as other areas of teaching, is *telecommunications*. Telecommunications can be classified in several

FIGURE 6-12. Whale sizes.

WHALE		SIZE
1> C-MINKE	1>	9
2> M-MINKE-AVE	2>	22
3> F-MINKE-AVE	3>	22
4> C-HUMPBACK-AVE	4>	14
5> M-HUMPBACK-AVE	5>	42
6> F-HUMPBACK-AVE	6>	40
7> C-BOWHEAD	7>	13
8> M-BOWHEAD	8>	51
9> F-BOWHEAD	9>	51
10> C-GRAY	10>	14
11> M-GRAY	11>	50
12> F-GRAY	12>	48
13> C-RIGHT-AVE	13>	15
14> M-RIGHT-AVE	14>	42
15> F-RIGHT-AVE	15>	42

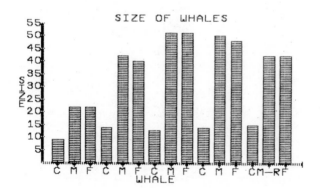

ways. One set of categories applicable to the classroom includes electronic mail systems, teleconferencing, and commercial databases.

Electronic mail systems.   *Electronic mail systems* can be carried out at several different levels. The simplest can be operated within a single classroom. Suppose a class is studying pets. When a question arises for which one group of students would like more information, they can leave the question on their class bulletin board. In determining a healthy pet environment, this group might decide the number of hours pets spend with humans is important. A questionnaire can be placed on the class bulletin board. Each classmate can provide information to this group on his or her pet interactions.

This same computer arrangement can also be used as a general class message center. Research on the *Quill* project (see Chapter 4) suggests that a classroom electronic mail center encourages students' writing. These uses might not seem particularly unique, but they are straightforward ways of introducing a new technology. A piece of software designed just for this purpose is the *Electronic Mailbag* by Exsys, which simulates, with one computer, an electronic mail system.

At a more complex level, a school building or school system can have a common electronic mail system. The simplest way to tie together computers in different locations is through *modems*. These devices, which readily attach to a computer and a telephone jack, take the digital electronic signal sent by the computer and turn it (that is, *mo*dulate it) into an analogue signal that can be sent over a telephone line. At the other end, the modem takes the telephone analogue signal and *demo*dulates it for the computer. Modems are reasonably inexpensive, ranging around $100. The cost of the hardware is not usually an issue for schools. The telephone and other commercial costs, however, might be a problem.

Given an electronic mail system, any school person—student, teacher, or staff—can communicate with any other person. the advantages to this kind of communication is that it can happen at any time people have access to a computer and modem. People can read their mail and respond, or not, during the day or evening, or on weekends. Moreover, it is much more likely that a student will have a conversation with a principal or teacher in another building through an electronic mail system than by any other current way. In many instances a specialist in the school system, such as one on local fauna, will be able to dialogue easily with a particular class as they study the topic.

If we now extend this electronic bulletin board to a broader geographic area, the potential for talking directly to all kinds of other people becomes almost unlimited. When using electronic mail, the user does not necessarily know much about the other people involved. It often happens, for example, that an adult becomes involved in a discussion with someone quite his or her junior. The environment for students to dialogue with experts on scientific topics is now available. In addition, the potential for building shared databases on topics of mutual interest is exciting from both a research and educational perspective.

Teleconferencing. The next level of telecommunications can be termed *teleconferencing*. This is essentially organizing electronic mail by topic. Someone who wishes to carry on a focused dialogue, perhaps with a limited number of people, but wants to avoid the hassle of finding a common meeting place or time finds that teleconferencing meets his or her needs. Electronic conferencing can be done at a variety of times, or at the same time, whichever is more appropriate for the particular situation. At the student level this provides a means for carrying out joint projects with classes in different geographical locations or communicating with a scientific research group at a particular university or laboratory.

A particularly exciting project incorporating this technology was conducted by TERC. (Mokros, May, 1986). Fourth through sixth-graders in nine sites around the country—rural Nebraska, suburban California, New York City, Washington, D.C., Pennsylvania, and Massachusetts—were linked together electronically to share data each class collected on the amount of acid rain in their location. The project was overwhelmingly successful, as illustrated by the following comments collected from participants in concluding interviews:

> Scientists have been doing this for 5 million years, and just think, we're only kids, and we can do it. (Jeff, 12 years, California)

> The worst was finding out that we had the most acid in our rain and that it is going to kill our fish. In a hundred years, it's not going to be too swift, for everything is going to slowly die. This project is good because it makes us aware. California has nothing to worry about, but we do, and we have to do something about it. (Megan, 11 years, Pennsylvania)

> It is very important for kids to know about acid rain. We should try to keep the rain cleaner in the next years, or it is only going to get worse. We must fix it, we have to fix it now. We plant corn, and water it. The pheasants are eating it, which is very bad for them. (Ryan, 13 years, Nebraska)

> This is much more interesting than reading about it [in a textbook]. Because the writer who wrote the book might not really be interested in a topic, but when we get to try it ourselves we might see that it's really interesting. Also the writer might not have all the right answers. You have to do it yourself to find the answers. (Tom, 12 years, Massachusetts)

> We are sharing among the other schools and we are helping the United States. It's not just for schools. (Matthew, 12 years, California)

> We got to find out about other schools, and it's like amazing that there's a one-room school in Nebraska, and they can do this too. I was surprised they even had a computer. (Karen, 11 years, Massachusetts)

I never dreamed that all teachers and all kids could be brought together to share their ideas. I learned that we are not all that different, although we come from different areas. (Priscilla, teacher, Pennsylvania)

This has tied our school in with the rest of the United States. Before they felt as if they were a small school and no one cared about them. (Sally, teacher, Nebraska)

They got the message that science is a collective enterprise as opposed to an individual one. That message came through very strong. (Bruce, teacher, Massachusetts) (Mokros)

Looking at all the data collected, Mokros concluded that the project was so universally appealing because of, "the importance and relevance of the topic; their own involvement and control over data collection; and the ability to share and compare data with others in the network." Teleconferencing is clearly a tool to look at carefully for changing the way teaching and learning occur in science as well as other areas of the curriculum.

Commercial databases.   The third category of telecommunications for the classroom is accessing a *commercial database.* Now on-line or available by subscription are encyclopedias that are updated far more often than those in print, news services, and a host of specialized electronic information service. The catch here is the cost. To become involved in computer networking, a school needs a modem to enable the computer to send and receive information over telephone lines. In addition there is usually a monthly subscription fee for a commercial networking service and sometimes an added fee for access to certain electronic databases. In spite of these added costs, more and more schools are piloting telecommunications in some way. Of course, this is as powerful a resource for the social studies as it is for the natural sciences.

CONCLUSIONS

Reconsidering the six reasons given at the beginning of this chapter for the crisis in science education, let's see if computers might alleviate some of the problems. The first point was the lack of reeducation when teachers were introduced to the curricula developed in the fifties. Is integrating computers into the curricula going to be an easier task for teachers than learning to use the kits? Quite frankly, the new challenge requires at least twice the effort for most teachers. However, learning to use a computer (half the task) is useful for many aspects of a teacher's life—not just in the classroom. Moreover, obtaining computer literacy is generally considered an appropriate goal for anyone, and therefore has the support of society.

The second reason given is that kits are difficult to use in the classroom because of the large numbers of pieces needed to create a hands-on experience for all students. Computers certainly cut down on the number of pieces needed. However, the cost rises if the goal is to provide hands-on experience for everyone. Let's suppose schools will, in a reasonable time, have enough computer resources and count this problem as resolved by computer integration.

The current crisis is to some extent caused by the lack of qualified teachers. If history teaches anything, it certainly suggests that when there are large numbers of unfilled jobs, salaries tend to increase, thereby attracting people to those employment opportunities. Will the people who are attracted to science education be qualified? This is a complex issue. In some way this depends on the prestige attached to teaching. Since teaching, at least in recent years, has been low on the professional prestige ladder, it will take some time yet to raise society's view of it. On the other hand, if teaching becomes an even more rewarding profession because of the infusion of technology, it might again attract the young, idealistic person or rejuvenate the excellent, but burned-out experienced teacher.

The fourth reason suggested for the current crisis, the large amount of reading required in the traditional science curriculum, is certainly lessened with the increased use of computers.

1. Most software is designed to have a minimum of text on the screen. Even when wordy manuals accompany software, students inevitably learn what is needed without opening them.

2. Students usually work at computers in pairs or teams. Tasks can be divided by giving heavy reading jobs to the good readers and other assignments to students with other strengths.

3. Computer work is motivating enough for students to do the necessary reading, thereby improving their reading skills.

4. The computer provides many different options for learning—through data collection and analysis, simulations, and telecommunication.

The difficulty in starting students off at their current level of understanding, the fifth reason, is perhaps mitigated by the use of computers. Computers have a way of making abstract concepts concrete because of their ability to display dynamic graphics. Software can much more easily be matched to children's levels of understanding than can textbooks. Most software described in this chapter has several levels of difficulty. Because software usually represents a limited number of hours of classroom use, or, in the case of tools, is almost completely open-ended, teachers have more flexibility in matching each student to an appropriate computer activity.

The last problem impacting on science education today is sex discrimination. Although it is a very subtle and hard-to-measure variable, sex discrimination still exists but is gradually lessening. It will truly take a new generation of teachers, brought up in a more aware society, to eliminate such discrimination. Computers, however, are helping because they appeared in schools after society had generally agreed that sex discrimination needed to be eliminated. Concerted efforts are being made by schools to give girls equal access to computers and encourage them to use technology—and the results are noticeable.

Science involves the study of the world around us. Teaching science means engaging students in what they see, hear, feel, and smell. If we are successful, students will find that exploring the world can be both satisfying and stimulating. Students' explorations do not have to be limited by traditional definitions of ability, since these definitions are rapidly changing with the increased availability of technological educational tools.

REFERENCES

BARCLAY, WILLIAM. "Graphing Misconceptions." TERC Technical report 85-5, November 1985.

BORK, ALFRED, AUGUSTO CHIOCCARIELLO, AND STEPHEN FRANKLIN. "Scientific Reasoning via the Computer." Working paper. University of California at Irvine, December 1985.

BREDDERMAN, TED. "Effects of Activity-Based Elementary Science on Student Outcomes: A Quantitative Synthesis." *Review of Educational Research*, vol. 53, no. 4 (Winter 1983), 499–518.

ECCLES, ISABEL. Activity developed for final project in graduate class, Lesley College, 1982.

MOKROS, JANICE. "The Impact of Microcomputer-Based Labs on Children's Graphing Skills." TERC working paper, February 1986.

MOKROS, JANICE. "KidNet." TERC working paper, May 1986.

ROCKCASTLE, V., F. SALAMON, V. SCHMIDT, AND B. MCKNIGHT. *Elementary School Science.* Menlo Park, Calif.: Addison-Wesley, 1973.

TINKER, ROBERT. "Problem-Solving Tools." NSF Grant No. MDR-8550373. Technical Education Research Centers, Cambridge, Mass., 1986–88.

WATTS, J. W., AND D. W. PEACEMAN. "The Simulation of Petroleum Reservoirs." *Perspectives in Computing*, vol. 5, no. 1, (Spring 1985), 14–23.

SEVEN
LOGO PROGRAMMING IN THE CURRICULUM

PROGRAMMING IN THE SCHOOLS

It's the early 1960s and I am a senior in high school. Today my teacher brought in a large packet of fan-fold computer paper. As he unfolded it he told us that it was a computer printout from a program that instructed the computer to start at 1 and repeatedly multiply by 2. The first number was 1, the next 2, then 4, 8, 16, 32, 64, 128, and so forth. Each number was on a separate line. Very quickly we saw a single number that spread across the whole width of the paper. Before we got halfway down the first sheet, the numbers were twenty or thirty digits long! Together we identified the numbers that represented the population of the United States, then the world, and even the number of atoms in the universe! Even these large numbers did not get us very far down the packet of printout. The teacher then showed us the punch cards used to program the computer to do this task. We spent the next couple of weeks learning a few elementary FORTRAN commands in order to write simple programs. The unit culminated with a trip to M.I.T., where we used a punch-card machine to type our programs. The teacher then submitted our sets of cards to the computer center operator. The next week we got printouts of the results.

In college two years later, I took an introductory programming course and my high school experience was repeated. I wrote elementary mathematical calculation programs for such tasks as figuring interest, typed the programs onto cards, handed the cards in to be run, and got a printout the next day. Computing had an esoteric quality, and for the young neophyte the mechanics were as important and as interesting as the actual content. I remember more vividly learning to use the punch-card machine than learning to program.

The advent of the interactive programming language BASIC was the first step away from the domination of the mechanics over the process. It was at this time that some school systems joined together to access time sharing on a mainframe computer by using telephone lines. For the first time a student could sit at a terminal, type in a program, and run it all in one session. The cost of this process limited the teaching of programming to a small number of high schools.

BASIC was developed at Dartmouth College. The original motivation was to create a language that would make it easy for professors and students to write their own programs for course-related tasks. BASIC was written to fit into a small amount of computer memory, since memory was then an expensive resource. The authors of BASIC used the science-and-mathematics-oriented language FORTRAN (FORmula TRANslation) as their model.

Microcomputers, the next advance, were cheaper and made programming accessible to a much larger range of people. Some mathematics teachers in elementary schools tried to teach their students BASIC. Their goals were generally simple. Programming was seen as a skill of the future, and most of the programming tasks involved mathematical problem solving such as, "Write a program to print out all the odd numbers from 1 to 100."

The Development of Logo

At about the same time another language-development project, called Logo, was occurring at M.I.T. and Bolt Beranek and Newman. The M.I.T. part was led by Seymour Papert and the BBN part by Wallace Feurzeig. Logo was very different both in purpose and in approach from BASIC. Logo's developers were looking towards the future. They envisioned a time when computers would be more available and more powerful than they were currently. They wanted to create a language that would be both powerful and accessible to many people.

For Logo's authors accessible meant not only being easy to begin programming, but also personally interesting to students. The ability to create new commands in Logo and to give these commands unique names is an example of making an environment that a student can personalize.

Logo's developers believed that students had too little control over their own learning in most schools. They wanted an environment that placed students' own ideas at the center, making students initiators of their own learning. The Logo development team created a language that allows the user to begin with a few simple programs—such as drawing lines by moving forward or back, and turning right or left—and use them as tools to create, extend, and explore their own ideas for making shapes or pictures.

Logo's developers also felt that too much time in schools was spent on repetitive, isolated drill and too little on activities that might support the development of better ways of thinking, problem solving, and learning. In an early paper Papert contrasted teaching students mathematics (memorizing facts and formulas) with teaching students how to *be* mathematicians (exploring, inventing, trying out ideas, discovering patterns, developing hypotheses, and figuring out why things don't work). Logo was designed to support different styles of problem solving (for example, it incorporated both a "top-down" hierarchical approach and a "bottom-up" constructive approach) and to support the analytical process of "debugging" programs that do not seem to work. Papert and his colleagues also believe that a good learning environment should support students' inventions—that is, the creation of something new that they had never been told how to do. They not only wanted to create computer environments that reinforced these new kinds of learning, but in addition they wanted to foster new ways of thinking about traditional subject matter.

Turtle geometry. One result of this was Logo's *turtle geometry,* an engaging set of activities that allow students to command a "turtle" to create pictures and shapes on the screen with natural commands such as FORWARD, BACK, RIGHT, and LEFT. In a turtle geometry environment, students are encouraged to devise their own projects, but to carry them out they often have to grapple with or invent a range of geometric ideas.

The original Logo, developed on a DEC (Digital Equipment Corporation) computer in the early 1970s, did not have a turtle or any graphics capability because the DEC computer did not support graphics. The turtle was the result of Norbert Weiner's studies of cybernetics, or self-adjusting systems, at M.I.T. in the 1940s and 1950s. It is told that Weiner, using a mechanical turtle, taught it to navigate through the corridors of M.I.T. by "knowing that if it bumped into the wall it should turn away and keep going." Weiner's work in creating the field of cybernetics was important to later developments in guidance systems. However, the concrete turtle also fit quite well with Piaget's theories of how children learned. Papert brought these two ideas together in the Logo turtle. The programming of a "real" turtle (connected to a computer using Logo) to draw on the floor was one of the first applications of Logo in the elementary classroom. Today's Logo screen turtle is a more flexible, more powerful, and only slightly more abstract version of the original floor turtle. Microcomputer

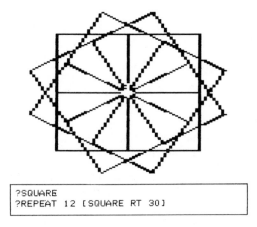

```
?SQUARE
?REPEAT 12 [SQUARE RT 30]
```

FIGURE 7.1   A Logo Screen with a turtle drawn design and the commands that created it.

versions of Logo provide engaging activities that allow students of all ages to command a "turtle" to create shapes and pictures on the screen.

For those unfamiliar with Logo, here is a peek at Logo in a classroom:

> A small group of students is clustered around a computer screen. Using a series of FORWARD and RIGHT commands, they have just figured out how to make the small, white triangle in the center of the screen (the turtle) draw a square. The students have decided to call their square "BOX" and now they want to teach the computer to draw the same shape. Turning to the keyboard, one student types in:

```
TO BOX
    FORWARD 50
    RIGHT 90
    FORWARD 50
    RIGHT 90
    FORWARD 50
    RIGHT 90
    FORWARD 50
    RIGHT 90
END
```

> From now on the computer will dutifully draw a square whenever a student in the group types the new command BOX.

> That accomplished, another child discovers how to combine the box with a TRIANGLE command she has just defined to form a house. She types in:

```
TO HOUSE
    BOX
    FORWARD 50
    RIGHT 30
    TRIANGLE
END
```

Meanwhile, yet another child decides that a sun would be a nice addition to the picture, so the group begins to explore the geometry involved in using FORWARD and RIGHT commands to make a circle.

Later on, these students learn that they can make Logo repeat patterns of instructions using the REPEAT command. Using REPEAT they can make a more efficient BOX procedure:

```
TO BOX
    REPEAT 4 [FORWARD 50 RIGHT 90]
END
```

They also learn that they are not limited to a box of size 50. Just as they can tell FORWARD how far to go (FORWARD 50), they can write their own procedures, allowing for a variable input for size. They can control the size of their box by replacing the 50 in FORWARD 50 with a named variable (the name itself is up to them, of course) and placing their variable name in the title line as well:

```
TO BOX :SIZE
    REPEAT 4 [FORWARD :SIZE RIGHT 90]
END
```

(*Note:* the colon before the word SIZE tells Logo that SIZE is a variable name.) Now they can type commands such as BOX 20, BOX 100, or BOX 5 to get different-sized boxes or to make different-sized houses.

Logo Enters the Schools

In 1978 the first versions of microcomputer Logo found their way into schools. Logo took many elementary school classrooms by storm. In the earliest years it was often initiated by an interested teacher who managed to introduce Logo to a class of elementary school children with only one computer. Interest and excitement was often so high that teachers set up special all-day computer schedules to allow every student a chance at a machine. In some classes the day would be divided into half-hour blocks and students would be scheduled one after another. When their time came, students would stop whatever they were doing and go to the computer. When their time was up, the next person on the schedule would simply tap them on the shoulder. Students were expected to make up missed work by copying the notes of fellow students.

What is it about Logo that led teachers to change their normal daily schedule so radically? In the words of one teacher:

> It's the children. I have never seen them so excited and so committed to anything in school. They come in early, they want to stay in at recess, and they stay after school to work on their projects! And they feel so good about themselves.

It seems that the level of excitement, engagement, and commitment to learning shown by students was one reason teachers were willing to modify business as usual. One teacher describes the change Logo brought about for one of her students:

> For the first time Susan has been willing to take on a complex project and work on it over a long period of time. She is willing to have something not work, go back over it, try to fix it, ask others for help, and keep on trying. She's learning to take risks! I've never seen her do this in school before.

When teachers are asked, "Why Logo?" the answers are much more varied and complex than, "to develop computer literacy," or "to teach computer programming." Below are the responses of a group of ex- perienced Logo-using classroom teachers when asked, "What do your students get from learning Logo?" The responses cluster in two general categories: What students learn about the process of learning, and what students learn about problem solving.

Learning About Learning

My students are learning to take initiative in their own learning.

They are learning to invent and discover.

They have become both solvers of new problems and new problem setters. A set of questions have become automatic in my classroom: "What else can you do or try?" "How can we change the problem?" "What can we discover?"

For the first time for many of my children mistakes are OK! We've even discovered that mistakes or bugs can be interesting and useful. I've even instituted a bug collection book where we share interesting or common mistakes.

My children are experiencing directly that there can be more than one right answer to a question. They are also experiencing that the teacher (that's me) isn't the only one with The Right Answer. I love it and they love it. They can invent something brand new! One of my fourth-graders invented a new way to make a circle that really mirrors the way they'll do it in high school geometry. A catch phrase that we use is, "Here's one way, let's have another!"

I like what you said about the teacher not always having all the answers. My students are learning to experience each other (and themselves) as resources.

A phrase I read in a Logo article and I use to get kids to ask each other questions is, "Ask three before you ask me."

Logo has allowed my students to experience and enjoy what I call "intellectual exploration," the pleasure of getting an idea and trying things out to see what happens.

What you have said has made me realize that using Logo in my classroom has created an environment where we talk about problem solving, about thinking, and about learning in ways we never did before. During our sharing meetings when students share both projects and bugs, we now talk about things that are hard to learn.

Learning About Problem Solving

The whole process of debugging programs that do not work. The process of finding something that does not work and figuring out how to fix it rather than the "fail-give up" process that is usually so common with my students.

A variation I see is the development of a process that moves from trial and error to trial and revision. You try something, you see how it's off, and then try to fix it, based on what you've found out.

One thing I like is the idea of breaking a complex problem down into small parts. I find it hard to get kids to think this way, but once they see it, it really changes the way they do things.

We compare "top-down" and "bottom-up" approaches to problem solving. I think it's important for kids to try out different ways of solving problems.

Another idea I use with them a lot is, "If it's too hard, try to simplify it. Solve a simpler version of the problem." For some students it helps a lot.

My favorite is PLAY TURTLE. If you want to solve a problem, think about exactly what you would have to do, step by step, to do it. Try acting it out in some way.

Other Ideas

I like Logo because I have a wide variety of abilities in my class and Logo has enough flexibility so that students of varying levels and learning styles can profit. I learn a lot about my students from watching them work. I often discover strengths I didn't know they had.

I'm not sure I can articulate exactly what the kids are getting out of it, but I can tell you I like the atmosphere when Logo work is going on. Rather than the old "get-the-next-workbook-page-done" feeling, there is a kind of project-oriented atmosphere. Students are using their knowledge to create a product they have designed themselves. They are applying their knowledge to something new.

In the middle of this discussion, one teacher pointed out that of all the learnings that had been listed, almost none fit a standard elementary school scope-and-sequence chart. In response to this, several teachers suggested mathematics topics that their students had picked up from doing Logo programming.

It provides younger students with direct, "concrete," meaningful experience with numbers up into the 100s, particularly a sense for the relative sizes of different numbers.

In the geometry curriculum Logo helped with the idea of angles and the characteristics of shapes.

Logo helped my students understand parallel lines.

Older children are introduced to the idea of a variable.

In making procedures to draw shapes, my students got a lot of useful experience with the mathematics of 360 (to make a regular six-sided shape, each external angle is 360/6, or 60 degrees; to make a five-sided shape, each angle is 360/5, or 72 degrees, and so forth).

Once I introduced variables, there were several situations where my students got to use decimals and negative numbers to solve what were (to them) real problems—for example, "I need a number between 1 and 2 to make my shape fit in my design."

When Logo first entered schools, there was not much focus on its relation to traditional standard curriculum. Logo was a programming language and was usually seen by administrators as part of computer literacy, or it was introduced because it would help kids with problem solving (something that was almost never a formal part of the scope-and-sequence charts anyway). But a change is under way. As more people discover the power and capabilities of Logo, they are beginning to integrate it into work in the standard curriculum. Let's look now at three teachers who have integrated Logo, both as a programming language and as a philosophy of learning, into the area of mathematics, language, and science.

LOGO IN THE CURRICULUM

Logo and Mathematics

Temple Ary works in a school outside Boston teaching math to third-through sixth-graders. For her, Logo is the perfect tool to help students explore and master mathematical ideas. She uses Logo to give her young students some experience with arithmetic operations that grow out of problem-solving activities. Once her students have been introduced to Logo and to defining procedures, she develops two simple Logo procedures with them:

```
TO F
   FORWARD 2
END
```

```
TO B
   PENCOLOR 0
   BACK 1
   PENCOLOR 1
END
```

She explains that if the student types F, the turtle moves forward two turtle steps and draws a line two turtle steps long. If the student types B, the turtle goes back one turtle step and erases the line (PENCOLOR 0 turns the turtle's pencolor to black [0] so that the line becomes the same color as the screen. PENCOLOR 1 resets the pencolor to white [1]). Giving the turtle an F command followed by a B command produces a line one turtle step long.

All the lessons that Temple has developed with Logo have the following format:

- She presents some problems to solve with Logo.
- She asks students to make up their own variations of the problems.
- She asks students to think about and discuss the math skills or ideas that a particular exercise helps them practice.

Temple began this unit by discussing the F and B procedures with her students. Then she gave them the following challenges. Using F and B, can you get the turtle to draw a line:

  1 unit long?
  2 units long?
  3 units long?
  5 units long?
  10 units long?
  25 units long?

Record how you do each one!

The students already knew how to use Logo's REPEAT command. For example, to draw a line 15 units long, type:

```
REPEAT 8 [F] B
```

This makes the turtle execute eight Fs (each of which are two turtle steps long) followed by 1 B. As an extension, she asks students who finish quickly if there are any lengths they cannot draw with Fs and Bs.

After working on these, students share and discuss their solutions. Some examples for making a line five turtle steps long are:

```
F B F F
F F F B
F F F F B B B
REPEAT 3 [F] B
```

Presented with these alternate solutions, the students explored the question of whether the B can be in any position, and whether a person can use more than three Bs. When actually trying these out on the computer, F is rewritten as FD 20 so that students can clearly see the movements of the turtle (single turtle steps are very small).

Next, Temple asks the students to make up their own problems. Some begin to do this spontaneously. Students come up with other lengths to make with her F and B, as well as invent their own versions of F and B such as:

```
TO MYF
    FORWARD 4
END

TO MYB
    PENCOLOR 0
    BACK 2
    PENCOLOR 1
END
```

and their own problems: Can you make a line 18 units long using MYF and MYB?

Everyone tries each other's procedures and problems. Temple also explores the fact that there are many ways to solve most of the problems. "How many different ways can you find to make a line 18 units long?"

Finally, Temple asks the students what arithmetic is involved in doing these problems. An obvious response is addition and subtraction, but many students discovered that they also used multiplication to create commands like

```
REPEAT 5 [MYF] MYB
```

for an eighteen-unit line.

Temple has also extended the F and B activities to get older students to explore common factors:

Write an F procedure that can be used to efficiently create all these lines:

18
54
36
24

Of course, there are many solutions, but Temple has found that discussing the possibilities leads quite naturally into a discussion of common factors.

Temple also uses Logo to have her students work out the solutions to perimeter problems. First, these problems provide a context for using basic skills that goes beyond workbook exercises. Second, the activities engage the students in exploring the relation between multiplication and division. She begins with problems such as:

- Make a Logo procedure to draw a square whose perimeter is 44 turtle steps. How much is each side?
- Create a procedure that draws a square with sides 4 turtle steps long. What is the perimeter?

She then extends this work by having the students do similar problems with triangles, hexagons, and pentagons. And, as always, she challenges students to make up their own problems for each other. Some students have spontaneously extended the work themselves, making up problems for twelve-sided shapes (duodecagons). This leads them into multiplication and division by 12, which is a new experience for many of them.

Temple also has students construct Logo procedures to illustrate word problems from their textbooks that involve perimeter:

Henry walked around a building. Each wall was 25 feet long. How long was his walk? Write a Logo procedure that shows the length of Henry's walk.

Another area of mathematics in which Temple uses Logo is fractions. In describing her Logo fraction unit, she says that one of the most important things that Logo provides is a visual model that kids can both build themselves and manipulate. For fractions she uses a rectangle as the model. She asks each student to write a Logo procedure to draw a large rectangle such as:

```
TO RECT
    RT 90
    FD 100
    LT 90
    FD 50
    LT 90
    FD 200
    LT 90
    FD 50
    LT 90
    FD 100
    LT 90
END
```

Because her students are familiar with the way an inch is divided up on a ruler, she talks about this as the "build-your-own-giant-inch" project. Once every student has a rectangle procedure, she asks them to write a procedure called HALF, which divides the rectangle in half. Once this is accomplished, the students are challenged to write a FOURTH procedure that divides the rectangle into four equal parts. Temple reports that there is much valuable discussion about the variety of methods students invent. "Was dividing the half in half the same as dividing the rectangle into four equal parts?" After FOURTHS, students complete their inch-construction project with an EIGHTHS procedure.

Here are some typical student procedures based on the RECTANGLE procedure used above (the turtle starts in the middle of the base of the rectangle):

```
TO HALF
    FD 50
    BK 50
END

TO FOURTHS
    RT 90
    BK 100
    FD 50
    LT 90
    FD 50 BK 50
    RT 90
    FD 50
    LT 90
    FD 50
    BK 50
    RT 90
    FD 50
    LT 90
    FD 50 BK 50
  END

TO EIGHTHS
    RT 90 BK 100
    REPEAT 8 [FD 50/2 LT 90 FD 50 BK 50 RT 90]
END
```

Once each student has constructed her or his own Giant Inch, Temple works with them to develop some fraction-exploration procedures:

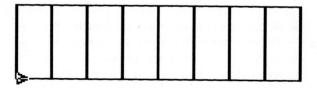

FIGURE 7.2. A "Giant Inch" created with Logo's RECT, HALF, FOURTHS, and EIGHTHS procedures.

START, which always moves the turtle to the lower left-hand corner of the rectangle, and a series of MOVE procedures that move the turtle along the inch in fractional steps:

```
TO START
    PENUP HOME
    RT 90
    BK 100
END

TO MOVE.HALF
    FD 100
END

TO MOVE.FOURTH
    FD 50
END

TO MOVE.EIGHTH
    FD 25
END
```

FIGURE 7-3. "Giant Inch" with Logo's SETSHAPE and STAMP procedures for labelling fractional values.

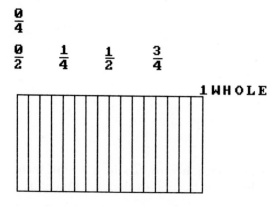

The next step is to create a generalized MOVE procedure that takes a fraction as an input and moves the turtle that fractional value along the rectangle. For example, MOVE 1/2 moves the turtle from its start position to halfway across the rectangle. Temple notes that although some of the children do not fully understand the variable MOVE procedure, they all use it successfully to explore fractional relationships.

```
TO MOVE :HOWFAR
    FD :HOWFAR * 200
END
```

Once they have defined MOVE, students can give commands like:

```
START
MOVE 1/4
MOVE 3/8
```

to get the turtle to actually move along the bottom of their inch in fractional amounts—the MOVE 1/4 and MOVE 3/8 commands move the turtle a total of five-eighths of an inch.

When the students have constructed the new MOVE procedure, it becomes an exploration tool for problems in areas such as:

- *Equivalent fractions:* What are all the ways you can use your MOVE procedure to get the turtle to the halfway point of your rectangle (MOVE 2/4, MOVE 4/8)?
- *Adding fractions:* What happens when you use MOVE to add fractions with the same denominators (MOVE 1/8 + 3/8)? (In this case Logo simply does the operation 1/8 + 3/8 and then uses the sum 4/8, or 1/2, as input to MOVE and moves the turtle the sum of 1/8 + 3/8!)
- *Comparing fractions:* Which is bigger—5/8 or 1/2? Here Temple has her students make predictions and then use their MOVE procedures to test out their hypotheses. She also asks them to invent their own comparison problems.

In all these situations Temple mixes the giving of specific and general problems. For adding fractions she might give a couple of specific problems such as, "What happens when you add 1/4 + 1/4 or 3/8 + 2/8?" Then she gives a general problem, "What can you find out about adding fractions with the same denominators?" and asks her students to explore. She finds that this allows her to give direction to students who need it and allows students who are ready to explore and discover to work on their own. Some students quickly extended the work on adding like fractions to discovering what happens when the sum of the numerators is more than the denominator; and what happens when one fraction is subtracted from another.

These activities provide a rich set of experiences for class discussions about mathematical ideas. After using their MOVE procedures to explore what happens when fractions with like denominators are added, the students articulated the idea that you simply add the numerators. It is exciting for them to discover and test this idea themselves rather than being told by the teacher to memorize an abstract rule.

After using Logo with her math students for two years, Temple says she is more convinced than ever that students need to be given a chance to manipulate, explore, and discover mathematical ideas. Logo provides an ideal functional tool that can be used by students to manipulate ideas and to better understand mathematical concepts through exploration, invention, and discovery.

Teaching Logo to Spell

Logo is well known for the powerful geometric capabilities of its turtle graphics, and we have just looked at some of its potential as a tool in mathematics. What is less well known is Logo's power for dealing with language. Logo is based on a computer language called LISP, which stands for LISt Processing. One type of list is simply a list of words or letters. Logo has a set of commands that allows the manipulation of words and sentences. Here is an example of how one teacher has used Logo's language-manipulation power to help his students think about spelling.

The focus of the activity is on getting students to articulate rules for pluralizing nouns and to articulate them well enough so that the rules can be "taught" to Logo. The idea is to start with the simplest rule for pluralization and slowly build a smarter and smarter Logo plural procedure.

The lesson begins with Bob Schwartz telling a class that he wants to teach Logo to spell. "Let's begin by trying to teach Logo to change nouns into their plurals." As the students know that teaching Logo involves creating a new procedure, Bob suggests calling this new procedure TO PLURAL. "What do we want PLURAL to do? We want to be able to input a singular noun and have it print its plural for us. Since we want PLURAL to be able to work with any singular noun, we need to use a variable as our input.

```
TO PLURAL :NOUN
```

[A note to those not familiar with Logo programming: A Logo procedure can take an input variable, which allows you to hand it different pieces of information when you give a command (e.g., handing PLURAL different nouns for it to pluralize). You create an input variable by giving it a name (in this case, :NOUN) and placing it in the title line of the procedure. The colon is used as punctuation to let Logo know something is a variable. To let Logo know that you are referring to the actual word HAT, you must use a quotation mark.

This tells Logo that you are referring to a literal letter or word. Thus, while :NOUN refers to the variable named NOUN and tells Logo to retrieve the word stored as the NOUN variable, "HAT tells Logo that you mean the actual word HAT.]

so now if we type:

```
PLURAL "HAT
```

what do we want the computer to do?"

At this point students readily respond, "Print HATS" or, "add an 's' onto HAT." Schwartz then asks, "What is the simplest rule for making a plural?" Students respond, "add an 's'." He continues, "So how do we get Logo to do that? Well, we want it to PRINT a WORD made up of the value of the noun (:NOUN) and the letter S (in Logo "S)." As Bob leads this discussion, he begins creating the procedure for PLURAL on the board:

```
TO PLURAL :NOUN
     PRINT WORD :NOUN "S
END
```

Schwartz explains, "There is a Logo command called WORD that takes two things and glues them together into a word. In this case it simply takes the value of our noun HAT and adds S to make it plural. That is why the line reads:

```
PRINT WORD :NOUN "S
```

Bob now types it into the computer, defines PLURAL, and tries it:

```
PLURAL "HAT
HATS
PLURAL "DOG
DOGS
```

Then he gives it a word that does not follow the rule:

```
PLURAL "BABY
BABYS
```

"Oops! What's the problem?" The students correct the spelling, BABIES, and are helped to articulate the generalization that if a word ends in -Y, take off the last letter and add -IES. The class now adds this rule to their

PLURAL procedure. In Logo the rule "if a word ends in Y, take off the -Y and add -IES" starts out:

```
IF "Y=LAST :NOUN
```

The teacher explains that LAST is a Logo command that gives you the last element of the input. The LAST of "BABY = "Y. If the last letter of :NOUN is a Y, THEN we want to PRINT a WORD made up if everything BUT the LAST letter of :NOUN plus IES. The rest of the Logo line is:

```
IF "Y=LAST :NOUN THEN PRINT WORD BUTLAST :NOUN "IES STOP
```

BUTLAST is another Logo command that returns everything BUT the LAST item of its input, BUTLAST BABY is BAB. The only thing we want to add is to tell Logo to STOP if it prints an -IES plural so it won't go on and print the "S plural as well.

```
TO PLURAL :NOUN
    IF "Y=LAST :NOUN THEN PRINT WORD BUTLAST :NOUN "IES STOP
    PRINT WORD :NOUN "S
END
```

Note that the PLURAL procedures are written in the M.I.T. Terrapin version of Logo. There are some differences in commands and syntax between different versions of Logo. If you are using a different version of Logo, you may have to make some changes in some of the lines. For example, in the LCSI version of Logo, all IF lines need to be rewritten with brackets ([ ]) rather than THEN:

```
Terrapin: IF "Y=LAST :NOUN THEN PRINT WORD BUTLAST :NOUN
              "IES STOP
LCSI Logo: IF "Y=LAST :NOUN [PRINT WORD BUTLAST :NOUN
              "IES STOP]
```

This is true for all the programs in this chapter.
 Schwartz defines this and then tries it:

```
PLURAL "BABY
BABIES
PLURAL "FLY
FLIES
```

and just to make sure it still works in the simple case:

```
PLURAL "HOUSE
HOUSES
```

Some students suggest trying PLAY:

```
PLURAL "PLAY
```

produces:

```
PLAIES
```

a misspelling. A failure? No, the challenge now becomes for students to discover a new rule to handle PLAY and articulate it clearly enough so that they can "teach it to Logo." The activity becomes a double challenge for students. "Find words the program misspells and then figure out a rule, if one applies, and add it to the plural procedure." Of course, some words are exceptions and do not follow any rules, such as "child-children," but these can be collected and placed in an exception list that the plural procedure can check. Figure 7-4 gives a version of PLURAL that can handle such exceptions.

From here the activity can go in many directions. The class can continue as a whole developing the PLURAL procedure as students find words and rules it does not respond to correctly. Students can work alone

FIGURE 7-4. A Logo program for pluralizing irregular nouns.

<u>PLURAL PROCEDURES THAT INCLUDE EXCEPTIONS</u>

```
TO PLURAL :NOUN
    IF MEMBER?  :NOUN  :EXCEPTIONS.LIST  THEN PRINT GET.EXCEPTION
        :NOUN :EXCEPTION.LIST STOP
    IF "Y = LAST :NOUN THEN PRINT WORD BUTLAST :NOUN "IES STOP
    PRINT WORD :NOUN "S
    END
```
(Note: the first line and the second indented line in PLURAL are to be typed as one line. **Do not** press Return after typing GET.EXCEPTION.)

```
TO GET.EXCEPTION  :NOUN   :EXCEPTIONS.LIST
    IF :NOUN = FIRST  :EXCEPTIONS.LIST THEN OUTPUT ITEM 2
        :EXCEPTIONS.LIST
    OUTPUT GET.EXCEPTION  BUTFIRST :EXCEPTIONS.LIST
    END
```
(Note: the first line and the second indented line in GET.EXCEPTION are to be typed as one line. **Do not** press Return after typing ITEM 2.)

```
MAKE "EXCEPTIONS.LIST [ CHILD CHILDREN LEAF LEAVES FISH FISH ]
```
New exceptions are added to the exceptionlist by editing the names and adding new singular and plural pairs to the exceptionlist list.

(Note: people using LCSI versions of Logo will need to replace MEMBER? with MEMBERP and change the syntax of the IF lines as described earlier in the chapter.)

or in small groups trying to build the best PLURAL procedure. One class developed an ongoing focus on exceptions; as a side activity, students queried parents and other teachers and looked in dictionaries in order to collect as complete an exception list as possible. These students, under their own initiative, learned a great deal both about spelling and finding information, as well as creating a "smarter and smarter" program.

Logo and Science: A Reaction Timer

A final example of integrating Logo into the curriculum comes from a science teacher. Beverly Brown believes that studying science not only involves learning scientific facts and ideas, but also having students directly experience how scientists go about discovering those ideas in the first place. She believes that students should not only *do* experiments but also *design* their own experiments. Brown believes that a fundamental aspect of learning science involves inquiry, having students come up with their own questions and hypotheses to investigate. She wants her class to have the atmosphere of a research lab and she finds Logo to be an ideal tool.

Using Logo, Beverly creates a series of procedures that set the stage for experimentation. One of her Logo experiment procedures focuses on reaction time. To use it, students type in the word REACT and press the <RETURN> key. The screen goes blank for a short amount of time and then an **X** appears in the middle. The student presses the space bar as quickly as possible, once she or he sees the **X**. The program then prints out the amount of time it took between the appearance of the **X** and the press of the <RETURN> key (in sixtieths of a second).

Brown begins the class by explaining the reaction-time experiment. She asks for a volunteer and has the other students make predictions of how quickly the volunteer will respond. The class then tries the experiment to see how accurate their guesses are. Reaction time is usually much faster than students predict. They are next asked to predict how much improvement will occur over five trials? This can also be tried as a group. Brown then asks students what other questions they might ask and brainstorms a list such as:

- How do the left hand and right hand differ?
- How much better would your nondominant hand get with practice?
- How long will it take to reach a maximum speed?
- What differences are there between people? Are girls faster than boys?

The students go off and try these experiments in groups. After a while, the class gets back together and shares the data. Usually there are discrepancies in the results and this leads to discussion about experimental design and uncontrolled variables. As the discussion progresses, students come up with new questions like:

- What if we used a dot (a period) instead of an *X?*
- Does the length of the wait between pressing <RETURN> and the appearance of the *X* make a difference? (In the original program the waiting period varied randomly.)
- How would random placement of the **X** each time affect the results?
- Would you respond faster to a sound than to an **X** on the screen?

Many of these questions demand changes in the REACT procedure, and the power of using Logo here is that changing the procedure is relatively simple (see below). With only a rudimentary knowledge of Logo, students can begin to design and carry out their own experiments by rewriting the REACT procedure to fit their needs. If need be, the teacher can also supply simple tools such as a sound-producing CLICK procedure for students to use.

Simple REACT:

```
TO REACT
    CLEARTEXT               ;clears the screen
    WAIT 25 + RANDOM 100 ;waits for a random amount of time
    CURSOR 10 10            ;places the cursor in the middle of
                             the screen
    PRINT [X]               ;prints the X
    PRTIME 0                ;counts the time until user presses
                             a key and when key is pressed
                             prints elapsed time.
    PRINT [IS THE TIME IT TOOK YOU.]
END

TO PRTIME :TIME
    IF RC? THEN PRINT :TIME STOP   ;RC? checks key press.
    PRTIME :TIME + 1               ;adds one to the time
                                     variable.
END

TO WAIT :NUM
    IF :NUM = 0 THEN STOP
    WAIT :NUM - 1
END
```

REACT with randomly placed **X**:

```
TO REACT
    CLEARTEXT
    WAIT 25 + RANDOM 100
    CURSOR RANDOM 39 RANDOM 23
    PRINT [X]
    PRTIME 0
    PRINT [IS THE TIME IT TOOK YOU.]
END
```

REACT with tone instead of **X**:

```
TO REACT
    CLEARTEXT
    WAIT 25 + RANDOM 100
    CURSOR 10 10
    CLICK
    PRTIME 0
    PRINT [IS THE TIME IT TOOK YOU.]
END

TO CLICK
    .DEPOSIT .EXAMINE 49200 49200
END
```

One of the things that delights this teacher about Logo is the support it provides for a real experience of the scientific process. Using REACT, students come up with questions to investigate, design experiments, gather data, and then share and argue about findings. This leads to further hypotheses that lead to further experiments. In using REACT, her students are not only learning about human reaction time but are getting important lessons on the process of scientific inquiry.

Logo, because of its simplicity, its flexibility, and its participatory nature, is an ideal tool for creating exploratory, initiative-based activities in a variety of curriculum areas. Logo is often thought of as solely a tool for computer literacy and programming; but, as these examples show, its power extends well into the standard curriculum.

REFERENCES

ARY, TEMPLE. "Exploring Fractions with Logo." *The Computing Teacher,* vol. 13, no. 9 (June 1986), 47–50.

PAPERT, SEYMOUR. "Teaching Children to be Mathematicians vs. Teaching About Mathematics." Logo Memo No. 4, AI Memo No. 249, M.I.T., Cambridge, Mass., July 1971.

EIGHT
CREATING AN
INTERDISCIPLINARY
CURRICULUM

One of the complaints about current educational practice is that each subject is treated as a totally separate entity. In the real world neither jobs nor problems come in such neat, isolated units. The result is that students tend to develop an unrealistic view of knowledge. The only time they think about history is during history class and the only time they "do math" is during math class. Skills become separated from actual applications, and students do not become as effective problem solvers as they might. Most often in school students work in isolation at their desks. Most problems in real life, however, are solved by groups of people working together. In addition, because the educational world is usually divided into forty-five-minute "classes," students often do not get the chance to immerse themselves in a problem or an area of study.

Some schools and curriculum projects have pursued a very different model. One approach, developed in the 1930s in the University of Chicago lab school, is called *central subject*. In a central-subject classroom, activities in language arts, literature, history, and geography are centered around a year-long theme such as Eskimos, the Greeks, the Middle Ages, or whales and the Nantucket whalers. The idea is for students to immerse themselves in the culture they are studying and to build as much of the curriculum as possible out of activities related to the central subject. The approach usually involves one or more large whole-class projects or events such as a play, a mock Olympics, or a medieval fair.

Some advantages of organizing the curriculum in this way have been described by teachers as follows:

• Studying a rich and general topic such as the Greeks gives a teacher the ability to provide materials to suit a variety of abilities and interests yet have a common area for understanding and discussion.

• Combining a variety of disciplines allows students to spend significant amounts of time becoming engaged with the subject matter and enough breadth to allow almost all students to find something of special interest.

• Using writing, art, and drama allows students to express their ideas and understandings in a variety of ways, again based around a common set of ideas and experiences.

• Many basic skills activities can be related to, or grow out of, the central-subject theme and as such become an integral part of something that is significant to the student.

• Students experience the interrelationships of many areas of knowledge.

Although very rewarding, implementing a cross-disciplinary curriculum is hard work. Opening up the rigid confines of isolated subjects presents a whole new way of looking at curriculum. It demands flexibility. Teachers have found they are not always able to predict what will grow out of the intense involvement and interest students often show in these projects. Working on colonial history may lead to areas as diverse as exploring the effect of salt in preserving food and the mathematics of the cost of supplying a family with a year's worth of food.

EXAMPLES OF CROSS-DISCIPLINARY CURRICULUM EFFORTS

Computers and good educational software can play an important role in this process. Some software, by engaging students in real-world activities, lends itself naturally to interdisciplinary activities and extensions. For example, the *Sell Series* of simulations (described in Chapter 3) focuses on economic concepts such as best price and the effects of advertising. This software also provides a wonderul opportunity for mathematical analysis and scientific investigation (Friel). Students are challenged to figure out how the underlying mathematical model that controls the simulation behaves. How does advertising affect sales? How do changes in prices affect profit? Does increasing the price one cent have the same effect, no matter what the starting price is? What begins as a social studies investigation ends with students making charts and graphs and looking for mathematical relationships. In the process, students also have to identify, isolate, and control variables.

Lemonade and the other *Sell* series simulations can be used to combine the disciplines of economics and mathematics, as well as provide lessons in the process of scientific investigation. This can be extended to include a critical look at the topic of computer simulations by asking questions such as, Just how accurate is the program's model of a lemonade stand? and, In what way is the program an incomplete model? By considering how questions like these might be answered, students are introduced to a whole new world of critical inquiry.

The *Mimi* Curriculum Project

We are just beginning to see a few examples of larger-scale curriculum materials that use the computer as a focal point for integrated studies. Currently, the preeminent example is a curriculum project called *The Voyage of the Mimi*, developed by Bank Street College in New York. *Mimi*'s developers set out to create curriculum materials that would integrate math and science, appeal to both boys and girls, and take advantage of current technology. After extensive research they found whales to be a topic of general appeal. They decided to use video to create a dramatic adventure about some students who join a whale research project aboard a sailing ship named *Mimi*. To go along with the thirteen episodes of the story, the producers also created thirteen related documentaries in which the young actors who play the characters in the dramatic story visit and interview scientists at their work. These visits include everything from a meteorologist on top of Mt. Washington, to a ship architect, to the scientist, Katy Paine, who does research on the songs of humpback whales.

In the dramatic story the researchers aboard the *Mimi* use all kinds of technology—from computers to record ocean temperatures to radio direction finders to locate their position when they get lost. The published materials include four computer-based curriculum modules: "Introduction to Computers," "Maps and Navigation," "Whales and Their Environment," and "Ecology." These modules use computers to allow students to participate directly in many of the activities they watched on the video screen, whether navigating a ship or graphing changes in water temperature. Learning is no longer a matter of reading about what some scientist has done or doing predigested unidimensional exercises in a workbook. Students can now participate fully in a real-life activity such as locating a whale, using skills and concepts from both math and science. The material is full of intertwined math and science topics; from the mathematics of sampling to measure the size of whale populations, to rate, time, and distance problems in navigating a ship.

Although the focus of *Mimi* is on integrating math and science, teachers who have used *Mimi* materials have found it very hard to limit their classwork to these two disciplines. The drama of the thirteen episodes and the personalities of the characters are so strong that work in other areas such as language arts is a natural outgrowth of the video material. For example, record keeping and diaries are a theme in the story. The scientists keep records of the whales they spot. When C.T., the captain's grandson, learns that his great grandfather was a whaler from reading his diary, C.T. begins to keep his own diary of the voyage and to plot their position daily. It is a natural extension to ask students to pick a character and keep a diary of the voyage from that character's point of view. In one fifth-grade classroom, the students asked how they could go on such a research trip. The teacher suggested they might apply by writing a letter. He initiated an activity in which he asked his students to write a letter on the word processor to Captain Granville applying for a place on the next voyage of the *Mimi*. Once the letters were written, a team of students reviewed and criticized them, and the class discussed the strengths and weaknesses of different approaches. Following this, each student used the word processor to revise his or her letter.

Curriculum Webbing

Planning an interdisciplinary curriculum is not an easy task. One technique many teachers have found useful, especially in working with the *Mimi* materials, is called *curriculum webbing*. The webbing technique can be a useful tool for breaking out of the narrow perspective of traditional curriculum guidelines. This technique is built on the brainstorming process, in which a teacher and students begin with a central topic such as whales and generate a variety of ideas connected to whales in a web diagram (see Figure 8-1). Some teachers engage students in this process in order to build a curriculum from the students' particular interests and questions. An interdisciplinary curriculum involves an attempt to take a broader and less linear view of the subject matter. The web therefore becomes a planning tool that allows the teacher to organize possible activities and to make connections within the existing curriculum or to create entirely new connections between and among curricular areas.

Most current computer software for organizing and processing information, such as word processors and databases, although flexible in design is linear in nature. We are just beginning to see programs that support a more free-flowing, idea-generating process. A person can take notes with a word processor and reorganize them as he or she goes along; however, the ability to go off in a variety of possible directions implicit in the curriculum-webbing diagram is not really well-supported on standard word processors. The technology of visual-spatial mapping and idea extension found in a webbing diagram is just beginning to be explored. Programs that present a more flexible approach in generating ideas have been called

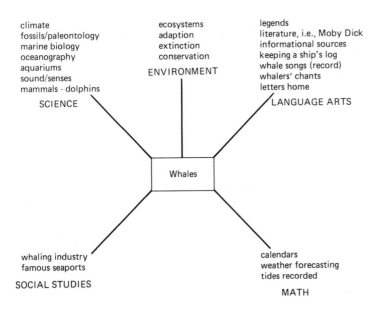

climate
fossils/paleontology
marine biology
oceanography
aquariums
sound/senses
mammals - dolphins

SCIENCE

ecosystems
adaption
extinction
conservation

ENVIRONMENT

legends
literature, i.e., Moby Dick
informational sources
keeping a ship's log
whale songs (record)
whalers' chants
letters home

LANGUAGE ARTS

Whales

whaling industry
famous seaports

SOCIAL STUDIES

calendars
weather forecasting
tides recorded

MATH

FIGURE 8-1. The curriculum-webbing technique.

idea processors. Currently there are two: one called *Ideamap* by Mitch Development Corporation in Canada; the other, called *Calliope,* by David Thornberg. It is exciting to see technology supporting such alternatives to thinking and curriculum development. In this capacity the computer shows itself as a powerful integration tool for thinking about and organizing of information in creative ways.

Integrated Software

The ability to present students with more integrated activities is one power of the computer. Another is to provide teachers with tools for interdisciplinary study and investigation. A current trend in business software is *integrated software*—programs that combine several tools such as a word processor, a database, and a spreadsheet into one integrated package. *Lotus* 123 and *AppleWorks* are two well-known examples.

The "Immigrants" project. So far there has been very little use of integrated tools in education. An exciting exception is a project developed by the Educational Technology Center at Harvard University called "Immigrants." "Immigrants" is an attempt to use the integrated computer power of *AppleWorks* to create interdisciplinary curriculum materials. "Immigrants" focuses on the movement of Irish immigrants to Boston in the late 1800s. Students are provided with a computer data disk. They use *AppleWorks'* word processor to read an introductory story explaining that the students' job is to take on the role of an Irish family coming to America, decide on a dream they want to fulfill, and try to achieve that dream. To choose a family, they are directed to *AppleWorks'* database and several files of ships' passenger lists on the data disk. Students must search through this primary source, choose an actual historical family, and collect as much data as they can about it, such as the names, ages, and professions of family members and cash on hand.

Students then begin a diary about their family, using *AppleWorks'* word processor. Their next step is to choose housing. Students again go to the database and look at housing lists taken from the period. Once the students have chosen housing, they must then find jobs. They turn to the database once more but now must also begin to plan a budget. Here the students use *AppleWorks'* spreadsheet program. From the database documents they can calculate how much their family's housing, food, and clothes cost and enter the amounts into a prepared budget on the spreadsheet. Students must also figure in transportation to their jobs if they have picked a place to live that is far from their place at work. Knowing how much their family makes at their jobs, they can then use the spreadsheet program to figure out what they can afford and if they can save anything toward their "dream," such as a farm in the rural town of Lexington.

Students can also build other budgets based on different jobs and housing. The spreadsheet program allows them not only to try various budgets but project the budgets into the future. How long would it take for the family to afford to move to a "better" neighborhood? How much difference would it make if the children went to work?

This multifaceted use of the computer allows students to enter into the world of an Irish immigrant family; it combines the study of history and economics with the mathematics involved in maintaining a family in the late 1800s. At the same time, the students are using the word processor to keep a diary about their family's experience. Using the computer allows students to examine original source material, role-play, collect and organize data, do mathematical calculations and analysis, and write up their findings in one integrated computer environment.

The "Sturbridge" project.   Another project that began with the study of a historical period provides a different example of the interdisciplinary role a computer can play. At the Phoenix School, in Cambridge, Massachusetts, students have been studying historical periods in the life of different Massachusetts communities. Currently they are looking at the village of Sturbridge and the life of people who lived there in the late 1600s. Sturbridge is a rich site because the village has been restored and many original records from earlier times have been collected.

The class is doing a project similar to "Immigrants." Each group has taken on the role of a family, but this time the students must collect the data to enter into a program their teacher has written in Logo. The teacher was concerned about this part of the unit. He worried that the students would get bored entering data into his database program. As it turned out, exactly the opposite occurred. The program became a center of interest, and students eagerly read diaries, tax records, and various inventories to gather data to go into what they saw as their personal database.

Preparing data for the program became a catalyst for all kinds of activities. First the class often had to decide on how they wanted to enter a piece of data—for example, what units to use. If someone found a citation that said eight barrels of salt was worth two dollars, they had to decide how to enter this information. Should the unit be one barrel? If so, how much would one barrel cost if eight barrels cost two dollars? Furthermore, how much salt was in a barrel? Many mathematical problems such as these arose from their research into the items used in Sturbridge and the items' costs. The students were fascinated. But this particular example led beyond mathematics. The next question was, Why would anyone want a barrel of salt, anyway? This led into some work in science on the preservation of foods and an investigation of how much salt people today use in a year.

Once a large amount of data is collected and entered into the database, the students begin to provision their Sturbridge families. Then they use the database to plan each family's weekly and seasonal purchases. Here the computer provides the students with a sense of ownership of their work that functions as an important motivation for a range of interdisciplinary studies.

These students had used computer simulations such as "Oregon Trail" and "Hammurabi" (a simulation of the politics and economics of an old Sumerian Empire), and they now wanted to create one of the lives of their families in Sturbridge. Luckily, the database the students had been using was written in Logo by their teacher and he could modify the program to use all the data they had collected as part of the simulation. This computer project plunged them into an analysis of the economics of a farming community of the late 1600s. For example, the class had to find out how much wheat an acre of land produced, how much it might cost to harvest it, and how much money sales of the wheat would produce. They discovered that most economic exchange was done by a barter system based on careful record keeping. Planning the computer simulation, with their teacher's help, immersed these students in both historical research and mathematics.

A final example of how the computer became a tool to support the interdisciplinary curriculum also occurred during this Sturbridge simulation project. One student asked why it was warm in the summer and cold in the winter. The teacher took a globe and made a brief explanation about

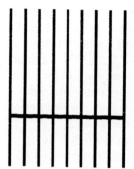

FIGURE 8-2. Sun's rays directly over Earth.

the angle of the sun during the different seasons. The students were not convinced. Why should the angle of the sunlight make a difference? The teacher worked with the students, using Logo's turtle graphics to construct a simulation of parallel rays falling on a strip of land. The students changed the angle of the sun's rays and counted the number of rays that fell on the simulated land for various angles. They found that when coming from an angle, fewer rays hit the strip of land than when coming from directly overhead. Having the students help construct this computer simulation of the sun's rays and try it out themselves made the ideas understandable. See Figures 8-2 and 8-3.

The "Inventions" project.   A final example of the development of an interdisciplinary curriculum project using computer database software occurred in a sixth-grade science class. The teacher wanted to do a unit on inventions; moreover, she wanted her students to understand that science is done by real people and that the work of scientists affects all our daily lives in a variety of ways. (Seeing scientists as real people is also a theme of the video documentaries in *The Voyage of the Mimi.*)

This intermediate-grade teacher began by having her students brainstorm about inventions: What were the most famous inventions the

FIGURE 8-3. Sun's rays hitting Earth at a 45° angle.

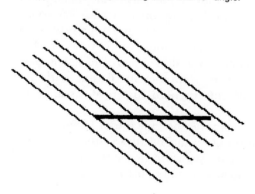

```
TO SUNS.RAYS :SUN.ANGLE
 MAKE "DIST 10 ; DISTANCE BETWEEN RAYS
 MAKE "LENGTH 150 ; LENGTH OF RAYS
 EARTH
 SUN.POS :SUN.ANGLE ; ANGLE FROM HORIZON
 RAYS :DIST :LENGTH
END

TO EARTH
 BK 1 RT 90 FD 40 BK 80 FD 40 LT 90
 BK 1 RT 90 FD 40 BK 80 FD 40 LT 90
 FD 2 RT 90 FD 40 BK 80 FD 40 LT 90
END

TO SUN.POS :ANGLE
 LT 90 PU FD 100 RT 90
 ARCR 100 :ANGLE ; ARC DRAWING TOOL PROCEDURE
END

TO RAYS :DIST :LENGTH
 PD REPEAT 5 [RT 90 PD FD :LENGTH BK :LENGTH PU LT 90 FD :DIST] PU BK :DIST * 5
 RT 180 FD :DIST
 REPEAT 4 [LT 90 PD FD :LENGTH BK :LENGTH PU RT 90 FD :DIST] PU BK :DIST * 5
END

TO ARCR :RADIUS :DEGS
 RT 5
 ARCR1 :RADIUS * 0.0174 :DEGS
 LT 5
END

TO ARCR1 :RADIUS :DEGS
 REPEAT ( QUOTIENT :DEGS 10 ) [FD :RADIUS*10 RT 10]
 CORRECTARC :RADIUS ( REMAINDER :DEGS 10 )
END

TO CORRECTARC :RADIUS :AMOUNT
 FD :RADIUS * :AMOUNT
 RT :AMOUNT
END
```

FIGURE 8–4. Logo program to generate sun's rays diagrams.

class knew of? and, Did they know the names of any people associated with the inventions? The class generated a large list and they talked about how some of these inventions might have affected their lives. Several students noted that some of the inventions such as the telephone had been invented before they were born and wondered what life was like before there were things like telephones. Wanting her students to do some informal research, the teacher asked the students how they could find out more about the origins of the inventions they had listed. To her surprise, the students suggested doing interviews with older people.

At this point the science teacher conferred with the language arts teacher and in their next language arts class the students (with teacher assistance) brainstormed an interview form entitled, "How Have Inventions Affected Your Life?" A word processor was used to record the brainstorming ideas. The students were able to criticize their ideas and discuss what would make a final list of useful questions. When there was disagreement, a student could use the word processor to create his or her own individualized interview form. They then practiced interviewing one another and made final changes in their interview forms. Next, they went into the community and interviewed grandparents and older neighbors, asking them what inventions had affected their lives in the most significant way. When all the students had completed at least one interview each, they shared their findings. As a group they used the word processor to write and edit a class book that they entitled, "The Impact of Inventions on People's Everyday Lives."

While these activities were going on in language arts, the class continued working on the impact of inventions in science. They took their growing list of inventions based on their work in language arts and began a database. To do this, they had to discuss what they wanted to include about each invention. The students thought about all the different ways they might want to categorize inventions such as by date, inventor, company affiliation, country, city, and area of impact such as medicine, transportation, households. These categories became fields in their record form for the inventions database. Next the students did research to gather the pertinent information on each invention chosen. The particulars they found were added to the database program.

Once they had a number of records, they began to use their database to ask questions such as:

- What periods of time could be called the "most inventive" and the "least inventive," and what might have contributed to this?
- What geographic areas had the most inventions?
- Were inventions in a particular discipline, such as medicine or electronics, clustered around certain dates?
- Was one country or city the "most inventive"?
- Were most inventors independent or did they work for a company?

This was a rich project that resulted from a science teacher's willingness to look beyond the confines of her discipline and explore the possibility of building an interdisciplinary cooperative project. Towards the end of this project, Scholastic Publishing came out with a commercial database on inventions. This turned out to be a wonderful coincidence because it gave the teacher the opportunity to let her students compare their work to that of the prepared database. They were excited about this and even found some errors in the commercial database. The teacher decided that her students' explorations into areas and inventions of interest were a more valuable learning experience than "plugging" into a commercial database. She decided that in the future she would not show the commercial database to the students until they had done their own searching, recording, and decision making on the topic of inventions.

CROSS-DISCIPLINARY SOFTWARE TOOLS

The flip side of looking at software that supports interdisciplinary work is looking at general software tools that can be used in a variety of disciplines. The preeminent example, of course, is the word processor—a general-purpose writing tool that can be used in any subject involving students in writing. Based on the power of a word processor, a new set of tools is appearing. One of these is an outlining program called *Think Tank*. *Think tank* is described as a planning tool. It allows a person to dynamically make and revise an outline. For example, let's say a class is setting up a travel agency and each student is to choose a country. The student's job is to find out about the country and why someone might want to travel there. Let's watch a student who has chosen Spain as his country and is using *Think Tank* to plan his work.

He begins with a blank screen. He types "Spain" as the title of his outline. He thinks a moment and then types "Sights" and "Weather" as two subheadings under Spain.

```
SPAIN
      Sights
      Weather
```

He then thinks to himself, "Maybe I'd better start with a brief description." He moves his cursor up and inserts "Brief Description" above "Sights." He looks at "Weather." "How hot *is* it in Spain?" he asks himself. He moves the cursor to "Weather" and gives the INDENT command. The cursor opens up an indented space under "Weather." He types in "average temperature chart."

```
SPAIN
      Brief Description
      Sights
      Weather
            Average Temperature Chart
```

Then he thinks, "Where can I get that? I should check the encyclopedia and that book Mr. Thompson showed us, *The World Almanac*. I'd better make a list of things to do." He presses a key and the cursor jumps to the bottom of his outline. He types "Things to Do," gives the INDENT command, and begins his list: "check encyclopedia, check almanac." As he is making this list, it occurs to him that some people like Spanish food and he ought to include something about that. He moves the cursor back up in his outline and inserts "Food." He remembers that his friend Paulo's

grandmother used to live in Spain and thinks he ought to interview her.
He jumps back to his "To Do" list and adds "interview Paulo's grandmother."
He now goes back up to "Sights," indents, and types "Bullfights," the
reason he chose Spain. He now indents again and begins to write a
paragraph describing the excitement of a Spanish festival in which bulls
run through the city streets and brave people run with them, risking their
lives. After a couple of paragraphs of this, he presses a key, the paragraphs
disappear, and his main outline reappears on the screen. He reviews what
he has done and decides to work on finding out about the weather
tomorrow. He then reopens his "To Do" entry and adds a series of
questions he wants to investigate. Next, he moves all of the "check
almanac" headings to the top of the "To Do" list. Finally, satisfied, he
closes up some of his subheadings and quits *Think Tank* for the day.

```
SPAIN
        Brief Description
        Sights
            +Bullfights
                The most thrilling event . . .
        Food
        Weather
            Average Temperature Chart
                compare to here
            rainfall
            when best to go?
        Things to do
            Check encyclopedia
            Check almanac
            Interview Paulo's Grandmother

    SPAIN
        Brief Description
        Sights
        Food
        Weather
        Things to do
            Check almanac
            Check encyclopedia
            Interview Paulo's Grandmother
```

The *Think Tank* outline grows and changes with the development of his
project. Its structure allows this student to work on separate details

(writing up paragraphs of text, making lists of places to visit, and what to do at each place) and at any time, as ideas occur. He can move quickly to another part of the project plan at whatever level of detail he wishes. By closing up the subheadings, he can also, at any time, get an overview. If he needs to refer to books and keep notes, he can use *Think Tank* to keep his notes and record bibliographic information. Once he has done this, he can even use *Think Tank* to print out his bibliography.

Although *Think Tank* was designed as an outlining and planning tool, it has another integrative capability that is ideally suited for schools. All through school people study social studies and history. Rarely, however, are the different courses taken at different times related or integrated in any way. *Think Tank* can be a wonderful tool for each student to keep a personally developed *time line,* from dinosaurs to the present day. The time line can be developed year by year as students study new eras. The details of specific events can be stored under subheadings that can be hidden, so when the *Think Tank* file is opened the student sees a general outline of history.

```
B.C.
0-500
500-1000
1000-1500
1500-1600
1600-1700
1700-1800
1800-1900
1900-present
```

To get to specific events, a student can simply open various headings to reveal a more detailed outline of major heading years. These might also have subheadings, going down to whatever level of detail the student has developed for that period of history. This time line can also be used in the long run to connect the study of things like literature with the study of history. For example, what else was going on in the world when Lewis Carroll wrote *Alice's Adventures in Wonderland?*

CONCLUSIONS

The authors believe that tools like these can open up the possibility of engaging students in rich interdisciplinary investigations that ask them to use all the standard academic skills as well as a new set of information-processing skills. If students have access to large database capabilities as well as word processing and spreadsheets, they can pursue a whole range of investigations. For example, the Sears catalog for 1920 can be stored in the database along with the current one. Students can then ask questions such as, How much did it cost to furnish a house in 1920 compared to today? and, What were the major technological differences between the two times? Or, How are men and women represented differently in the two catalogs? Students can be asked to gather data on the questions, do appropriate calculations, and present their findings.

Contemporary problems that are of general interest to students, such as the predicted arrival of killer bees, can be studied. Resources such as maps, information about habits, habitats, history, and life cycles can be stored on the computer in databases and word-processing files. Students can be asked for predictions about the problem and suggestions for a solution. To do this, students need to work together and, in the killer bees example, draw on materials from geography, biology, ecology, and mathematics, as well as use a variety of research skills.

The best learning comes from things that engage students' interest and are experienced as part of a larger, meaningful whole. Much learning in today's schools is needlessly fragmented. Today's students desperately need to develop skills for tackling complex, multifaceted problems and they need to be equipped with tools, both intellectual and technological, that can help them collect, organize, analyze, synthesize, and evaluate new information. Isolated subject matter is one major barrier to learning these important skills.

Computers, through their power to simulate, can create engaging real-world environments in which students can use academic skills to explore multifaceted, multidisciplinary problems. Computers can also provide tools that allow students to manipulate information in ways that have not been practical before. These two capacities can put students in situations in which they have to both initiate new ideas and compare and evaluate different and unique results, something that rarely happens in current classrooms. If we can take advantage of these capabilities, we have the possibility of transforming the process of studying and learning: a chance to break out of the world of forty-five-minute isolated lessons and engage in extended projects that draw on a broad range of skills and interests. We have the possibility of bridging school work to the non-academic world and the chance to challenge students to develop the large-scale integrated skills they need to deal with the growing complexity of the world they inhabit.

REFERENCES

FRIEL, SUSAN. "Lemonade's the Name, Simulation's the Game." *Classroom Computer News*, vol. 3, no 3 (1983), 34–39.

NINE
NEXT STEPS

Throughout this book we have been examining how a microcomputer can be used as a powerful tool to support learning in today's classrooms. Much of what we have described would not have been possible with the first microcomputers produced in the early 1970's. The memories, speed, and graphic capabilities of those machines were too limited. There has been an incredible change in a relatively few years, but the change has not been simply technological. Part of the change has to do with vision, the vision of what education might be. Whether it involves allowing students to design their own science experiments, invent their own geometric theories, or produce their own newspaper, the microcomputer has brought with it an expanded vision of how education can be transformed.

Such visions are created through the accumulation of many positive experiences over a long term. Teachers do not become skilled computer users overnight. Successful integration takes several years with many possible paths to follow. Given a supportive principal, reasonable resources, and access to education courses or knowledgeable consultants, how might the process of integrating technology into the curriculum occur over, say, a five year period for a middle school teacher? Following is a description of one such possible path.

YEAR	RESOURCES AVAILABLE	CURRICULUM OBJECTIVES
1	1 computer in the classroom; lab of 15 computers nearby.	Introduce database software and build one database for one social studies unit. Use a computer simulation in conjunction with a science unit.
2	2 classroom computers and a large monitor; plus the computer laboratory.	Expand the use of databases to a science unit. Introduce word processing to the class as a method for taking notes during a brainstorming session and then to the whole class in the computer lab. Introduce Logo as a mathematics tool and tool-builder. Use tutorials for students needing basic skill strengthening.
3	Adds a videodisc player to the classroom.	Extends use of Logo as a tool in science. Acquires one interactive science videodisc. Introduces spreadsheets for use in both mathematics and social studies.
4	Adds a modem and telephone jack to classroom equipment.	Experiments with telecommunications by subscribing to a commercial service that provides access to databases and worldwide electronic mail. Begins sharing scientific data with schools across the country as part of a nationally funded project.
5	School system installs a local area network (LAN) tieing together all computers within the town. Upgrades some of its computer equipment to provide high quality sound and graphics capability.	Initiates electronic mail within the school system and homes with computers and modems. Begins experimenting with having students who are at home sick participate in class through the computer network. Offers an enriched computer-based art and music program.

If this class continues on the path outlined above, where might it be in the late 1990s? Let us close the book with a look at where continuing changes in technology coupled with this expanding vision of education might find our students in the late 1990s.

SCHOOL DAYS 1999*

Terry and Susan Smith are on their way to school. It is a sunny day in May of 1999. Terry is 15 years old and Susan is 6. Each one is carrying a *dynabook*—a small, book-sized electronic device with a display screen and a touch-sensitive keyboard. This is the first year that children as young as

*This section is adapted from Ricky Carter, "School Days 1991: A Vision of Student Life in the Next Decade," *Classroom Computer News* (Jan.-Feb. 1982), pp. 17-27.

Susan have been given dynabooks. Terry did not have one when he first entered school.

Susan is particularly excited about having a dynabook because of its capacity to generate music. Susan loves music. When she got her dynabook last week, Terry promised to teach her how to use it. After finishing his work last night, in which he used his dynabook to edit and illustrate his own story, Terry listened to Susan read a personalized computer-generated story her teacher had entered into her dynabook. It was about a girl named Susan who loved music. The story contained words Susan knew plus a few she was just learning. Then Terry taught Susan how to use the dynabook as a music machine so that she could compose her own tunes.

The dynabook contains a database of musical phrases. To compose tunes a person selects a set of musical phrases and puts them together in any order that sounds pleasing. The music phrases can be continually rearranged in the same way word phrases can be rearranged with a word processor. In addition, as students acquire an understanding of measures and notes, they can add their own phrases to the database. The dynabook music system provides an environment in which Susan can continuously experiment with sound.

Although school does not formally begin until 8:30 A.M., the children arrive at 8:00. The school is open early for students who want to work on special projects. Susan plans to make an animated picture to go with the tune she has created. Terry wants to find out if the baseball game he and three other students have been working on has been accepted for distribution on the Computer Games Network. They are supposed to hear today.

After saying good-bye to Susan, Terry goes to his classroom. It does not look like a traditional classroom at all. Instead of desks facing a chalkboard, clusters of workstations are situated around the room. Each workstation consists of a large computer screen "desk" with a built-in keyboard; underneath is a series of switches and plugs that enable the user to connect his or her station to that of any other student or teacher in the school, the resource library, or one of the national information networks. There is also a place to plug in a dynabook.

The center of the class is divided into a series of flexible areas that can be adapted for small or large discussion groups. At one end of the room are several large tables where children can work with a variety of math, science, or art materials that are stored on shelves. At the classroom's opposite end is a large video screen for displaying movies or for interclass communications. Next to the screen is a printing terminal.

Terry comes into the classroom and goes to his workstation. After turning it on and signing in he types:

```
>Mail?
```

to see if anyone has left him any messages. There are in fact several. One is from the resource library telling him that a new film on sharks—a particular interest of Terry's—has become available. He types:

>Schedule

and his schedule for the day is displayed. The message says there will be a group showing of the film at 10:00 A.M., or it could be shown on Terry's workstation at his convenience. Since he has a free period, he signs up to see it with the other members of the shark interest group at 10:00 in the Discussion Center.

Terry clears his screen and asks for his next message. It is from a friend who moved to California last month. Jose's note says that no, he hasn't seen any sharks but that one of the girls in his new class knows a lot about them and said she would be glad to connect with him.

These were the only messages—nothing from the game distribution center. Next, Terry checks to see if any of the game's coauthors are "on-line" by typing:

>Listusers

but none of them are, so he plugs in his dynabook and transfers the new, illustrated version of his story to the memory of his workstation. He then starts a program named *Spell* that checks the spelling of each of the words in his story and displays any misspelled ones. Terry corrects them and adds them to his individual spelling list. Later in the day he will do some spelling exercises using these words.

Now he wants to see what his story looks like, so he displays it on his screen. He decides to change the background color of one of his illustrations. After doing so, he uses a light pen to enlarge the tail of a shark in one picture. Finally, he decides to add one more shark to his illustration. At his request a grid is projected over his picture and Terry types in the coordinates of the place for the new shark. He then reproduces a shark, but half-size. This looks too small, so he erases the new shark and asks for a two-thirds reproduction. This still looks too small so he tries five-sixths: just right. After finishing he types:

>Save
>Sendcopy: Mrs. Feldman

to store the story in his workstation and also send a copy to his teacher's workstation for comments.

Looking up from his work now, Terry sees that several of his friends have arrived. He joins them and they talk until 8:30, when Mrs. Johnson, their homeroom teacher, calls a whole-class meeting. She begins with an outline of group activities for the day and then makes a few announcements. The last one is about a group of high school students who have been creating a simulation of the settling of their town and would like a few students to evaluate it. Terry wants to try it, thinking it might give him some ideas for the baseball simulation game, but remembers his busy schedule. He then sees Jeff, one of his coauthors, signing up and feels relieved.

After the meeting Terry returns to his workstation to plan his day. He asks the station to display his schedule and his "things to do" list. The shark film has already been entered into his schedule at 10:00. He decides to invite his friend David from another class to watch it with him. After checking to see if David is receiving messages, he types an invitation, which is automatically transferred to David's workstation. But David types back that he can't attend because he wants to do a science lab.

Tomorrow at 1:30 P.M. Terry and two other reporters from the school newspaper are scheduled for a half-hour teleconference interview with a man in California who has set a world hang-gliding record. They will meet with their faculty advisor, Mr. Parrish, at noon today to select their interview questions. Each reporter has made a list of questions, and Terry recalls that the others sent him their lists yesterday. He decides to set aside 11:30 to 12:00 to review them.

In history, Terry is studying the early explorers and has been involved in a simulation of Columbus' first voyage for the past week. He is in charge of provisions for one of the ships and will need to do some preparation before the next session, which is scheduled for 2:00. He sets aside 11:00 to 11:30 for this.

His writing group meets at 1:00 and Terry wants to do some final editing of his story, so he schedules 12:30 to 1:00 for that, hoping Mrs. Feldman will have a chance to go over his story before then. Next on Terry's "to do" list are some math exercises to finish and a worm dissection to perform by the end of the week for biology. He types:

```
>General Schedule
>Science Dissection Lab
```

to connect to the school master schedule and the science lab dissection chart. He sees that a dissection lab is scheduled for 10:00 A.M. tomorrow with two open spaces, checks his schedule, and signs up.

It is now 8:45. Terry decides to work on his math in the time left before the shark movie. He connects to the resource library, identifies himself, and is given the choice of a shape-generating geometry activity or an algebra project in which he has to work out equations to navigate a rocket to the Moon. He chooses rocket algebra. After he completes the exercise, the computer prints some questions asking how he was trying to solve the problem. Based on his answers, it recommends a particular review lesson (math is not one of Terry's strengths). He decides to put this off until afternoon because he notices that his message light is on. He asks for the message.

It is a note from Mrs. Feldman saying she has looked at his story and made a few comments. Terry asks for the message to continue and reads the comments. Since he still has a half-hour before 10:00, he decides to work on editing his story now. He asks that the latest version of his story be displayed on his screen with Mrs. Feldman's comments in bold type. Because the workstation screen is touch-sensitive, Terry is able to erase and insert words and even move sentences around, by touching the screen with his fingers. He is trying to work out a conclusion. Mrs. Feldman suggested combining his current conclusion with one from an earlier version of the story that is still stored in his workstation's memory. He asks for this to be displayed next to the version on which he is working. Terry goes to work using pieces of each version.

After a half-hour the light flashes at the top of the screen, telling him it is five minutes to 10:00. Still undecided between the two versions of his conclusion, Terry decides to take both of them to his writing group for other opinions. He saves his two current versions and also requests that they be printed in multiple copies for his writing group.

Terry turns off his workstation and goes across the room to his friend Jeff, who is also in the sharks special-interest group. Jeff has his earphones on. He is just finishing the town settlement simulation game with his friend Nancy, who is home recovering from a cold but has connected her dynabook through her home telephone to Jeff's workstation. They have composed a critique of the simulation and Jeff is sending it to the authors.

Terry asks if Jeff got any new ideas from the game. As they walk to the room where the shark group is meeting, Jeff explains that the simulation gave him a whole new idea about how to use probabilities to determine whether someone gets put out or not. Terry suggests that the high school students who wrote the simulation might be willing to help them apply it to their game.

When Terry returns to his workstation at 11:00 A.M., and turns it on, he finds his message light on. Terry asks for his message. It is from the Game Distribution Center. He calls Jeff over and they read it. The center has not accepted their baseball game for distribution, but has accepted it for review. They will send it out to a number of reviewers for comments. Jeff and Terry are very excited and immediately contact Steve, the third member of their group. He is in English class, so they leave him a message.

The Columbus simulation is next on Terry's schedule, and he sits down to work. In the simulation, his group has been at sea for a couple of months and the navigator, his friend Sandy, thinks they will reach land soon. In his job as provisioner, Terry is in charge of rationing food and gathering more once they reach land. To prepare for the simulation Terry studied nutrition to decide what provisions to take. He now has to figure out how much food and water they have left and what they will need for the return voyage. First, he wants to get some sense of what might be available when they reach land. He types:

```
>Library
>Data
```

to connect to the resource library and request a database search. He then types in a set of descriptors to indicate the information he is looking for:

```
:tropical environment
:plant life
:animal life
:edible
:food
```

The database responds with a list of possible sources that are at Terry's academic level. From the list Terry chooses a short film on tropical plants. Because the Columbus simulation includes a lot of video material, he wants to be able to recognize edible plants. He asks for the film to be shown at his workstation and he takes notes. His next step is to look up the nutritional value of each plant. . . .

This is a picture of what elementary and middle schools might be like in the 1990s. In terms of what is possible, this forecast is conservative. Almost all of the technologies described here actually exist now. Whether the picture becomes a reality depends on how schools, communities, and teachers respond to these technologies as their costs decline and they become more generally available.

Will schools respond by simply entrenching old practices in a new electronic garb? Will they use the power of these new technologies to create electronic workbooks, push-button page turners, and digital managers that lead the student through narrow sets of skill sequences? Or will schools adapt their vision of learning to the new potential for variety and independence offered by these technologies? The answers to these questions will depend on the decisions we make here and now; they will depend especially on our capacity to explore the use of computers and educational software in our classrooms today.

RESOURCE SECTION

This Resource Section includes annotations and specific information about the commercial software discussed throughout the text. The listings have been arranged alphabetically within the major content areas dealt with in the book—social studies, language arts, math, and science—and a separate section has been devoted to the various tools mentioned.

Each entry includes the name and address of the current distributor, the age or grade level most likely to benefit from the software, a brief description of the program, the type or category the software falls into, the grouping most likely to use it, and the chapter references. In a few cases where a point of reference is missing, it is because there was no clear-cut information available or, in the case of the tools, the category was readily apparent.

In several instances an author examined the use of a component of a total program rather than the program as a whole. In those cases the alphabetical listing uses the component's name, but indicates in the annotation its source such as *Island Survivors*, which is a part of *The Voyage of the Mimi*. Additionally, when a program is part of a series of related materials, those related programs are listed within the program description, such as *Classics Old and New*, which is listed with *M-ss-ng L-nks*. Finally, asterisks are used to indicate those pieces of software that are dealt with in depth in the text.

SOCIAL STUDIES

Name: *Geography Search**
Distributor: McGraw-Hill/Webster Division
                 1221 Avenue of the Americas
                 New York, NY 10020
Grade Level: 5-9
Description: Students work in explorer teams to search for the New World and
                 learn cooperation as well as skills related to mapping, navigation,
                 climate, effective record keeping and more.
Type: Simulation
References: Chapters 1, 2, and 3

Name: *Grolier's Electronic Encyclopedia*
Distributor: Grolier Electronic Publishing, Inc.
                 95 Madison Avenue
                 New York, NY 10016
Grade Level: 5-12
Description: The complete text of Grolier's *Academic American Encyclopedia* on a
                 CD-ROM. Allows students to interactively search any topic using sin-
                 gle or combinations of words and save information on a floppy disk to
                 be read into a word processor.
Type: Resource
References: Chapter 3

Name: *Hammurabi*
                 What Would You Do? Simulations in Social Studies
Distributor: MECC (Minnesota Educational Computing Corporation)
                 3490 Lexington Avenue North
                 St. Paul, MN 55112-8097
Grades: 5-8
Description: Students are immersed in the role of the ruler of a small, ancient king-
                 dom that is faced yearly with problems of land use, food production,
                 pests, and starvation. Gives students a chance to see how decisions are
                 made, and gives practice in manipulating variables to achieve a de-
                 sired goal. Explores disciplines of government, economics, geogra-
                 phy, and anthropology.
Type: Simulation
Grouping: Individual; small group
References: Chapter 8

Name: *Historian*
Distributor: Harcourt Brace Jovanovich
                 Orlando, FL 32887
Grade Level: High school
Description: Presents raw data about nine important issues in U.S. history; acting
                 as historians, students collect other relevant information, generate
                 and test hypotheses, and publish their findings.

Type: Simulation
Grouping: Individual
References: Chapter 3

Name: *Oregon Trail*
Distributor: American Peripherals
               122 Bangor Street
               Lindenhurst, NY 11757
Grade Level: 5-10
Description: The students must try to complete a trip in 1847 from Independence,
               Missouri, to Oregon City (a 2,000-mile trip). They have a five- to
               six-month time frame and must survive the hazards presented as clues
               along the way.
Type: Educational game; simulation
Grouping: Individual; small group
References: Chapters 2 and 8

Name: *The Other Side*
Distributor: Tom Snyder Productions
               123 Huron Avenue
               Cambridge, MA 02138
Grade Level: 7-adult
Description: A two-team computer/board game that teaches peace and conflict
               resolution. The two teams enter a world of scarce resources and
               sensitive national defense systems. Limited communications lead to
               misunderstanding. Only cooperation and negotiation can achieve the
               goal: to build a unifying bridge between two nations. Cable or modem
               required for playing with two computers.
Type: Simulation
Grouping: Small group
References: Chapter 3

Name: *Social Studies Fact Finder*
Distributor: Human Relations Media Software
               175 Tompkins Avenue
               Pleasantville, NY 10570
Grade Level: 7-12
Description: Three databases, "States," "Working America," and "Explorers,"
               provide students with actual historical and sociological data to
               promote the generating and testing of hypothesis, analysis of data,
               and detection of trends in the same way that historians and social
               scientists do. Activity cards are provided that guide students through
               self-directed inquiries, introduce them to the use of *PFS: File* (which
               must be used with the databases), and help them to build their own
               databases.
Type: Resource
Grouping: Individual
References: Chapter 3

LANGUAGE ARTS

Name: *Cloze Plus*
Distributor: Milliken Publishing Company
               1100 Research Boulevard
               St. Louis, MO 63132
Grade Level: 3-8
Description: Develops reading comprehension skills and vocabulary through structured cloze and context analysis activities. Develops skills such as identifying time/order, same/opposite meanings, and definitions. Monitors performance in eleven skill areas for up to five different classes with 100 students per class. Two packages, levels C-E and F-H. Stores and reports user performance.
Type: Skills practice; tutorial
Grouping: Individual
References: Chapter 4

Name: *Galaxy Search*
Distributor: Learning Well
               200 S. Service Road
               Roslyn Heights, NY 11577
Grade Level: Elementary (grades 3-6, Blue; and grades 2-4, Red)
Description: Plunging deep into space, players search for remote alien groups. Each group has invented valuable new robot parts that the players must collect in order to build their robots and win the game. Answering predicted outcome questions is the only way to obtain the desired robot parts. Program can be printed.
Type: Skills practice; educational game
Grouping: Individual; small group
References: Chapter 4

Name: *Gapper*
Distributor: HRM Software
               175 Tompkins Avenue
               Pleasantville, NY 10570
Grade Level: K-16
Description: Complete system of language arts instruction for any grade level. Consists of: "The Game Program," an interactive learning environment for encouraging effective reading strategies such as reading speed and comprehension; "Gapper Writer," an easy-to-use way of preparing texts; and "Game Command," which provides score reports and adjusts difficulty level.
Type: Tutorial; educational game
References: Chapter 4

Name: *How to Read in the Content Areas*
Distributor: Educational Activities, Inc.
               P.O. Box 392
               Freeport, N.Y. 11520

Grade Level: 3–8
Description: Four disks—literature, mathematics, social studies, and science—each with five content area selections. Teaches and reinforces the reading skills of vocabulary, words in context, main idea, inference, details and pronoun referents, as well as survey techniques. Word-find puzzles are provided and a summary of performance is available at the end of each program.
Type: Skills practice
Grouping: Individual
References: Chapter 4

Name: *Instant Zoo*
Distributor: Apple Computer, Inc.
20525 Mariani Avenue
Cupertino, CA 95014
Grade Level: 1–5
Description: A set of four educational, fast-moving games to develop a range of visual skills associated with reading. "Instant Zoo," visual perception; "Quick Match," visual discrimination; and "Scramble," word decoding and spelling.
Type: Educational game
Grouping: Individual
References: Chapter 4

Name: *Juggles' Rainbow*
Distributor: The Learning Company
4370 Alpine Road
Portola Valley, CA 94025
Grade Level: Preschool–1
Description: The user plays with dancing rainbows, butterflies, and windmills while learning how to use the computer. Very young children learn important reading- and math-readiness skills. Features nine different games.
Type: Skills practice; educational game
Grouping: Individual; small group
References: Chapter 4

Name: *Magic Spells*
Distributor: The Learning Company
4370 Alpine Road
Portola Valley, CA 94025
Grade Level: 1–5
Description: Sharpens spelling skills. Provides eight demon lists with commonly misspelled words. Students spell and unscramble words with fourteen prepared word lists. Players or teachers can tailor the game to any level by creating their own lists.
Type: Skills practice; educational game
Grouping: Individual; small group
References: Chapter 4

Name: *Microzine*
Distributor: Scholastic, Inc.
                730 Broadway
                New York, NY 10003
Grade Level: 4–10
Description: A magazine on a disk that features high-interest programs with opportunities for students to use the skills that form the cornerstone of computer literacy: programming, word processing, problem solving, filing, and database management. Each issue has four programs, a back-up disk, a student handbook, a teaching guide, and a newsletter.
Type: Multiple type
Grouping: Individual, small group, class
References: Chapter 4

Name: *M-SS-NG L-NKS*
Distributor: Sunburst Communications, Inc.
                Rm BN 39, Washington Avenue
                Pleasantville, NY 10570–9971
Grade Level: 4 and up
Description: Designed to encourage students to play with language and improve their reading, writing, and spelling. Nine Cloze formats are available. Students can alter the number of guesses they want to have, move around passages, and check their scores at any time while a game is in progress. A summary and score are available at the conclusion. A number of versions are available: *Young People's Literature, Classics Old and New,* and *Microencyclopedia.*
Type: Educational game
Grouping: Individual; group
References: Chapter 4

Name: *Newbury Winners*
Distributor: Sunburst Communications, Inc.
                39 Washington Avenue, Room VF414
                Pleasantville, NY 10570–9971
Grade Level: 3–8
Description: Fifteen packages, each containing a Newbury Award book in paperback, a courseware diskette, an instructional manual, and a teacher's guide. The four sections of the program provide an opportunity for students to work on extensions to the book: comprehension, vocabulary, sequencing, and a synonym puzzle.
Type: Skills practice
Grouping: Individual
References: Chapter 4

Name: *Spelling Wiz*
Distributor: DLM (Developmental Learning Materials)
                One DLM Park
                Allen, TX 75002
Grade Level: 1–6

Description:	Students place missing letters into words commonly misspelled from grade levels 1–6.
Type:	Drill and practice; educational game
Grouping:	Individual
References:	Chapter 4

Name:	*Story Tree*
Distributor:	Scholastic, Inc.
	730 Broadway
	New York, NY 10003
Grade Level:	5–12
Description:	A story processor that enhances writing skills by encouraging children to read, write, and extend their own stories with unlimited endings. Helps children to read more, write better, use their imagination, and think. Optional print feature makes it possible to reproduce stories.
Type:	Skills practice; computational tool
Grouping:	Individual
References:	Chapter 4

Name:	*Suspect Sentences*
Distributor:	Ginn and Company
	Lexington, MA 02173
Grade Level:	4 and up
Description:	A game of over fifty literary passages in which students practice and sharpen reading, writing, and thinking skills. The player acts as a "forger," who inserts sentences in a text, or a "detective," who picks out forged sentences. Particularly improves writing and the ability to evaluate the writing of others. Teacher has a utility disk to create own database of literary passages; quick-reference cards are provided for users; and blackline masters are also provided for practice off the computer.
Type:	Skills practice; educational game
Grouping:	Pairs; small groups
References:	Chapter 4

Name:	*Troll's Tale*
Distributor:	Sierra On-Line, Inc.
	36575 Mudge Ranch Road
	Coarsegold, CA 93614
Grade Level:	3–6
Description:	A journey into troll territory in search of hidden treasure; fosters skills in comprehension and following directions as well as in mapping and short-term memory.
Type:	Skills practice; educational game
Grouping:	Individual; small group
References:	Chapter 4

Name: *Verb Viper*
Distributor: DLM (Developmental Learning Materials)
              One DLM Park
              Allen, TX 75002
Grade Level: K-6
Description: Part of *Arcademic Skill Builders in Language Arts;* arcade game format for practice in selecting singular and plural forms of "to be" verbs, forms of irregular verbs, and so on. The speed, content, and difficulty level can be controlled by the user or the teacher. Record-keeping sheets and worksheets are provided.
Type: Educational game; drill-and-practice
Grouping: Individual
References: Chapter 4

Name: *Word Invasion*
Distributor: DLM (Developmental Learning Materials)
              One DLM Park
              Allen, TX 75002
Grade Level: 2-6
Description: Provides practice in identifying words representing six parts of speech: nouns, pronouns, verbs, adjectives, adverbs, and prepositions. *Word Invasion* is one of six programs included in *Arcademic Skill Builders in Language Arts.*
Type: Rote drill; educational game
Grouping: Individual
References: Chapter 4

Name: *Writing a Narrative*
Distributor: MECC (Minnesota Educational Computing Corporation)
              3490 Lexington Avenue North
              St. Paul, MN 55112-8097
Grade Level: 7-12
Description: In "Idea Storming One-Two-Three," students learn a story-starting technique and create the framework for a narrative. "Catch the Moments" focuses on key elements of narrative structuring by tracing the development of an event from a student's experience. "Point of View" encourages students to make conscious choices about voice of the narrator. Suitable for adult-ed.
Type: Skills practice; tutorial
Grouping: Individual
References: Chapter 4

Name: *Writing to Read*
Distributor: IBM Corporation
              P.O. Box 1329
              Boca Raton, FL 33432
Grade Level: K-3
Description: Pupils learn sounds and their corresponding symbols through a series

of words and pictures presented on the computer. They also practice writing in workbooks called journals and then move to a typewriter and compose words, sentences, and stories; students learn to write words according to the way they sound. Recordings of children's classics accompany books, which are included with this program.

Type:	Skills practice
Grouping:	Individual; pairs
References:	Chapter 4

MATHEMATICS

Name:	*Balance*
Distributor:	HRM Software
	175 Tompkins Avenue
	Pleasantville, NY 10570-9971
Grade Level:	3 and up
Description:	Focuses on equation-solving skills; includes illustrations of scales on which both sides of an equation must balance. Students experiment with different values of x in equations and observe how these values affect the balance of the equation.
Type:	Skills practice
Grouping:	Individual
References:	Chapter 2

Name:	*Bumble Games*
Distributor:	The Learning Company
	4370 Alpine Road
	Portola Valley, CA 94025
Grade Level:	Preschool-4
Description:	The user develops geometry skills by plotting positive numbers on grids. The program also presents the concepts of "greater than" and "less than" and introduces children to number pairs with positive numbers. Helps kids plot number lines or locations on maps and plot number pairs on arrays and grids. Features six different games for ages 4-10.
Type:	Skills practice; educational game
Grouping:	Individual; small group
References:	Chapter 5

Name:	*Bumble Plot*
Distributor:	The Learning Company
	4370 Alpine Road
	Portola Valley, CA 94025
Grade Level:	3-8
Description:	Contains games that build on math and computer skills introduced in *Bumble Games*. Players create original computer graphics by plotting positive and negative numbers on a four-quadrant grid; they also

learn mapping skills necessary for making charts and graphs. Features five different games.

Type:	Skills practice; educational game
Grouping:	Individual; small group
References:	Chapter 5

Name:	*Darts*
Distributor:	Control Data Publishing Co.
	P.O. Box 261127
	San Diego, CA 92126
Grade Level:	K-6
Description:	This game is designed to teach fractions. Balloons appear on a number line, and students guess where the balloons are by typing in mixed numbers. Each time they guess, an arrow shoots to the specified position. The arrow pops the balloon when the guess is correct.
Type:	Educational game
Grouping:	Individual
References:	Chapter 2

Name:	*Explorer Metros: A Metric Adventure*
Distributor:	Sunburst Communications, Inc.
	39 Washington Avenue, Room VF414
	Pleasantville, NY 10570
Grade Level:	4-6
Description:	Provides experience in metric measurements while developing estimation skills. While exploring a colorful alien planet, students learn to estimate metric capacity, mass, length, and temperature. Faced with randomly generated encounters, the student, as leader of an exploration party, makes decisions based on metric measurement. Speed is important.
Type:	Skills practice; educational game
Grouping:	Individual
References:	Chapter 2

Name:	*Exploring Tables and Graphs—Level 1*
Distributor:	Xerox Educational Publications
	245 Long Hill Road
	Middletown, CT 06457
Grade Level:	3-4
Description:	Students experiment with tables and picture, bar, line, and area graphs. Fun applications and topics include animals, languages, populations. Games and real-life uses are possible with topics like endangered species, world languages, and populations. Colorful tables and graphs can be modified right on the screen using simple arithmetic.
Type:	Skills practice; educational game
Grouping:	Individual; small group
References:	Chapter 5

Name: *Exploring Tables and Graphs—Level 2*
Distributor: Xerox Educational Publications
                   245 Long Hill Road
                   Middletown, CT 06457
Grade Level: 5-8
Description: Students experiment with tables and picture, bar, line, and area graphs. Applications and topics include satellites, women in industry, and incomes. Projects, colorful tables, and graph examples can be modified, reorganized, and redesigned right on the screen.
Type: Skills practice; educational game
Grouping: Individual; small group
References: Chapter 5

Name: *The Factory: Strategies in Problem Solving**
Distributor: Sunburst Communications, Inc.
                   39 Washington Avenue, Room VF414
                   Pleasantville, NY 10570
Grade Level: 4-12
Description: Challenges students to create geometric "products" programs. The components "Test a Machine," "Build a Factory," and "Make a Product" focus on several problem-solving strategies, including working backwards, analyzing a process, determining sequence, and applying creativity. Uses color graphics and animation.
Type: Skills practice; simulation
Grouping: Individual; small group
References: Chapter 5

Name: *Fraction Concentration*
Distributor: Agency for Instructional Television
                   Box A
                   Bloomington, IN 47402
Grade Level: 4-8
Description: Part of a series called *It Figures,* which is comprised of disks and videotapes to reinforce decimals, fractions, and fact finding.
Type: Skills practice
Grouping: Individual
References: Chapter 2

Name: *Fractions*
Distributor: Right On Programs
                   27 Bowdon Road
                   Greenlawn, NY 11740
Grade Level: 2-4
Description: Introduction to fractions provides randomized example plus incentives for correct answers.
Type: Tutorial
Grouping: Individual; small group
References: Chapter 2

Name:	*Gertrude's Puzzles*
Distributor:	The Learning Company
	4370 Alpine Road
	Portola Valley, CA 94025
Grade Level:	Preschool–4
Description:	Sharpens abstract thinking and reasoning skills. Features six different games that expand upon the skills and concepts presented in *Gertrude's Secrets*. Solving *Gertrude's Puzzles* involves early logic skills such as same/different relationships, and higher-level skills such as deductive reasoning and problem solving with a minimum of clues. Kids learn to analyze what they see. Requires color monitor.
Type:	Skills practice; educational game
Grouping:	Individual
References:	Chapters 1 and 5

Name:	*Gertrude's Secrets*
Distributor:	The Learning Company
	4370 Alpine Road
	Portola Valley, CA 94025
Grade Level:	Preschool–3
Description:	The user learns to recognize patterns and to categorize. Helps kids think logically, create order, and think ahead. Kids move puzzle pieces and guess secret rules to solve the puzzles, or create their own puzzle pieces. Features seven different games.
Type:	Educational game
Grouping:	Individual; small group
References:	Chapter 5

Name:	*Green Globs*
Distributor:	CONDUIT
	University of Iowa, Oakdale Campus
	Iowa City, IA 52242
Grade Level:	10–16
Description:	Two game levels, each displaying thirteen green globs scattered randomly over a set of coordinate axes. Student enters equations for graphs he or she thinks will hit these globs. Scoring encourages student to hit as many globs as possible with each shot.
Type:	Skills practice; educational game
Grouping:	Individual
References:	Chapter 2

Name:	*Guess My Rule**
Distributor:	HRM Software
	175 Tompkins Avenue
	Pleasantville, NY 10570-9971
Grade Level:	4–8
Description:	Problem-solving math environment in which the emphasis is to study what happens, to look for patterns, and to find ways to express these patterns. The activities provide an "experiential" basis

for such abstract concepts as variable, relations, function, and graph.

Type: Skills practice
Grouping: Individual
References: Chapter 5

Name: *Island Survivors*
Distributor: Holt, Rinehart & Winston
               School Marketing Department
               383 Madison Avenue
               New York, NY 10017
Grade Level: Intermediate
Description: A computer game based on the model of small, simple land and pond ecosystems presented in *The Voyage of the Mimi*. Changes in the abundance of the land and pond species are calculated, and students become aware of the factors that affect the size of populations. Students deal with information and issues such as seasonal changes, availability of food, and human food gathering that causes changes in the ecosystem.
Type: Simulation
Grouping: Small group
References: Chapters 5 and 6

Name: *The King's Rule**
Distributor: Sunburst Communications, Inc.
               39 Washington Avenue, Room VF414
               Pleasantville, NY 10570-9971
Grade Level: 4-13
Description: A challenging game that introduces students to the heart of scientific thinking: generating and testing hypotheses. Students work individually or in groups as they try to discover numerical rules that allow them to go to the center of a king's castle. They generate and test hypotheses by trying out as many combinations as they want. At the end students take a quiz. Six levels are available.
Type: Skills practice; educational game
Grouping: Individual; small group
References: Chapter 5

Name: *Math Mansions*
Distributor: Sunburst Communications, Inc.
               39 Washington Avenue, Room VF414
               Pleasantville, NY 10570-9971
Grade Level: 2-6
Description: Part of a program, *Challenge Math,* which fosters the practicing of basic whole-number and decimal operations. In this component, students make their way through a haunted house by constructing problems to produce given answers.
Type: Skills practice; educational game
Grouping: Individual
References: Chapter 2

Name: *Number Quest**
Distributor: Sunburst Communications, Inc.
                39 Washington Avenue, Room VF414
                Pleasantville, NY 10570-9971
Grade Level: 3-9
Description: Number lines involving whole numbers, decimals, and fractions require students to use binary search strategies and their knowledge of number order to locate a hidden number. Shows students graphically how searches actually locate a number.
Type: Skills practice; educational game
Grouping: Individual
References: Chapter 5

Name: *Power Drill**
Distributor: Sunburst Communications, Inc.
                39 Washington Avenue, Room VF414
                Pleasantville, NY 10570-9971
Grade Level: 4-9
Description: Reinforces basic computation but takes students into estimation and thinking about numbers. Four programs help students with addition of whole numbers and integers up to four places; with subtraction; with one-, two-, and three-digit multiplication; and with division.
Type: Skills practice
Grouping: Individual
References: Chapter 5

Name: *Teasers by Tobbs*
Distributor: Sunburst Communications, Inc.
                39 Washington Avenue, Room VF414
                Pleasantville, NY 10570-9971
Grade Level: 4-7
Description: Two programs reinforce mental arithmetic skills and help students construct relationships between mathematical operations. A grid and a character called Tobbs appear on the screen. The grid presents a series of math problems, each with a missing number. Students must decide which number cannot be, might be, or must be the correct solution. Both programs offer six levels of difficulty.
Type: Skills practice; educational game
Grouping: Individual; small group
References: Chapters 1 and 5

Name: *World Quest*
Distributor: Sunburst Communications, Inc.
                39 Washington Avenue, Room VF414
                Pleasantville, NY 10570-9971
Grade Level: 3-9
Description: In the first of two games, students deal with the concept of "between-ness" as they try to find a word that fits between two given words. In the second game (competition mode), one student picks a "mystery"

word, and the other has to guess what the word is by getting clues as to which words the mystery word fits between.

Type: Skills practice; educational game
Grouping: Individual; small group
References: Chapters 2 and 5

SCIENCE

Name: *Electronic Mailbag*
Distributor: EXSYS
               2728 23rd Street
               Greely, CO 80631
Grade Level: 3-12 and above
Description: *Mailbag* is an interactive electronic mail simulation for teaching telecommunications concepts. *Mailbag* has three levels of operation. A beginning level stresses simple log on and message system operation skills. The second level adds editing and printing functions. The third level simulates a commercial message base. *Mailbag* can also be used as a motivating technique in teaching writing skills.
Type: Simulation
Grouping: Individual; small group
References: Chapter 6

Name: *Experiments in Human Physiology/Science*
Distributor: HRM Software
               175 Tompkins Avenue
               Pleasantville, NY 10570-9971
Grade Level: 9-12
Description: Provides authentic science experiences for students in biology, physiology, health, and athletics programs. While all the experiments teach about physiological responses, many are also designed to teach students laboratory skills related to the use of computers as laboratory instruments.
Type: Tool
Grouping: Individual; small group
References: Chapter 6

Name: *Exploring Heat Through Lessons and Labs*
Distributor: Heath Courseware
               Collamore Educational Publishing
               125 Spring Street
               Lexington, MA 02173
Grade Level: 4-6
Description: Through the use of temperature probes and the ability to interact with the computer, students study a number of concepts concerning heat as a form of energy. The teacher's manual provides student worksheets, reinforcement activities for extra practice, and enrichment projects.

Type: Simulation
Grouping: Individual; small group
References: Chapter 6

Name: *Exploring Matter Through Lessons and Labs*
Distributor: Heath Courseware
              Collamore Educational Publishing
              125 Spring Street
              Lexington, MA 02173
Grade Level: 4-6
Description: With the use of temperature probes and the ability to interact with the
              computer, students study the effect heat energy has on molecules of
              solids, liquids, and gases. They learn to identify properties common
              to all matter, how molecules are composed of atoms, and how to
              describe the motion of molecules in solids, liquids, and gases. The
              teacher's manual provides student worksheets, reinforcement activi-
              ties for extra practice, and enrichment projects.
Type: Simulation
Grouping: Individual; small group
References: Chapter 6

Name: *Geology Search**
Distributor: McGraw-Hill Book Company
              1221 Avenue of the Americas
              New York, NY 10020
Grade Level: 5-9
Description: Students learn new vocabulary and organize information in the
              scientific mode of geology, focusing on principles of energy
              management in the context of the history of oil exploration. Sup-
              plementary materials provided; user support.
Type: Simulation (problem solving)
Grouping: Individual; small group
References: Chapter 6

Name: *Incredible Laboratory**
Distributor: Sunburst Communications, Inc.
              39 Washington Avenue
              Suite RMS
              Pleasantville, NY 10570-9771
Grade Level: 4 and above
Description: Focuses on the scientific process (i.e., inferring and hypothesizing)
              and teaches basic scientific concepts of quantification, cause and
              effect, interaction, change, models, validation, and significance.
              Problem solving is emphasized; students practice note taking for
              scientific purposes.
Type: Game; problem solving (simulation)
Grouping: Individual; small group
References: Chapter 6

Name: *Operation Frog**
Distributor: Scholastic, Inc.
               P.O. Box 7502
               2931 E. McCarty Street
               Jefferson City, MO 65102
Grade Level: 4-11
Description: Students become familiar with the structure and functions of the
               major organs of the body (anatomy) and develop an understanding of
               dissection procedures and tools through the simulated dissection and
               reconstruction of a frog. Resource reference information included, as
               well as worksheets for students.
Type: Tutorial; simulation (problem solving); game
Grouping: Individual
References: Chapter 6

Name: *Scientific Reasoning*
               (Series for IBM Personal Computer)
Distributor: IBM Corporation
               1000 NW 51 Street
               Boca Raton, RL 33432
Grade Level: 7-12
Description: Places students in situations similar to those encountered by scientists
               in order to help them think and reason using various scientific
               methods. Students will be able to form simple scientific theories and
               through experimental evidence will be able to determine if their
               theories are reasonable. Two components are available: "Measure-
               ment Process: Distance and Area" and "Theory Formation: Reflec-
               tions and Patterns."
Type: Simulation; problem solving
Grouping: Individual; small group
References: Chapter 6

Name: *Search Series*
Distributor: McGraw-Hill/Webster Division
               1221 Avenue of the Americas
               New York, NY 10020
Grade Level: 5-9
Description: Five sets of programs are available in this series. Each set includes
               software, student workbooks, and a teacher's manual: *Geology
               Search, Geography Search, Community Search, Archaeology Search,*
               and *Energy Search.*
Type: Simulation
Grouping: Small groups
References: Chapters 1, 2, and 3

Name: *Sell Series*
Distributor: MECC (Minnesota Educational Computing Corporation)
               3490 Lexington Avenue North
               St. Paul, MN 55112-8097
Grade Level: Varies with each program

Description: Four simulations designed to teach economics: *Sell Apples, Sell Plants, Sell Lemonade,* and *Sell Bicycles.*
Type: Simulation
Grouping: Small group
References: Chapters 3 and 8

Name: *Sir Issac Newton's Games*
Distributor: Sunburst Communications, Inc.
    39 Washington Avenue, Room VF414
    Pleasantville, NY 10570-9971
Grade Level: 4-adult
Description: Through easy-to-understand games students gain an initial understanding of the laws of motion, and they also come to understand how friction and other forces affect motion.
Type: Game
Grouping: Individual; small group
References: Chapter 6

Name: *The Voyage of the Mimi**
Distributor: Holt, Rinehart & Winston
    School Marketing Department
    383 Madison Avenue
    New York, NY 10017
Grade Level: 4-8
Description: An integrated curriculum for science and math that uses a scientific minilab, computer simulations, an adventure on video, and printed materials. The curriculum focuses on a group of young scientists studying humpback whales in the Gulf of Maine.
Type: Simulations; problem solving
References: Chapter 8

COMPUTER TOOLS

Name: *AppleWorks**
Distributor: Apple Computer
    20525 Mariani Avenue
    Cupertino, CA 95014
Grade Level: 5-adult
Description: Package includes word-processing, database, and spreadsheet programs.
Type: Tool
Grouping: Individual; pairs
References: Chapters 3 and 8

Name: *Bank Street Filer*
Distributor: Broderbund Software
    17 Paul Drive
    San Rafael, CA 94903

Grade Level: 4 and up
Description: An easy-to use data management and filing program for small busi-
nesses, schools and homes. With the *Filer* you can collect, explore and
manipulate data and information in a flexible way. Because the *Bank
Street Filer* is compatible with the *Bank Street Writer*, reports created
by the *Filer* can be automatically inserted into *Writer* text files.
Type: Tool
Grouping: Individual
References: Chapter 3

Name: *Bank Street Writer**
Distributor: Scholastic, Inc.
730 Broadway
New York, NY 10003
Grade Level: 4–12
Description: Word processor designed for the young writer; emphasizes ease of use;
simplifies editing and redrafting; disk includes detailed interactive
tutorial, and the manual includes twenty learning activities.
Type: Tool
Grouping: Individual
References: Chapter 4

Name: *The Computer Chronicles Newswire*
Distributor: InterLearn, Inc.
P.O. Box 342
Cardiff by the Sea, CA 92007
Grade Level: 3–12
Description: A writing system that enables students to become reporters for a
national news network. Stories are written with help of program
prompts and are sent either via *Mail-disk* or *The Source* to other
participating sites that produce their own local version of *Computer
Chronicles*. Available in English or Spanish. Requires *Writer's
Assistant* as the word processor.
Type: Tool
Grouping: Small group
References: Chapter 4

Name: *Crossword Magic*
Distributor: Mindscape
3444 Dundee Road
Northbrook, IL 60062
Grade Level: 3–adult
Description: Allows you to create crossword puzzles customized with your words to
any topic of your choosing. Clues of "across" and "down" can then be
added. Puzzles can be saved on the disk or printed out.
Type: Tool
Grouping: Individual; small group
References: Chapters 1 and 4

Name: *Data Plot*
Distributor: MUSE Software
              347 No. Charles Street
              Baltimore, MD 21201
Grade Level: 6–12
Description: User can create, edit, store, and print colored and labeled bar and pie charts and line graphs.
Type: Tool
Grouping: Individual
References: Chapters 5 and 6

Name: *Friendly Filer*
Distributor: Grolier Educational Corporation
              Sherman Turnpike
              Danbury, CT 06816
Grade Level: 3 and up
Description: Features easy-to-use menus that help the user get organized and manage information more productively. An interactive on-screen tutorial teaches the concepts and basic terminology of database management.
Type: Tool
Grouping: Individual
References: Chapter 3

Name: *The Geometric Supposer*
Distributor: Sunburst Communications
              Room B.N., 39 Washington Avenue
              Pleasantville, NY 10570–9971
Grade Level: Intermediate and above
Description: Students explore the properties of geometric constructions; they make measurements, change scale, and repeat experiments; and they are encouraged to make conjectures about geometric theorems. The three programs include: *The Presupposer, Triangles,* and *Quadrilaterals.*
Type: Tool
Grouping: Individual
References: Chapter 5

Name: *Kidwriter*
Distributor: Spinnaker Software
              215 First Street
              Cambridge, MA 02142
Grade Level: K–4
Description: Provides format for story writing and illustrations, encourages creativity, and introduces the fundamentals of word processing. Children choose from a variety of objects to make a picture on the screen; they then type in a story about the picture.
Type: Skills practice; tool
Grouping: Individual; small group
References: Chapter 4

Name: *Magic Slate*
Distributor: Sunburst Communications, Inc.
               39 Washington Avenue, Room VF414
               Pleasantville, NY 10570–9971
Grade Level: 2–adult
Description: Transforms the Apple into an easy-to-learn word processor that
               makes editing a pleasure. Includes 20-, 40-, and 80-column levels to
               provide flexibility for different ages and levels of ability.
Types: Teacher aid; word processor
Grouping: Individual
References: Chapter 4

Name: *The Newsroom*
Distributor: Springboard Software, Inc.
               7807 Creekridge Circle
               Minneapolis, MN 55435
Grade Level: Junior high and above
Description: Program features a word processor with five different fonts and a
               library of more than 600 pieces of clip art that can be combined and
               modified into original graphics using the keyboard, a joystick, or a
               Koala Pad. Manual provides a great deal of information on how to use
               the program as well as tips on producing a newspaper and a glossary
               of news terms. It requires a great deal of time to set up and use, with
               constant switching between disks.
Type: Tool
Grouping: Individual; small group
References: Chapter 4

Name: *PFS: File**
Distributor: Software Publishing Company
               1901 Landings Drive
               Mountain View, CA 94043
Grade Level: Adult
Description: An easy to use database software package that is menu driven. The
               user can easily retrieve and update information and print information
               on user-defined forms.
Type: Tool
References: Chapters 3 and 4

Name: *PFS: File/Life Science Databases*
Distributor: Scholastic, Inc.
               730 Broadway
               New York, NY 10003
Grade Level: 6–12
Description: The package is intended to help students become more creative in
               their approach to studying the life sciences through the sample "Bird
               Migration." The units and datafiles should help students become
               more actively involved in organizing, retrieving, and interpreting
               scientific data as well as helping them build their own files through a
               study of "Wild Flowers" or "Drugs."

Type:	Tool
References:	Chapter 6

Name:	*PFS: File/Physical Science Databases*
Distributor:	Scholastic, Inc.
	730 Broadway
	New York, NY 10003
Grade Level:	6-12
Description:	The package helps students become more actively involved in organizing, retrieving, and interpreting scientific data; it also helps them build their own files through a study of the physical sciences, particularly with chemistry and its common substances. Three substantial files, "Chemical Elements," "The Common Substances," and "Chemical Tests," are provided.

Type:	Tool
References:	Chapter 6

Name:	*PFS: Graph*
Distributor:	Software Publishing Company
	1901 Landings Drive
	Mountain View, CA 94043
Grade Level:	Adult
Description:	This product takes information from *PFS: File* forms or *VisiCalc* files to create pie, line, or bar charts and integrates this information into the body of a letter or report.

Type:	Tool
References:	Chapters 5 and 6

Name:	*The Print Shop*
Distributor:	Broderbund Software
	17 Paul Drive
	San Rafael, CA 94903
Grade Level:	6 and up
Description:	Write, design, and print as though you owned your own personal print shop. Create invitations, greeting cards, signs, personal stationery, banners, and advertising material. Designs created with joystick, Koala Pad, or keyboard. All directions are on the screen.

Type:	Tool
Grouping:	Individual; pairs
References:	Chapter 4

Name:	*Quill**
Distributor:	D. C. Heath
	125 Spring Street
	Lexington, MA 02173
Grade Level:	3-9
Description:	Three programs designed to promote prewriting, composition, and revision—"Planner," "Library," and "Mailbag"—as well as a program to edit text—"Writer's Assistant." Using the "Mailbag" component, students can send and receive messages in a format similar to an electronic mail system.

Type: Tool
Grouping: Individual; small group
References: Chapter 4

Name: *SemCalc**
Distributor: Sunburst Communications, Inc.
               39 Washington Avenue, Room VF414
               Pleasantville, NY 10570
Grade Level: 6-12
Description: The *Semantic Calculator (SemCalc)* is an innovative tool that helps
               students explore and solve word problems. It has two teaching
               objectives: to help students focus on correct unit names to avoid
               inappropriate computations (adding apples and oranges), and to help
               students focus on units rather than numbers, which enables them to
               choose the appropriate mathematics operation in a word problem.
               Keeps notes on the individual's process so user can see how answers
               were reached.
Type: Skills practice; computational tool
Grouping: Individual
References: Chapter 5

Name: *Story Maker*
Distributor: Scholastic, Inc.
               2931 E. McCarty Street
               P.O. Box 750
               Jefferson City, MO 65102
Grade Level: 3 and up
Description: Students can write, illustrate, and print out text. A picture gallery as
               well as eight type faces (fonts) add to the appeal. Uses a Koala Pad,
               Applemouse, or joystick for graphics and is driven from a single
               menu.
Type: Tool
Grouping: Individual; small group
References: Chapter 4

Name: *Survey Taker**
Distributor: Scholastic, Inc.
               730 Broadway
               New York, NY 10003
Grade Level: 3 and up
Description: With *Survey Taker* children make and take their own surveys or polls
               and analyze the results. Survey questions can include anything from
               the frivolous "Who is your friends' favorite rock star?" to the serious
               "Which candidate do your friends believe will win the presidential
               election?" Encourages children to think inquisitively and communi-
               cate effectively. Survey results are displayed on both colorful bar
               graphs and detailed table graphs that children read and analyze.
               School version contains teacher's manual, student handbook, and a
               back-up disk. Program can be printed.

Type: Tool
Grouping: Individual
References: Chapters 1 and 3

Name: *Terrapin LOGO*
Distributor: Terrapin, Inc.
              222 Third Street
              Cambridge, MA 02142
Grade Level: Primary to adult
Description: A simple language that enables children to draw pictures and make music. It can also be used with an assembly language interface, full-screen editor, and other advanced features. Older students and adults can use *Terrapin Logo* to write complex programs and learn about artificial intelligence.

Type: Tool
Grouping: Individual; pairs
References: Chapter 7

Name: *Think Tank*
Distributor: Living Videotext
              2432 Charleston Road
              Mountain View, CA 94043
Grade Level: 6-adult
Description: An "idea processor" that enables students and teachers to create, expand, and revise outlines. The program performs editing functions quickly and can be used to organize any kind of written material.

Type: Tool
Grouping: Individual
References: Chapter 8

Name: *VisiCalc*
Distributor: John Wiley Sons, Inc.
              605 3rd Avenue
              New York, NY 10158-0012
Grade Level: 9-12
Description: *VisiCalc* is an electronic spreadsheet with a matrix of 260 rows by 75 columns. The computer is like a window through which the user can view any part of the sheet. Each row and column name can contain a label, value, or formula. As these variables are defined, *VisiCalc* automatically computes numerical values as needed by the user.

Type: Tool
Grouping: Individual
References: Chapter 5

INDEX